A Note to Students   xviii

Preface   xix

PART ONE **College Thinking, Reading, and Writing**   1

1. **Critical Thinking, Reading, and Writing:** Making Connections   1
2. **Getting Ready to Write:** Purpose, Form, and Process   20
3. **Organizing Your Main Point and Support**   33
4. **Drafting and Revising Paragraphs and Essays**   49

PART TWO **Writing Different Kinds of Paragraphs and Essays**   66

5. **Narration:** Writing That Tells Stories   66
6. **Illustration:** Writing That Gives Examples   77
7. **Description:** Writing That Creates Pictures with Words   90
8. **Process Analysis:** Writing That Explains How Things Happen   101
9. **Classification:** Writing That Sorts Things into Groups   112
10. **Definition:** Writing That Tells What Something Means   124
11. **Comparison and Contrast:** Writing That Shows Similarities and Differences   136
12. **Cause and Effect:** Writing That Explains Reasons or Results   148
13. **Argument:** Writing That Persuades   161
14. **Research:** Writing That Explores a Question and Synthesizes Information   174

PART THREE **Grammar, Punctuation, and Mechanics**   189

15. **Basic Grammar:** An Overview   189
16. **The Four Most Serious Errors:** Fragments, Run-Ons, Subject-Verb Agreement Problems, and Verb-Tense Problems   197
17. **Other Grammar and Style Concerns**   223
18. **Punctuation and Capitalization**   245

Index   263

Useful Editing and Proofreading Marks   *inside back cover*

Real
Writing
ESSENTIALS

Real Writing
ESSENTIALS

From Paragraph to Essay

Miriam Moore
Lord Fairfax Community College

Susan Anker

bedford/st.martin's
Macmillan Learning

Boston | New York

For Bedford/St. Martin's

Vice President, Editorial, Macmillan Learning Humanities: Edwin Hill
Senior Program Director for English: Leasa Burton
Program Manager: Karita France dos Santos
Executive Marketing Manager: Joy Fisher Williams
Director of Content Development: Jane Knetzger
Senior Development Editor: Gillian Cook
Assistant Editor: Suzanne H. Chouljian
Content Project Manager: Andrea Cava
Senior Workflow Project Manager: Jennifer Wetzel
Production Supervisor: Brianna Lester
Senior Media Project Manager: Rand Thomas
Project Management: Lumina Datamatics, Inc.
Composition: Lumina Datamatics, Inc.
Permissions Editor: Angela Boehler
Permissions Assistant: Allison Ziebka
Permissions Associate: Claire Paschal
Permissions Manager: Kalina Ingham
Photo Researcher: Donna Ranieri, Lumina Datamatics, Inc.
Text Researcher: Mark Schaefer, Lumina Datamatics, Inc.
Text Design: Claire Seng-Niemoeller
Cover Design: John Callahan
Cover image: FlamingPumpkin/Getty Images
Printing and Binding: LSC Communications

Manufactured in the United States of America.

3   2   1   0   9   8
f   e   d   c   b   a

For information, write: Bedford/St. Martin's, 75 Arlington Street, Boston, MA 02116

ISBN 978-1-319-15344-1

Acknowledgments

Text acknowledgments and copyrights appear at the back of the book on page 261, which constitutes an extension of the copyright page. Art acknowledgments and copyrights appear on the same page as the art selections they cover.

Contents

A Note to Students   xviii

Preface   xix

PART ONE

College Thinking, Reading, and Writing   1

1. Critical Thinking, Reading, and Writing: Making Connections   1

Critical Thinking   1

   Recognize and Question Assumptions   1

   Be Aware of Bias   3

Critical Reading   5

   2PR Preview the Reading   5

   2PR Read the Piece: Find the Main Point and the Support   6

      Read Actively   6

      Main Point   6

      Support   7

   2PR Pause to Think   8

   2PR Review and Respond   9

      Paraphrase   9

   A Critical Reader at Work   11

   Reading: Amanda Jacobowitz, *A Ban on Water Bottles: A Way to Bolster the University's Image*   11

Writing Critically about Readings   13

   Summary   14

   Analysis   16

   Synthesis   16

   Evaluation   19

2. Getting Ready to Write: Purpose, Form, and Process   20

■■ Four Basics **of Good Writing**   20

First Basic: Audience and Purpose   20

    Paragraph and Essay Form   22

        Paragraph Form   22

        Essay Form   23

Second Basic: The Writing Process   24

Finding, Narrowing, and Exploring Your Topic   25

    Narrowing a Topic   26

        Divide It into Smaller Categories   26

        Think of Specific Examples from Your Life   27

        Think of Specific Examples from Current Events   27

        Question Your Assumptions   27

    Exploring Your Topic   29

        Freewriting   29

        Listing / Brainstorming   30

        Discussing   30

        Clustering / Mapping   30

        Keeping a Journal   31

        Research Your Topic Further   31

        Avoid Plagiarism   32

    CHECKLIST: Evaluating Your Narrowed Topic   32

3. Organizing Your Main Point and Support   33

Third Basic: Topic Sentences and Thesis Statements   33

    Consider the Size of the Assignment   34

    State a Single Main Point   36

    Be Specific   37

    Choose a Point You Can Show, Explain, or Prove   38

    CHECKLIST: Evaluating Your Main Point   39

Fourth Basic: Support for Your Main Point   40

    Key Features of Good Support   40

    Support in Paragraphs versus Essays   41

    Generating Support   42

    Selecting the Best Primary Support   43

    Adding Secondary Support   43

    CHECKLIST: Evaluating Your Support   44

Arrange Your Ideas   44

    Use Time Order to Write about Events   44

    Use Space Order to Describe Objects, Places, or People   45

    Use Order of Importance to Emphasize a Particular Point   46

Planning Your Draft   46
CHECKLIST: Evaluating Your Outline   48

4. Drafting and Revising Paragraphs and Essays   49

Drafting Paragraphs   49
Use Complete Sentences   49
Consider Introductory Techniques   49
End with a Concluding Sentence   50
Title Your Paragraph   50
Sample Student Paragraph   50
CHECKLIST: Evaluating Your Draft Paragraph   51
Drafting Essays   52
Write Topic Sentences, and Draft the Body of the Essay   52
Write an Introduction   52
Write a Conclusion   53
Title Your Essay   53
Sample Student Essay   54
CHECKLIST: Evaluating Your Draft Essay   56
Revising Paragraphs and Essays   56
CHECKLIST: Revising Your Writing   57
Revise for Unity   58
Revise for Development of Support   59
Revise for Coherence: Transitions and Key Words   59
Sample Student Paragraph: Revised   61
CHECKLIST: Evaluating Your Revised Paragraph   62
Sample Student Essay: Revised   62
Peer Reviewing   64
CHECKLIST: Questions for Peer Reviewers   65
CHECKLIST: Evaluating Your Revised Essay   65

PART TWO
Writing Different Kinds of Paragraphs and Essays   66

5. Narration: Writing That Tells Stories   66

Understand What Narration Is   66
Four Basics of Good Narration   66
First Basic: Main Point in Narration   67
Second and Third Basics: Support in Narration   68
Fourth Basic: Organization in Narration   68

Read and Analyze Narration   69

Narration in the Real World: Anne Terreden, *Nursing Note*   69

Paragraphs vs. Essays in Narration   70

Student Narration Paragraph: Jelani Lynch, *My Turnaround*   72

Professional Narration Essay: Amy Tan, *Fish Cheeks*   73

Write Your Own Narration   75

CHECKLIST: How to Write Narration   76

6. Illustration: Writing That Gives Examples   77

Understand What Illustration Is   77

Four Basics **of Good Illustration**   77

First Basic: Main Point in Illustration   78

Second and Third Basics: Support in Illustration   79

Paragraphs vs. Essays in Illustration   80

Fourth Basic: Organization in Illustration   82

Read and Analyze Illustration   82

Illustration in the Real World: Karen Upright, *Memo*   82

Student Illustration Paragraph: Casandra Palmer, *Gifts from the Heart*   84

Professional Illustration Essay: Susan Adams, *The Weirdest Job Interview Questions and How to Handle Them*   85

Write Your Own Illustration   87

CHECKLIST: How to Write Illustration   89

7. Description: Writing That Creates Pictures with Words   90

Understand What Description Is   90

Four Basics **of Good Description**   90

First Basic: Main Point in Description   91

Paragraphs vs. Essays in Description   92

Second and Third Basics: Support in Description   94

Fourth Basic: Organization in Description   94

Read and Analyze Description   95

Description in the Real World: James C. Roy, *Incident Report: Malicious Wounding*   95

Student Description Paragraph: Alessandra Cepeda, *Bird Rescue*   96

Professional Description Essay: Oscar Hijuelos, *Memories of New York City Snow*   97

Write Your Own Description   99

CHECKLIST: How to Write Description   100

8. Process Analysis: Writing That Explains How Things Happen 101

Understand What Process Analysis Is 101

▪▪▪ Four Basics **of Good Process Analysis** 101

First Basic: Main Point in Process Analysis 102

Second and Third Basics: Support in Process Analysis 103

Fourth Basic: Organization in Process Analysis 103

    Paragraphs vs. Essays in Process Analysis 104

Read and Analyze Process Analysis 106

    Process Analysis in the Real World: Stephen Martin, *How to Practice Simple Meditation* 106

    Student Process Analysis Paragraph: Charlton Brown, *Buying a Car at an Auction* 107

    Professional Process Analysis Essay: Eric Rosenberg, *How to Start Your Service Based Side Hustle* 108

Write Your Own Process Analysis 110

    CHECKLIST: How to Write Process Analysis 111

9. Classification: Writing That Sorts Things into Groups 112

Understand What Classification Is 112

▪▪▪ Four Basics **of Good Classification** 112

First Basic: Main Point in Classification 114

Second and Third Basics: Support in Classification 115

Fourth Basic: Organization in Classification 115

    Paragraphs vs. Essays in Classification 116

Read and Analyze Classification 118

    Classification in the Real World: Leigh King, *Prom Fashions* 118

    Student Classification Paragraph: Lorenza Mattazi, *All My Music* 119

    Professional Classification Essay: Frances Cole Jones, *Don't Work in a Goat's Stomach* 120

Write Your Own Classification 122

    CHECKLIST: How to Write Classification 123

10. Definition: Writing That Tells What Something Means 124

Understand What Definition Is 124

▪▪▪ Four Basics **of Good Definition** 124

First Basic: Main Point in Definition   125

   Paragraphs vs. Essays in Definition   126

Second and Third Basics: Support in Definition   128

Fourth Basic: Organization in Definition   129

Read and Analyze Definition   129

   Definition in the Real World: Walter Scanlon, *Employee Assistance Program*   129

   Student Definition Paragraph: Corin Costas, *What Community Involvement Means to Me*   130

   Professional Definition Essay: Janice E. Castro with Dan Cook and Cristina Garcia, *Spanglish*   131

Write Your Own Definition   133

   CHECKLIST: How to Write Definition   135

11. Comparison and Contrast: Writing That Shows Similarities and Differences   136

Understand What Comparison and Contrast Are   136

   Four Basics **of Good Comparison and Contrast**   136

First Basic: Main Point in Comparison and Contrast   138

Second and Third Basics: Support in Comparison and Contrast   138

Fourth Basic: Organization in Comparison and Contrast   139

   Paragraphs vs. Essays in Comparison and Contrast   140

Read and Analyze Comparison and Contrast   142

   Comparison and Contrast in the Real World: Brad Leibov, *Who We Are*   142

   Student Comparison/Contrast Paragraph: Said Ibrahim, *Eyeglasses vs. Laser Surgery: Benefits and Drawbacks*   143

   Professional Comparison/Contrast Essay: Mark Twain, *Two Ways of Seeing a River*   144

Write Your Own Comparison and Contrast   146

   CHECKLIST: How to Write Comparison and Contrast   147

12. Cause and Effect: Writing That Explains Reasons or Results   148

Understand What Cause and Effect Are   148

   Four Basics **of Good Cause and Effect**   148

First Basic: Main Point in Cause and Effect   150

Second and Third Basics: Support in Cause and Effect   150

   Avoid Logical Fallacies   150

Fourth Basic: Organization in Cause and Effect   151

Paragraphs vs. Essays in Cause and Effect   152

Read and Analyze Cause and Effect   154

Cause and Effect in the Real World: Mary LaCue Booker, *School Rules*   154

Student Cause/Effect Paragraph: Caitlin Prokop, *A Difficult Decision with a Positive Outcome*   156

Professional Cause/Effect Essay: Kristen Ziman, *Bad Attitudes and Glowworms*   157

Write Your Own Cause and Effect   159

CHECKLIST: How to Write Cause and Effect   160

13. Argument: Writing That Persuades   161

Understand What Argument Is   161

Four Basics **of Good Argument**   161

First Basic: Main Point in Argument   162

Second and Third Basics: Support in Argument   163

Types of Evidence   163

Paragraphs vs. Essays in Argument   164

Testing Evidence   166

Fourth Basic: Organization in Argument   166

Read and Analyze Argument   167

Argument in the Real World: Diane Melancon, *The Importance of Advance Directives*   167

Student Argument Essay 1: "Yes" to Social Media in Education: Jason Yilmaz, *A Learning Tool Whose Time Has Come*   169

Student Argument Essay 2: "No" to Social Media in Education: Shari Beck, *A Classroom Distraction—and Worse*   170

Write Your Own Argument   172

CHECKLIST: How to Write Argument   173

14. Research: Writing That Explores a Question and Synthesizes Information   174

Understand What Research Is   174

Four Basics **of Good Research**   174

First Basic: Begin with a Question   175

Second Basic: Find Appropriate Sources   175

Third Basic: Evaluate and Synthesize Sources   176

Synthesize Information to Support a Thesis Statement   177

Fourth Basic: Cite and Document Sources to Avoid
Plagiarism   177

Use MLA Format to Cite and Document Sources   179

Use In-Text Citations within Your Essay   179

Use a Works Cited List at the End of Your Essay   180

Write Your Own Research   180

Read and Analyze Research: Student Research Essay   181

Dara Riesler, *Service Dogs Help Heal the Mental Wounds
of War*   181

CHECKLIST: How to Write Research   187

PART THREE

Grammar, Punctuation, and Mechanics   189

15. Basic Grammar: An Overview   189

The Parts of Speech   189

The Basic Sentence   190

Verbs   190

Action Verbs   191

Linking Verbs   191

Helping Verbs   192

Subjects   193

Complete Thoughts   194

Six Basic English Sentence Patterns   195

**16. The Four Most Serious Errors: Fragments, Run-Ons,
Subject-Verb Agreement Problems, and Verb-Tense
Problems**   197

Fragments   197

1. Fragments That Start with Prepositions   198

2. Fragments That Start with Dependent Words   199

3. Fragments That Start with *-ing* Verb Forms   200

4. Fragments That Start with *to* and a Verb   201

5. Fragments That Are Examples or Explanations   201

Run-Ons   203

1. Correct Run-Ons by Adding a Period or a Semicolon   204

2. Correct Run-Ons by Adding a Comma and a Coordinating
Conjunction   205

3. Correct Run-Ons by Adding a Dependent Word   206

Problems with Subject-Verb Agreement   208
  1. The Verb Is a Form of *Be, Have,* or *Do*   209
  2. Words Come between the Subject and the Verb   211
    Prepositional Phrase between the Subject and the Verb   211
    Dependent Clause between the Subject and the Verb   211
  3. The Sentence Has a Compound Subject   212
  4. The Subject Is an Indefinite Pronoun   213
  5. The Verb Comes before the Subject   215
Problems with Verb Tense   216
  Regular Verbs   216
    Present-Tense Endings: -s *and No Ending*   216
    Regular Past-Tense Ending: -ed *or* -d   217
  Irregular Verbs   217
  Past Participles   221

17. Other Grammar and Style Concerns   223
Pronouns   223
  Check for Pronoun Agreement   224
    Indefinite Pronouns   225
    Collective Nouns   226
  Make Pronoun Reference Clear   227
    Repetitious Pronoun Reference   227
  Three Important Types of Pronoun   227
    Subject Pronouns   228
    Object Pronouns   228
    Possessive Pronouns   229
  Use the Right Pronoun   229
    Pronouns Used with Compound Subjects and Objects   229
    Pronouns Used in Comparisons   229
    Choosing between Who *and* Whom   230
  Make Pronouns Consistent in Person   230
Adjectives and Adverbs   231
  Choosing between Adjectives and Adverbs   231
  Adjectives and Adverbs in Comparisons   232
    Good, Well, Bad, and *Badly*   233
Misplaced and Dangling Modifiers   233
  Misplaced Modifiers   234
  Dangling Modifiers   235
Coordination and Subordination   235
  Coordination   236
  Subordination   237

Parallelism   238

Sentence Variety   239

   Start Some Sentences with Adverbs   239

   Join Ideas Using an *-ing* Verb   240

   Join Ideas Using a Past Participle   240

   Join Ideas Using an Appositive   240

   Join Ideas Using an Adjective Clause   241

Word-Choice Problems   241

   Vague and Abstract Words   241

   Slang   242

   Wordy Language   242

   Clichés   243

   Sexist Language   244

18. Punctuation and Capitalization   245

Commas [,]   245

   Commas between Items in a Series   245

   Commas between Coordinate Adjectives   245

   Commas in Compound Sentences   246

   Commas after Introductory Words   246

   Commas around Appositives and Interrupters   246

   Commas around Adjective Clauses   246

   Commas with Quotation Marks   247

   Commas in Addresses   247

   Commas in Dates   247

   Commas with Names   248

   Commas with *Yes* or *No*   248

Apostrophes [']   248

   Apostrophes to Show Ownership   248

   Apostrophes in Contractions   249

   Apostrophes with Letters, Numbers, and Time   250

Quotation Marks [" "]   251

   Quotation Marks for Direct Quotations   251

   Setting Off a Quotation within Another Quotation   252

   No Quotation Marks for Indirect Speech   252

   Quotation Marks for Certain Titles   253

Semicolon [;]   253

   Semicolons to Join Closely Related Sentences   253

   Semicolons When Items in a List Contain Commas   253

Colon [:]   254

   Colons before Lists   254

Colons before Explanations or Examples   254

Colons in Business Correspondence and before Subtitles   255

Parentheses [( )]   255

Dash [—]   255

Hyphen [-]   255

Hyphens to Join Words That Form a Single Description   256

Hyphens to Divide a Word at the End of a Line   256

Capitalization   256

Capitalization of Sentences   256

Capitalization of Names of Specific People, Places, Dates, and Things   257

People   257

Places   257

Dates   258

Organizations, Companies, and Groups   258

Languages, Nationalities, and Religions   258

Courses   259

Commercial Products   259

Capitalization of Titles   259

Index   263

Useful Editing and Proofreading Marks   *inside back cover*

A Note to Students from Miriam Moore

Since 1991, I have taught writing, grammar, reading, and ESL in a variety of places, including a university, an Intensive English program, two community colleges, and even a chicken processing plant! In each place, I have tried to share my love of words with students, and I have learned by listening to their words, their rhythms of speech, their questions, and their frustrations.

Words, and the ways we put them together, help us accomplish ordinary tasks and (as our skills improve) some incredible feats: getting a date, making a sale, convincing the boss to try a new idea, changing a law, or solving a long-standing problem. The words we use to read and write can also help us to think more creatively, more deeply, and more effectively.

In *Real Writing Essentials*, I want to help you see the value of skills like reading, thinking, and writing. It takes time and attention to learn new words, understand them when you read, and master rules for combining and punctuating them accurately. But in the end, after working for these skills, you will begin to see *them* working for *you*. It will be worth the effort.

I applaud your decision to take this course, and I wish you every success.

A Note to Students from Susan Anker

For the last twenty years or so, I have traveled the country talking to students about their goals and, more important, about the challenges they face on the way to achieving those goals. Students always tell me that they want good jobs and that they need a college degree to get those jobs. I designed *Real Skills Essentials* with those goals in mind—strengthening the writing, reading, and editing skills needed for success in college, at work, and in everyday life.

Here is something else: good jobs require not only a college degree but also a college education—knowing not only how to read and write but how to think critically and learn effectively. So that is what I stress here, too. It is worth facing the challenges. All my best wishes to you, in this course and in all your future endeavors.

Preface

Curriculum redesign has transformed developmental English courses in recent years. For many instructors, this has led to classes with greater diversity in student preparedness than ever before. *Writing Essentials Online: A Macmillan LaunchPad* has been developed to enable instructors to meet the diverse needs of their students by providing flexible, modular writing instruction from sentence to essay level. It is supported by a series of three brief books, each of which focuses on a particular set of writing skills that build on each other, guiding students as they grow as writers.

- *Real Skills Essentials: From Sentence to Paragraph*
- *Real Writing Essentials: From Paragraph to Essay*
- *Real Essays Essentials: From Drafting to Revising*

Real Writing Essentials: From Paragraph to Essay

The goal of *Real Writing Essentials* is twofold: to show students that writing is fundamental to success in the real world and to help them develop the skills they need to achieve success in their own college, work, and everyday lives. In support of this message, the book provides both an engaging real-world context for writing and exercises and activities that help students write strong paragraphs and essays.

Core Features

Convenient and Affordable Format. The text offers what is essential for the paragraph-to-essay-level course in a concise, affordable, and easy-to-carry format. Targeted instructional content highlights what students need to know about paragraphs and essays: the writing process, paragraph unity, patterns of development, cohesion, and the grammar needed for effective editing.

Coverage of Critical Thinking and Reading. Chapter 1 discusses the importance of thinking critically as you read and identifying and questioning the assumptions and biases of both the reader and writer. It also outlines the steps in the Critical Reading Process (2PR: preview, read, pause, and review), providing students with strategies and practice for each step, and explains how to paraphrase and summarize effectively and write critically about readings. This focus on reading and thinking critically is displayed throughout the text.

Coverage of Writing Using Patterns and Research. Chapters 5–13 address structuring paragraphs and essays using different patterns of organization, including argument. Chapter 14 provides basic information on developing a research question, finding, evaluating, and synthesizing sources, and using MLA to cite and document sources. It also includes guidelines for writing a researched paper.

A Blend of Authentic Academic and Professional Writing Examples. Samples of real students' writing demonstrate the concepts covered and give students confidence that good writing skills are achievable and relevant. Additional examples from workplace communications and professional publications emphasize the relevance of patterns of organization for the real-world and academic success.

Four Basics Boxes. To present writing skills in manageable increments, these boxes break down the essentials of topics such as revision, good paragraphs, and cause-and-effect writing. The Four Basics approach to complex composition topics helps students target, remember, and apply concepts without feeling overwhelmed by them. For the rhetorical modes, the Four Basics boxes remind students of key concepts applicable to all good writing: a main point, major supporting points, effective use of detail, and a logical organization.

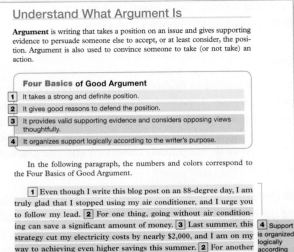

Understand What Argument Is

Argument is writing that takes a position on an issue and gives supporting evidence to persuade someone else to accept, or at least consider, the position. Argument is also used to convince someone to take (or not take) an action.

Four Basics of Good Argument

1. It takes a strong and definite position.
2. It gives good reasons to defend the position.
3. It provides valid supporting evidence and considers opposing views thoughtfully.
4. It organizes support logically according to the writer's purpose.

In the following paragraph, the numbers and colors correspond to the Four Basics of Good Argument.

1 Even though I write this blog post on an 88-degree day, I am truly glad that I stopped using my air conditioner, and I urge you to follow my lead. 2 For one thing, going without air conditioning can save a significant amount of money. 3 Last summer, this strategy cut my electricity costs by nearly $2,000, and I am on my way to achieving even higher savings this summer. 2 For another thing, living without air conditioning reduces humans' effect on the environment. 3 Agricultural researcher Stan Cox estimates that air conditioning creates 300 million tons of carbon dioxide (CO_2) 4 Support is organized logically according to the writer's purpose.

Visual Comparisons of Paragraphs and Essays.   For each rhetorical mode, *Real Writing Essentials* provides a side-by-side annotated example of a paragraph and an essay to emphasize the structural similarities between them.

Checklists.   Checklists throughout the text help novice writers know when a piece of writing is finished and ready for submission or distribution to a real-world audience.

Focus on the Four Most Serious Errors.   *Real Writing Essentials* concentrates first on the four types of grammatical errors that matter most: fragments, run-ons, errors in subject-verb agreement, and errors of verb tense and form. Once students master these four topics and start building their editing skills, they are better prepared to tackle the grammar errors treated in later chapters.

Find and Fix Boxes.   *Real Writing Essentials* includes concise, step-by-step instructions for fixing common problems in grammar and punctuation. Find and fix boxes walk students through the editing process, from identification of a problem to a solution, with examples.

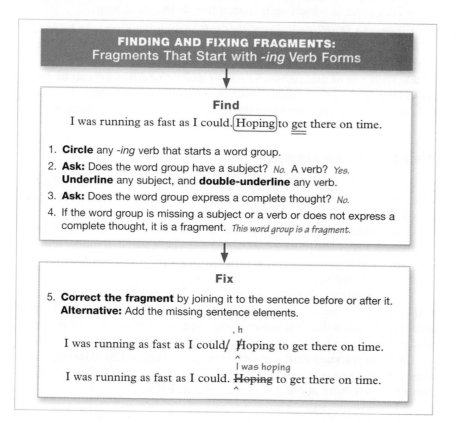

Writing Essentials Online: A Macmillan LaunchPad

An all-in-one resource, *Writing Essentials Online* combines a proven approach to developmental writing instruction with sentence-to-essay-level support in a single, flexible digital product.

- **Comprehensive instruction** from all three *Essentials* texts (*Real Skills Essentials, Real Writing Essentials,* and *Real Essays Essentials*) provides easy-to-customize modular content that addresses sentence-to-essay-level writing skills and includes additional readings, downloadable information sheets (common transitions, word parts, editing and proofreading marks, a guide to grammar terminology, and graphic organizers), and detailed information on MLA and APA documentation styles for quick reference.

- **Diagnostics** provide opportunities to assess areas for improvement and assign additional exercises based on students' needs. Visual reports show performance by topic, class, and student as well as improvement over time.

- **LearningCurve**, adaptive quizzing for targeted learning, focuses on the areas in which each student needs the most help.

- **Integrate *Writing Essentials Online*** with your school's learning management system so that your class is always on the same page.

As with any of the *Essentials* texts, *Real Writing Essentials* can be packaged with *Writing Essentials Online* at a significant discount. For more information, contact your Macmillan Learning sales representative.

We're all in. As always.

Bedford/St. Martin's is as passionately committed to the discipline of English as ever, working hard to provide support and services that make it easier for you to teach your course your way.

Find **community support** at the Bedford/St. Martin's English Community (community.macmillan.com), where you can follow our *Bits* blog for new teaching ideas, download titles from our professional resource series, and review projects in the pipeline.

Choose **curriculum solutions** that offer flexible custom options, combining our carefully developed print and digital resources, acclaimed works from Macmillan's trade imprints, and your own course or program materials to provide the exact resources your students need.

Rely on **outstanding service** from your Bedford/St. Martin's sales representative and editorial team. Contact us or visit **macmillanlearning .com** to learn more about any of the options below.

Choose from Alternative Formats of *Real Writing Essentials*

Bedford/St. Martin's offers a range of formats. Choose what works best for you and your students:

- *Paperback.* To order the print edition, use ISBN 978-1-319-15344-1.
- *Popular e-Book formats.* For details of our e-Book partners, visit **macmillanlearning.com/ebooks**.

Instructor Resources

You have a lot to do in your course. We want to make it easy for you to find the support you need—and to get it quickly.

The *Instructor's Manual for Real Writing Essentials* is available as a PDF that can be downloaded from **macmillanlearning.com**. Visit the instructor resources tab for *Real Writing Essentials*. In addition to chapter overviews and teaching tips, the instructor's manual includes sample syllabi and detailed information on working with developmental writers, integrating critical thinking into the course, facilitating cooperative learning, teaching ESL students, assessing student writing, and much more.

Acknowledgments

Real Writing Essentials grew out of a collaboration with teachers and students across the country and with the talented staff of Bedford/St. Martin's. I am grateful for the thoughtful contributions of all who shepherded this project from concept to completion, especially the support of Karita France dos Santos and the tireless effort and creativity of my editor on this project, Gillian Cook. I would like to acknowledge as well my colleagues at Lord Fairfax Community College and across the Virginia Community College System. Finally, thanks to my husband, Michael, for unwavering patience, and to Mandy, Mallory, and Murray.

Reviewers

I would like to thank the following instructors for their many good ideas and suggestions for this edition. Their insights were invaluable.

Jose Amaya, Marshalltown Community College; Nikki Aitken, Illinois Central College; Valerie Badgett, Lon Morris College; Michael Briggs, East Tennessee State University; Tara Broeckel, Oakland Community College; Andrew Cavanaugh, University of Maryland University College; Kim Davis, Oakland Community College; Dawna DeMartini, Sacramento City College; Debra Justice, Ashland Community College; Russell Keevy, Technical

College of the Lowcountry; Jeff Kosse, Iowa Western Community College; Mimi Leonard, Wytheville Community College; Lynn Lewis, Oklahoma State University; Trina Litteral, Ashland Community College; Katie Lohinski, Harford Community College; Leanne Maunu, Palomar College; Shannon McCann, Suffolk Community College; Loren Mitchell, Hawaii Community College; Jim McKeown, McLennan Community College; Virginia Nugent, Miami Dade College; Lisa Oldaker Palmer, Quinsigamond Community College; Anne Marie Prendergast, Bergen Community College; Robert Rietveld, William Penn University; Patricia Roller, Pellissippi State Community College; Gina Schochenmaier, Iowa Western Community College; Marcea Seible, Hawkeye Community College; Karen Taylor, Belmont College; Heather Weiss, Technical College of the Lowcountry; Elizabeth Wurz, College of Coastal Georgia; Svetlana Zhuravlova, Lakeland Community College

Students

Many current and former students have helped shape *Real Writing Essentials,* and I am grateful for all of their contributions.

Among the students who provided paragraphs and essays for the book are Shari Beck, Charlton Brown, Alessandra Cepeda, Corin Costas, Said Ibrahim, Amanda Jacobowitz, Jelani Lynch, Lorenza Mattazi, Casandra Palmer, Caitlin Prokop, Dara Riesler, and Jason Yilmaz.

I would also like to thank the nine former students who provided inspirational words of advice and examples of workplace writing which are central to the book. They are Mary LaCue Booker, Jeremy Graham, Celia Hyde, Leigh King, Kelly Layland, Brad Leibov, Diane Melancon, Walter Scanlon, and Karen Upright.

Critical Thinking, Reading, and Writing

Making Connections

In order to become a better writer, you need to use critical thinking and reading skills. This chapter explains critical thinking and reading strategies and explores the important connections among critical thinking, reading, and writing.

Critical Thinking

You are already a critical thinker. If you have ever questioned a claim made by a politician or second-guessed an advertisement, you were thinking critically about what you saw, heard, or read.

Critical thinking is a process of actively questioning what you see, hear, and read to come to thoughtful conclusions about it. Critical thinking also involves making connections between existing impressions and new ones, and among various beliefs, claims, and pieces of information.

Critical thinking requires you to recognize the **iceberg principle**. Only about 10 percent of an iceberg is visible above the surface of the ocean; the remaining 90 percent is hidden from view. But that 90 percent has a tremendous impact on what is going on above the surface. Similarly, you may not be fully aware of what is motivating your reactions and decisions in a situation. When you think critically, you pause to explore what is hidden below the surface of what you read or see, along with your reactions to it. Such pauses help you keep an open mind, see new perspectives, find alternatives, and make better decisions. Two potential troublespots you can uncover with critical thinking are assumptions and biases.

Recognize and Question Assumptions

Assumptions—ideas or opinions that we do not question and that we automatically accept as true—can get in the way of clear, critical thinking. Here is an example. Imagine you are the shift supervisor at the student union café, and you have been asked to train a new employee.

He shows up fifteen minutes late, seems a little dazed, and is not wearing his uniform. What do you think to yourself about this person? What assumptions do you make about the kind of employee he will be? Why do you think that? Here are some assumptions you might make:

- He is unreliable, because he showed up late.
- He is careless about his appearance, because he is not wearing his uniform.
- He has a problem with drugs or alcohol, as he looks dazed.

Everything you know here is based on first impressions, guesses. Without additional facts, you are going on surface appearances and your assumptions about them, which may not lead to a correct interpretation of the situation.

In college, work, and life, we all hold assumptions of which we are unaware. By recognizing and questioning them (are they accurate, fair, or factually based), we are able to move beyond quick judgments to think more critically, exploring and evaluating what we see, hear, and read. In the case of this employee, you might find when talking to him that he was given the wrong start time, found out at the last minute and raced across campus to get to work. Perhaps he then decided it was more important to get to work than to stop and put on his uniform. Maybe the dazed look in his eyes is the result of his being up all night with his sick child rather than the effect of drugs.

Questioning Assumptions

SITUATION	ASSUMPTION	QUESTIONS
COLLEGE: I saw from the syllabus that I need to write five essays for this course.	That sounds like too much work.	What obstacles might be getting in my way? What might be some ways around those obstacles? What have others done in this situation?
WORK: Two of my coworkers just got raises.	My own raise is just around the corner.	Did my coworkers accomplish anything that I didn't? When was their last raise, and when was mine?
EVERYDAY LIFE: My neighbor has been cool to me lately.	I must have done something wrong.	Is it possible that this has nothing to do with me? Maybe he is going through something difficult in his life?

When questioning assumptions, try to get a bit of distance from them. Imagine what people with entirely different points of view might say. You might even try disagreeing with your own assumptions. Take a look at the chart on page 2.

You need to be aware not only of your own hidden assumptions but also of any assumptions hidden in what you read, see, and hear. For example, look at the bottled water label that follows. Labels like this one might suggest directly or indirectly that bottled water is better than tap water. What evidence do they provide for this assumption? What other sources of information could be consulted to support, disprove, or call into question this assumption? However confidently a claim is made, never assume that it cannot be questioned.

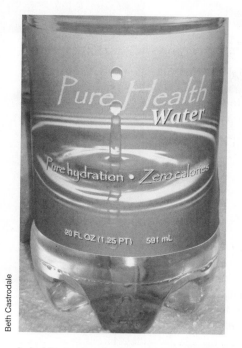

Label from a leading brand of bottled water

Be Aware of Bias

In addition to assumptions, be aware of **biases,** one-sided and sometimes prejudiced views that may prevent you and others from seeing multiple perspectives on a situation. Here is just one example:

I don't trust kids today; they are too lazy to read.

This is an extreme statement that others could contradict with their own experiences or additional information (for example, pointing out the success of the *Harry Potter* series, or giving examples of "kids" who *are* readers).

Be on the lookout for bias in your own views and in whatever you read, see, and hear. When a statement seems one-sided or extreme, ask yourself what facts or points of view might have been omitted.

. . . .

PRACTICE 1–1   Think Critically

Look at the images on this page and then answer the questions that follow.

Courtesy DiMassimo Goldstein, New York

Last year, plastic bottles generated more than 2.5 million tons of carbon dioxide. **Drink tap. tappening.com**

Advertisement from Tappening, a group that opposes bottled water

Beth Castrodale

Smaller Cap = Less Plastic

Our Eco-Slim cap is part of our ongoing effort to reduce our impact on the environment. This cap contains an average of 37% less plastic than our previous cap.

WE CAN ALL MAKE A DIFFERENCE. PLEASE RECYCLE.

WARNING: Cap is a small part and poses a CHOKING HAZARD, particularly for children.

Label from a leading brand of bottled water

- What is the main message of the advertisement? What is the main message of the bottled water label?
- Make a connection between the two images: How are they alike? How are they different?
- What assumptions are behind each of the images? Write down as many as you can identify. Then, write down questions about these assumptions, considering different points of view.

- Which image do you find more effective? Why?

- Collaborate: Do others in your group agree with the way you "read" each image? Why or why not? What makes you read them the way you do?

Critical Reading

Critical reading requires that you think critically. To do this, you need to read actively, pay close attention to the text, and ask yourself questions about the author's purpose: What is his or her main point? What support does he or she provide? How good is that support? Also, look out for assumptions and biases (both the writer's and your own) and consider whether you agree or disagree with the points the author is making.

Here are the four steps of the critical reading process:

2PR The Critical Reading Process

1 **Preview** the reading.

2 **Read** the piece, double underlining the <u>thesis statement</u> and underlining the <u>major support</u>. Consider the quality of the support.

3 **Pause** to think during the reading. Take notes and ask questions about what you are reading. Imagine that you are talking to the author.

4 **Review** the reading, your marginal notes, and your questions.

2PR Preview the Reading

The first step in the critical reading process is **previewing**. The roots of this word can help you understand what it means: you look ("view") before ("pre") to get a general sense of what a reading is about (topic), who it is written for (audience), and why it was written (purpose). You may also be able to determine the main ideas and supporting details as you skim through a text quickly. When you preview, you also make connections with the topic and identify your purpose for reading.

To preview a reading, skim through all of it quickly to identify the **rhetorical context** (topic, purpose, audience). Look for the following information:

- **Source:** The source or location of publication (online magazine, newspaper, Facebook, class handout) can help you identify the writer's purpose.

- **Author:** Information about the author can help you evaluate the purpose and accuracy of the information.

- **Title:** The title or subject line can help you determine the topic and main idea.

- **Headings:** Subtitles, headings, or captions often reveal the major supporting details.
- **Marginalia:** Definitions or comments in the margins (sidebars) often highlight key terms or major supporting details.
- **Visuals:** Charts, graphics, or photos illustrate the main idea by giving specific details.
- **Definitions:** Words or phrases in bold often show the ideas that the writer wants to emphasize and provide explanations of what terms mean.
- **Summaries and abstracts:** A short summary or abstract (provided in many scholarly publications) often gives the main idea and major support.

Once you have identified the rhetorical context of the piece, consider your own reasons for reading: Why are you reading the piece? What do you already know about the topic? What else do you need to know? Choose a guiding question—a question you think the reading might answer—to help you stay focused as you read.

2PR   Read the Piece: Find the Main Point and the Support

After previewing, begin reading carefully and actively for meaning, trying especially to identify the writer's main point and the support for that point.

Read Actively

If you have previewed a reading, you have already begun to read actively. Active readers recognize that *looking* at words or images on a page or screen is not the same as *reading* those words or images. As the name suggests, active readers act: they ask questions (using their minds, their voices, or their hands as they write or type), and they annotate—they personalize a reading by making notes and adding words or images that will help them make sense of what they are reading. Active readers often begin by identifying the main point of the reading.

Main Point

The **main point** of a reading is the central idea the author wants to communicate. The main point is related to the writer's *purpose*, which can be to explain, to demonstrate, to persuade, or to entertain, and to his or her intended *audience*, which can range from specific (say, a particular person) to general (any reader of a periodical). Use these hints to help you identify the writer's main point.

- *Don't confuse the topic and the main idea.* The main idea tells you what the writer says about the topic. To make sure you have identified the main idea and not just the topic, complete this sentence:
  - The writer is saying that _____

- *A main point is often the answer to the guiding question you created when previewing the reading.*

- *A reading has only one main point.* Make sure you identify the main idea of the entire reading, not a supporting detail. (Don't focus on only one or two paragraphs; look at the entire text.)

- *A main point or thesis may be stated in a single sentence that you can find in the reading.* We call this the stated main idea. When the main point is stated directly, you can double-underline it.

- *A main point or thesis may not be stated directly.* If a writer chooses not to state the main idea directly, we say that the main idea is *implied*. If there is an implied main idea, write the main point in your own words, using either the margins of the text or your notebook.

Support

Support is the evidence that shows, explains, or proves the main point. The author might use statistics, facts, definitions, and scientific results for support, or he or she might use memories, stories, comparisons, quotations from experts, and personal observations.

Not all support is good support. When you are reading, ask yourself: What information is the author including to help me understand or agree with the main point? Is the support (evidence) valid and convincing? If not, why not?

Here's an example of a well-constructed paragraph. The main point is double-underlined, and the support is underlined.

Making a plan for your college studies is a good way to reach your academic goals. The first step to planning is answering this question: "What do I want to be?" If you have only a general idea—for example, "I would like to work in the health-care

→

field"—break this large area into smaller, more specific subfields. These subfields might include working as a registered nurse, a nurse practitioner, or a physical therapist. <u>The second step to planning is to meet with an academic adviser to talk about the classes you will need to take to get a degree or certificate in your chosen field.</u> <u>Then, map out the courses you will be taking over the next couple of semesters.</u> Throughout the whole process, bear in mind the words of student mentor Ed Powell: "Those who fail to plan, plan to fail." A good plan boosts your chances of success in college and beyond.

PRACTICE 1–2   Find the Main Point and Support

Read the following paragraph. Double-underline the main point and underline the support.

Networking is a way businesspeople build connections with others to get ahead. Building connections in college also is well worth the effort. One way to build connections is to get to know some of your classmates and to exchange names, phone numbers, and email addresses with them. That way, if you cannot make it to a class, you will know someone who can tell you what you missed. You can also form study groups with these other students. Another way to build connections is to get to know your instructor. Make an appointment to visit your instructor during his or her office hours. When you go, ask questions about material you are not sure you understood in class or problems you have with other course material. You and your instructor will get the most out of these sessions if you bring examples of specific assignments that you are having trouble with.

2PR   Pause to Think

Active readers also take time to pause and think during the reading process. If you race through a reading without stopping to consider what you are reading, you may not fully understand the author's point, mistaking a minor detail for the main idea or misunderstanding the author's purpose.

Stop regularly as you read, and if needed, reread a sentence or paragraph. When you pause, do the following:

- Double-underline the <u>main idea</u> or write it in the margin.
- Note the <u>major support points</u> by underlining them.
- Note ideas that you agree with by placing a check mark next to them (✓).
- Note ideas that you do not agree with or that surprise you with an X or !.
- Note ideas you do not understand with a question mark (?).
- Note any examples of an author's or expert's assumptions or biases.
- Jot any additional notes or questions in the margin.
- Consider how parts of the reading relate to the main point.
- Make a note of new vocabulary words and definitions, if needed.

2PR   Review and Respond

After reading, take a few minutes to look back and review. First, make sure you can identify the main point and major supporting details of the piece.

For more on writing critically about readings, see pages 13–19.

Paraphrase

To make sure you understand the writer's point, paraphrase it. **Paraphrasing** means restating an idea using different language. When you have read carefully and critically, you can paraphrase what an author says, using your own words and style, to explain the writer's meaning for yourself and for others. Here are three tips to help you effectively paraphrase key points from your reading.

TIPS FOR EFFECTIVE PARAPHRASING

Tip 1: Do not copy the main idea (thesis) or major supporting details (topic sentences) when you take notes.

Tip 2: Think about what the writer says for each point, cover the source, and imagine you are explaining that point to one of your friends. Here is one way to begin your paraphrase: "In other words, the writer is saying that . . ." Write your explanation without looking back at the original.

Tip 3: Avoid cut-and-paste paraphrases. A cut-and-paste paraphrase copies the original and then just changes one or two words. For example, here is a point from Amanda's essay (p. 11 in this chapter) followed by a cut-and-paste paraphrase. The parts that are the same are highlighted.

Original

"Ideally, given the ban on selling water bottles, every student on campus should now take the initiative to carry a water bottle, filling it up throughout the day at the water fountains on campus. Realistically, we know this has not and will not happen."

Cut-and-paste paraphrase

Amanda says that given the ban on selling water bottles, it would be great if every student at the college took the initiative to carry their own water bottle, filling it up as needed during the day at the water fountains on campus. But she knows that realistically this is not going to happen.

Do you see how close the sentence structure and language are to the original? As a result, the cut-and-paste paraphrase is not acceptable. Now compare this to an appropriate paraphrase:

Appropriate paraphrase

In her essay "A Ban on Water Bottles: A Way to Bolster the University's Image," Amanda Jacobowitz explains that even though her college has decided not to sell water bottles on campus, most college students are not going to respond by purchasing their own water bottles to use during the day instead.

While some of the individual words are the same in this paraphrase, the student taking these notes has not borrowed Amanda Jacobowitz's structure or longer strings of words.

Once you have identified the writer's main point, go over your guiding question, your marginal notes, and your questions—and connect with what you have read. Consider, "What interested me? What did I learn? How does it fit with what I know from other sources?" When you have reviewed your reading in this way and fixed it well in your mind and memory, it is much easier to respond in class discussion and writing, because to write about a reading, you need to generate and organize your ideas, draft and revise your response, and above all, use your critical thinking skills.

A Critical Reader at Work

Read the following piece. The notes in the margin show how one student applied the process of critical reading to an essay on bottled water.

Amanda Jacobowitz

A Ban on Water Bottles: A Way to Bolster the University's Image

Amanda Jacobowitz is a student at Washington University and a columnist for the university's publication *Student Life,* in which the following essay appeared.

1   Lately, I am always thirsty. Always! I could not figure out why until I realized that the bottled water I had purchased continuously throughout my day had disappeared. At first I was just confused. Where did all the water bottles go? Then I learned the simple explanation: The University banned water bottles in an effort to be environmentally friendly.

Guiding Question: What does the author think about the ban on bottled water?

Larger main point (not stated directly): (1) the ban is ineffective, and (2) there are better ways to protect the environment.

2   Ideally, given the ban on selling water bottles, every student on campus should now take the initiative to carry a water bottle, filling it up throughout the day at the water fountains on campus. Realistically, we know this has not and will not happen. I have tried to bring a water bottle with me to classes—I do consider myself somewhat environmentally conscious—but have rarely succeeded in this effort. Instead, although I have never been too much of a soda drinker, I find myself reaching for a bottle of Coke out of pure convenience. We can't buy bottled water, but we can buy soda, juice, and other drinks, many of which come in plastic bottles. I am sure that for most people—particularly those who give very little thought to being environmentally conscientious—convenience prevails and they purchase a drink other than water. Wonderful result. The University can pride itself on being more environmentally friendly, with the fallback that its students will be less healthy!

Why not just drink from a water fountain? You don't have to have a bottle.

Examples of other drinks available in plastic bottles.

3   Even if students are not buying unhealthy drinks, any benefit from the reduction of plastic water bottles could easily be offset by its alternatives. Students are not using their hands to drink water during meals. They are using plastic cups — cups provided by the University at every eatery on campus. Presumably no person picks up a cup, drinks their glass of water, and then saves that same cup for later in the day. That being said, how many plastic cups are used by a single student, in a single day? How many cups are used by the total campus-wide population daily, yearly? This plastic cup use must equate to an exorbitant amount of waste as well.

Example of another common source of waste.

4   My intent is not to have the University completely roll back the water bottle ban, nor is my intent for the University to level the playing field by banning all plastic drink bottles. I'm simply questioning the reasons for specifically banning bottled water of all things? Why not start with soda bottles — decreasing the environmental impact, as well as the health risks. There are also many other ways to help the environment that seem to be so easily overlooked.

Example of another way to cut down on use of plastic bottles

5   Have you ever noticed a patch of grass on campus that's not perfectly green? I can't say that I have. The reason: the sprinklers. Now, I admit that I harbor some animosity when it comes to the campus sprinklers; I somehow always manage to mistakenly and inadvertently walk right in their path, the spray of water generously dousing my feet. However, my real problem with the sprinklers is the waste of water they represent. Do we really need our grass to be green at all times?

Another example of waste

6   The landscaping around our beloved Danforth University Center (Gold LEED Certified) is irrigated with the use of rainwater. There is a 50,000-gallon rainwater tank below the building to collect rain! I admit, this is pretty impressive, but what about the rest of the campus? What water is used to irrigate and keep green the rest of our 169 acres on the Danforth campus?

Town/city water, I assume.

7   I understand that being environmentally conscious is difficult to do, particularly at an institutional level. I applaud the Danforth University

Center and other environmental efforts the University has initiated. However, I can't help but wonder if the University's ban on the sale of water bottles is more about appearance and less about decreasing the environmental impact of our student body. The water bottle ban has become a way to build the school's public image: we banned water bottles, we are working hard to be environmentally friendly! In reality, given the switch to plastic cups and the switch to other drinks sold in plastic bottles, is the environmental impact of the ban that significant? Now that the ban has been implemented, I certainly don't see the University retracting it. However, I hope that in the future the University focuses less on its public image and more on the environment itself when instituting such dramatic changes.

Is it really about public image? What would a university administrator say?

PRACTICE 1-3   Make Connections

Look back at the advertisement on page 3 and the bottled water labels on page 4. Then, review the reading by Amanda Jacobowitz. What assumptions does Jacobowitz make about bottled water? What evidence, if any, is provided to support these assumptions? Based on your observations, would you like to see bottled water not banned or banned at your college? Why or why not?

Writing Critically about Readings

There are different types of writing in college. In Chapters 2 through 4, we examine the writing process in general and learn how to draft and revise paragraphs and essays. In Chapters 5 through 13, we explore the different techniques for developing an essay, such as narration and illustration.

In this section, we discuss the key college skill of writing critically about what you read. In any college course, your instructor may ask you to summarize, analyze, synthesize, or evaluate one or more readings to demonstrate your deep understanding of the material. When you do so, you answer the following questions.

Writing Critically

Summarize

- What is important about the text?
- What is the purpose, the big picture? Who is the intended audience?
- What are the main points and key support?

Analyze

- What elements have been used to convey the main point?
- Do any elements raise questions? Do any key points seem missing or undeveloped?

Synthesize

- What do other sources say about the topic of the text?
- How does your own (or others') experience affect how you see the topic?
- What new point(s) might you make by bringing together all the different sources and experiences?

Evaluate

- Based on your application of summary, analysis, and synthesis, what do you think about the material you have read?
- Is the work successful? Does it achieve its purpose?
- Does the author show any biases? Are there any hidden assumptions? If so, do they make the piece more or less effective?

Summary

A **summary** is a condensed or shortened version of something—often, a longer piece of writing, a movie or play, a situation, or an event. A summary paragraph presents the main idea, support, and organizational pattern of a longer piece of writing (or text), stripping the information down to its essential elements. A summary is a logical final step in the reading process: it expresses what you have learned about the important features of a text, in your own words.

A summary has these features:

- a topic sentence that states the title of the selection, the author, and the main idea
- the major supporting details
- references to the author with descriptive verbs which describe what the writer says and does in the text

- the author's final observations or recommendations
- original language (paraphrases)

Descriptive Verbs for a Summary	
Verbs followed by a complete idea (to introduce what the writer says)	**Verbs followed by a noun or nouns (to introduce what the writer does, or the strategies the writer uses)**
argues (that) denies (that) asks (that) explains (that) asserts (that) implies (that) claims (that) points out (that) demands (that) suggests (that)	analyzes evaluates classifies exemplifies compares expresses contrasts illustrates defines synthesizes describes

The following paragraph is a summary of "Don't Work in a Goat's Stomach" by Frances Cole Jones (p. 120). The main point of the essay is double-underlined, and the descriptive verbs used to introduce supporting ideas are underlined once.

In her essay, "Don't Work in a Goat's Stomach," Frances Cole Jones classifies items that may clutter our work environments, and she suggests that readers should clean out the clutter on a regular basis. Jones describes the office of a former colleague, whose workspace was so cluttered that the boss compared it to a goat's stomach. Jones then presents three categories of clutter as defined by psychologist Sam Gosling: items that show our identity, items which help us manage stress, and items leftover from our daily routines. Jones doesn't advocate getting rid of everything in our offices, but she divides these office items into two groups: those that should be removed immediately—including food, trash, dead plants, and toys—and those that should be managed carefully—including grooming tools, extra clothes, and photos. Jones concludes that a regular cleaning-out routine will keep the clutter at bay.

A summary is a useful way to record information from a reading in a course notebook. You can put the main points of an article into your own words for later review. You may also be asked to provide summaries in homework assignments or on tests in order to show that you read and understood a reading. In addition, summary is an important tool for keeping track of information for a research project.

Analysis

An **analysis** breaks down the points or parts of something and considers how they work together to make an impression or convey a main point. When writing an analysis, you might also consider points or parts that seem to be missing or that raise questions in your mind. Your analysis of a reading provides the main points as well as your own reaction to the piece.

Here is an analysis of the excerpt from the essay by Francis Cole Jones (pp. 120–122).

> Jones addresses the line between a comfortable workspace and consideration for other employees, including the boss. She presents a specific example: a colleague whose messy office was noticed by the boss and who ultimately lost his job. She also quotes an expert, Sam Gosling, who connects the clutter to three areas of life: identity, mood management, and leftovers from ordinary activities. She emphasizes that the problem is what the clutter communicates to those around us, and she gives a bulleted list of items to be removed immediately, as well as those that can remain after some careful thought.
>
> I understand what she is saying, but I wonder if demanding organization and neatness could interfere with creativity, especially in a tech company or new business. Do some people work better when surrounded by clutter? If so, should we really ask them to change?

In any college course, your instructor may ask you to write an analysis to show your critical thinking skills and your ability to respond to a reading.

Synthesis

A **synthesis** pulls together information from additional sources or experiences to make a new point. Here is a synthesis of the essay by Francis Cole Jones (pp. 120–122). Because the writer wanted to address some of the questions she raised in her analysis, she incorporated additional details from published sources and from people she interviewed. Her synthesis of this information helped her arrive at a fresh conclusion.

In her essay, "Don't Work in a Goat's Stomach," Frances Cole Jones classifies items that may clutter our work environments, and she suggests that readers should clean out the clutter on a regular basis. Jones then presents three categories of clutter as defined by psychologist Sam Gosling: items that show our identity, items which help us manage stress, and items leftover from our daily routines. Jones divides these office items into two groups: those that should be removed immediately—including food, trash, dead plants, and toys—and those that should be managed carefully—including grooming tools, extra clothes, and photos. Jones concludes that a regular cleaning-out routine will keep the clutter at bay. But are there situations where it might be better not to straighten up the mess?

First source

While Jones suggests that the messy workspace sends the wrong message to other employees'. Researcher Kathleen Vohs says that there may be some benefits to a messy desk. She and her colleagues conducted a series of studies to examine how a disorganized environment will affect those in it. In her first study, she found that people in an organized environment behave better; they also focus on the status quo. But those in a messy environment were more creative and more innovative. So while the clean office may send a clear message, as Jones suggests, it may also limit creativity.

Second source

The research that Vohs conducted was in a lab. What about the real world? Andrew Tate, who is a neuroscientist and writer, has looked at innovative people and their workspaces, including Albert Einstein, Mark Zuckerberg, and Steve Jobs. He has evidence from photos that these inventors worked at desks piled with papers and books, in offices where the furniture seems to have been swallowed by the papers, prototypes, and many other items.

Third source

I talked to a couple of friends about this issue. Callie, who is a junior at Tech, agrees with Vohs and Tate. She says she does her best work when she is surrounded by a mess. "There's all this stuff in front of me," she notes, "so I have all the raw materials to make something work. When I am writing a paper, all I have to do is turn my head, and I will find inspiration from something I see." Obviously, for a student like Callie, a cluttered workspace is a benefit.

Fourth source

Fifth source

But for Davis Matthews, an assistant manager in my father's insurance office, clutter actually interferes with his work. Davis says that he is easily distracted by photos or stacks of paper on others' desks. He begins to wonder about the people involved, and he finds it hard to stay focused on his own tasks. Smells, in particular, are a problem. If a colleague has left an empty pizza box in the office over the weekend, he finds it hard to concentrate when he begins work on Monday morning. "A clean desk," Davis says, "is like clean slate. It is inviting me to get something done."

Fresh conclusion

Looking at Jones's advice, the published research, and the experiences of Callie and David, I can conclude that the right balance of clutter and neatness varies according to the individual, the job, and the office environment. There is no "right way" to deal with office clutter. Instead, we need to look at what we are trying to accomplish and who else is working nearby. With a little thought and some consideration for those around us, we should be able to find a sweet spot for productive work for everyone involved.

Works Cited

Jones, Frances Cole. "Don't Work in a Goat's Stomach." *Real Writing Essentials*, Miriam Moore and Susan Anker, Bedford/St. Martin's, 2017, pp. 120–122.

Tate, Andrew. "5 Reasons Creative Geniuses Like Einstein, Twain and Zuckerberg Had Messy Desks – And Why You Should Too." *Creativity from Chaos*, Canva, 29 May 2015, https://designschool .canva.com/blog/creative-desks/.

Vohs, Kathleen. "It's Not 'Mess.' It's Creativity." *The New York Times*, 13 Sept. 2013, http://www.nytimes.com/2013/09/15/opinion/sunday/ its-not-mess-its-creativity.html.

Synthesizing is important for longer writing assignments and research papers, in which you need to make connections among different works. Many courses that involve writing, such as history and psychology, require papers that synthesize information from more than one source.

Evaluation

An **evaluation** is your *thoughtful* judgment about something based on what you have discovered through your summary, analysis, and synthesis. To evaluate something effectively, apply the questions from the Writing Critically box on page 14. Here is an evaluation of the essay by Francis Cole Jones on pages 120–122.

> In her essay, "Don't Work in a Goat's Stomach," Frances Cole Jones classifies items that may clutter our work environments, and she suggests that readers should clean out the clutter on a regular basis. Jones divides these office items into two groups: those that should be removed immediately—including food, trash, dead plants, and toys—and those that should be managed carefully—including grooming tools, extra clothes, and photos. She concludes that a regular cleaning-out routine will keep the clutter at bay. Jones's use of examples and expert opinions give her recommendations a lot of weight. However, her advice does not cover all workplaces and purposes. Additional research by Kathleen Vohs and Michael Tate suggests that there are times when some clutter or mess might actually be beneficial. While I am not sure that Jones's conclusions apply to all offices equally, she makes a strong case for cleaning up from time to time; if nothing else, we need to consider what message our office space sends to those who are working around us.

When you do college-level work, you must be able to evaluate the readings and other sources you encounter. Instructors may ask you to write evaluations in order to demonstrate your ability to question and judge sources.

PRACTICE 1-4   Make Connections

As you work through this exercise, refer to the Writing Critically box on page 14 and to your responses to Practice 3 (if you completed it).

1. **SUMMARY:** Summarize Amanda Jacobowitz's essay on pages 11–13.

2. **ANALYSIS:** Write a paragraph analyzing the points Jacobowitz presents.

3. **SYNTHESIS:** Read additional opinion pieces or blog postings on bottled water. In one paragraph, state your position on the subject according to your reading of these materials. Also, explain the range of opinions on the subject.

4. **EVALUATION:** Write a paragraph that evaluates Jacobowitz's essay.

2
Getting Ready to Write

Purpose, Form, and Process

Four elements are key to good writing. Keep them in mind whenever you write.

Four Basics of Good Writing

1 It reflects the writer's purpose and the needs, knowledge, and expectations of its intended audience.

2 It results from a thoughtful writing process.

3 It includes a clear, definite point.

4 It provides support that shows, explains, or proves the main point.

This chapter discusses the first two basics in more detail. It also shows you how to start the process by choosing something to write about. Chapter 3 explains the last two basics, while Chapter 4 focuses on finishing the process by revising and editing.

First Basic: Audience and Purpose

Your **audience** is the person or people who will read what you write. In college, your audience is usually your instructors. Whenever you write, always have at least one real person in mind as a reader. Think about what that person already knows and what he or she will need to know to understand your main point.

Your **purpose** is your reason for writing. Let's take a look at some different audiences and purposes.

Audience and Purpose

TYPE OF WRITING	AUDIENCE AND PURPOSE	TIPS
COLLEGE: A research essay about the environmental effects of "fracking": fracturing rock layers to extract oil or natural gas	**AUDIENCE:** The professor of your environmental science class **PURPOSE:** • To complete an assignment according to instructions • To show what you have learned about the topic	When writing to fulfill an assignment, never assume "My instructor already knows this fact, so what's the point of mentioning it?" By providing relevant examples and details, you demonstrate *your* knowledge of a subject.
WORK: An email to coworkers about your company's new insurance provider	**AUDIENCE:** Fellow workers **PURPOSE:** To make sure that coworkers understand all the important details about the new provider	Define or explain any terminology or concepts that will not be familiar to your audience.
EVERYDAY LIFE: An electronic comment about an online newspaper editorial that you disagree with	**AUDIENCE:** • The editorial writer • Other readers of the editorial **PURPOSE:** To make the editorial writer and other readers aware of your views	Keep all correspondence with others as polite as possible, even if you disagree with their views.

The tone and content of your writing will vary depending on your audience and purpose. In some cases, such as text messages or emails with friends, it makes sense to use informal English. However, in college, at work, and in your everyday life, when you are speaking or writing to someone in authority for a serious purpose, use formal English: people will take you seriously.

. . . .

PRACTICE 2-1   Writing for a Formal Audience

A student, Terri Travers, sent the following text message to a friend to complain about not getting into a criminal justice course. Rewrite the text as if you were Terri and you were writing an email to Professor Wexner. The purpose is to ask whether the professor would consider allowing you into the class given that you signed up early and have the necessary grades.

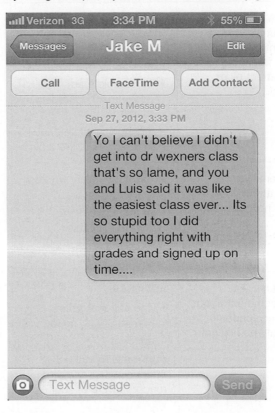

Paragraph and Essay Form

Your audience and purpose will also determine the form of your writing. In this course (and in the rest of college), you will write paragraphs and essays, each of which is a form of writing expected by instructors and academic audiences. Your professors will look for basic paragraph and essay structure in your writing.

Paragraph Form

A **paragraph** has three basic parts: a topic sentence, a body, and a concluding sentence.

PARAGRAPH PART	PURPOSE OF THE PARAGRAPH PART
1. The **topic sentence**	states the **main point**. The topic sentence is often the first sentence of the paragraph.
2. The **body**	supports (shows, explains, or proves) the main point with **support sentences** that contain facts and details.
3. The **concluding sentence**	reminds readers of the main point and often makes an observation.

Essay Form

An **essay** is a piece of writing that examines a topic in more depth than a paragraph. A short essay may have four or five paragraphs, totaling three hundred to six hundred words. A long essay may be many pages long, depending on the essay's purpose, such as persuading someone to do something, using research to make a point, or explaining a complex concept.

An essay has three necessary parts: an introduction, a body, and a conclusion.

ESSAY PART	PURPOSE OF THE ESSAY PART
1. The **introduction**	states the **main point**, or **thesis**, generally in a single, strong statement. The introduction may be a single paragraph or multiple paragraphs.
2. The **body**	supports (shows, explains, or proves) the main point. It generally has at least three **support paragraphs**, each containing facts and details that develop the main point. Each support paragraph has a **topic sentence** that supports the thesis statement.
3. The **conclusion**	reminds readers of the main point and makes an observation. Often, it also summarizes and reinforces the support.

The following diagram shows how the parts of an essay correspond to the parts of a paragraph.

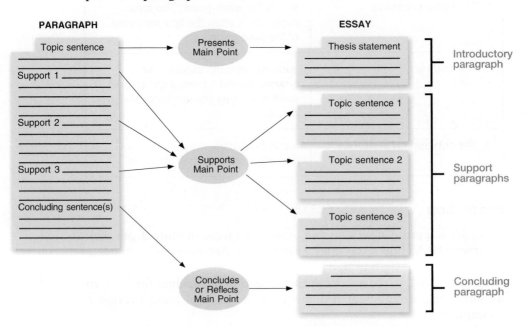

Second Basic: The Writing Process

Paragraphs and essays do not appear polished and ready for a reader all at once. Good academic writing is the result of a thoughtful process that includes four stages, illustrated in the chart that follows. Keep in mind that you may not always go in a straight line through the four stages; instead, you might circle back to earlier steps to further improve your writing.

THE WRITING PROCESS

Generate ideas

CONSIDER: What is my purpose in writing? Given this purpose, what interests me? Who will read this paper? What do they need to know?

- Determine your audience and purpose (pages 20–22).

- Find and explore your topic (pages 25–32).

- Make your point (pages 33–39).

- Support your point (pages 40–44).

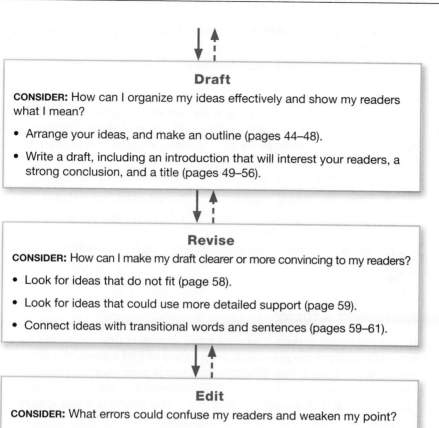

Draft

CONSIDER: How can I organize my ideas effectively and show my readers what I mean?

- Arrange your ideas, and make an outline (pages 44–48).

- Write a draft, including an introduction that will interest your readers, a strong conclusion, and a title (pages 49–56).

Revise

CONSIDER: How can I make my draft clearer or more convincing to my readers?

- Look for ideas that do not fit (page 58).

- Look for ideas that could use more detailed support (page 59).

- Connect ideas with transitional words and sentences (pages 59–61).

Edit

CONSIDER: What errors could confuse my readers and weaken my point?

- Find and correct the most serious errors in grammar (Chapter 16).

- Look for other errors in style and grammar (Chapter 17).

- Check your punctuation and capitalization (Chapter 18).

Finding, Narrowing, and Exploring Your Topic

The first step in the writing process is to identify an appropriate topic. A **topic** is who or what you are writing about. It is the subject of your paragraph or essay. Sometimes, your instructor will give you a topic or require you to write about reading. At other times, you will need to choose a topic (or select a topic from a list of approved choices). If you are allowed to choose, your topic should fit the requirements of the assignment.

QUESTIONS FOR FINDING A GOOD TOPIC

- Does this topic interest me? If so, why do I care about it?

- Do I know something about the topic? Do I want to know more?

■   Can I get involved with some part of the topic? Is it relevant to my life in some way?

■   Is the topic specific enough for the assignment (a paragraph or a short essay)?

Choose one of the following topics or one of your own and focus on one part of it that you are familiar with. (For example, focus on one personal goal or a specific problem of working students that interests you.)

Health or fitness concern	Financing education
Problems of working students	An essential survival skill
Privacy and technology	Urban or rural culture

Use the general topic you have chosen to complete the practice exercises on pages 28 and 32.

Narrowing a Topic

If your instructor assigns a general topic, it may at first seem uninteresting, unfamiliar, or too general. It is up to you to find a good, specific topic based on the general one. Whether the topic is your own or assigned, you next need to narrow and explore it. To **narrow** a general topic, focus on the smaller parts of it until you find one that is interesting and specific.

Here are some ways to narrow a general topic.

Divide It into Smaller Categories

One way to narrow a general topic is to consider specific categories or groups that make up the topic. Ask yourself this question: What are the different types of _____? For example, if your instructor has asked you to write about a personal goal, you might ask this: What are the different types of personal goals? Possible answers might include health goals, education goals, or career goals.

General Topic: A personal goal

Health Goals:	*Education Goals:* Get	*Career Goals:*
Lose weight, lower	a degree, keep a B	Make more money,
cholesterol	average in my major	get a job with flexible
		hours

Think of Specific Examples from Your Life

You can also narrow a topic by thinking of specific examples from your own life. Ask yourself how you have experienced the topic and what questions you have about the topic.

General Topic: Social media

- Snapchat and Instagram (Have they improved communication among my friends and family members?)
- Online dating — how it has worked for my friends (What are the dangers?)
- Google+ (is it just another Facebook, or is it truly different?)

Think of Specific Examples from Current Events

Another way to narrow a topic is by finding examples from current events. You might ask yourself this question: What have I seen or read about this topic recently?

General Topic: Heroism

The guy who pulled a stranger from a burning car
The people who stopped a robbery downtown

Question Your Assumptions

Questioning assumptions—an important part of critical thinking (see Chapter 1)—can be a good way to narrow a topic. First, identify any assumptions you have about your topic. Then, question them, playing "devil's advocate"; in other words, imagine what someone with a different point of view might say.

GENERAL TOPIC: Video Games

TOPIC	POSSIBLE ASSUMPTIONS	QUESTIONS
Video Game Pros	Kids get rewarded with good scores for staying focused	Does staying focused on a video game mean that a kid will stay focused on homework or in class?
	Video games can teach some useful skills.	Like what? How am I defining "useful"?

(continued)

TOPIC	POSSIBLE ASSUMPTIONS	QUESTIONS
Video Game Cons	They make kids more violent.	Is there really any proof for that? What do experts say?
	They have no real educational value.	Didn't my niece say that some video game helped her learn to read?

Next, ask yourself what assumptions and questions interest you the most. Then, focus on those interests.

When you have found a promising topic for a paragraph or essay, be sure to test it by using the Questions for Finding a Good Topic on page 25. You may need to narrow and test your ideas several times before you find a topic that will work for the assignment.

A topic for an essay can be a little broader than one for a paragraph because essays are longer than paragraphs and allow you to develop more ideas. But be careful: most of the extra length in an essay should come from developing ideas in more depth (giving more examples and details, explaining what you mean), not from covering a broader topic.

Read the following examples of how a general topic was narrowed to a more specific topic for an essay and an even more specific topic for a paragraph.

GENERAL TOPIC		NARROWED ESSAY TOPIC		NARROWED PARAGRAPH TOPIC
Internships	→	How internships can help you get a job	→	One or two important things you can learn from an internship
Public service opportunities	→	Volunteering at a homeless shelter	→	My first impression of the homeless shelter

PRACTICE 2-2   Narrowing a General Topic

Use one of the four methods above to narrow your topic. Then, ask yourself the Questions for Finding a Good Topic (from page 25).

Exploring Your Topic

Invention strategies (sometimes called **prewriting techniques**) can give you ideas at any time during the writing process: they help you identify what you know about the topic, what interests you about the topic, and what you want to say about the topic. They can help you to discover if you want to learn more through research and reading, and they can aid you in narrowing a general topic down into a specific one that you want to write about. No one uses all of these techniques; writers choose the ones that work best for them.

INVENTION STRATEGIES

- Freewriting
- Listing/brainstorming
- Discussing

- Clustering/mapping
- Using the internet
- Keeping a journal

When prewriting, your goal is to come up with as many ideas as possible. Do not say, "Oh, that's stupid" or "That won't work." Just get your brain working by writing down all the possibilities.

Freewriting

Freewriting is like having a conversation with yourself, on paper. To freewrite, just start writing everything you can think of about your topic. Write nonstop for five minutes. Do not go back and cross anything out, and do not worry about using correct grammar or spelling; just write. Here is a student's freewriting on the topic of getting a college degree:

So I know I want to get a college degree even though sometimes I wonder if I ever can make it because it's so hard with work and my two-year-old daughter and no money and a car that needs work. I can't take more than two courses at a time and even then I hardly get a chance to sleep if I want to do any of the assignments or study. But I have to think I'll get a better job because this one at the restaurant is driving me nuts and doesn't pay much so I have to work a lot with a boss I can't stand and still wonder how I'm gonna pay the bills. I know life can be better if I can just manage to become a nurse. I'll make more money and can live anywhere I want because everyplace needs nurses. I won't have to work at a job where I am not respected by anyone. I want respect, I know I'm hardworking and smart and good with people and deserve better than this. So does my daughter. No one in my family has ever graduated from college even though my sister took two courses, but then she stopped. I know I can do this, I just have to make a commitment to do it and not look away.

Listing / Brainstorming

List all the ideas about your topic that you can think of. Write as many as you can in five minutes without stopping.

GETTING A COLLEGE DEGREE

want a better life for myself and my daughter

want to be a nurse and help care for people

make more money

not have to work so many hours

could live where I want in a nicer place

good future and benefits like health insurance

get respect

proud of myself, achieve, show everyone

be a professional, work in a clean place

Discussing

Many people find it helpful to discuss ideas with another person before they write. As they talk, they get more ideas and immediate feedback.

If you and your discussion partner both have writing assignments, first explore one person's topic and then explore the other's. The person whose topic is being explored is the interviewee; the other person is the interviewer. The interviewer should ask questions about anything that seems unclear and let the interviewee know what sounds interesting. In addition, the interviewer should identify and try to question any assumptions the interviewee seems to be making (see page 27). The interviewee should give thoughtful answers and keep an open mind. He or she should also take notes.

Clustering / Mapping

Clustering, also called mapping, is like listing except that you arrange your ideas visually. Start by writing your narrowed topic in the center. Then, write the questions "Why?" "What interests me?" and "What do I want to say?" around the narrowed topic. Write at least three answers to each question. Keep branching out from the ideas until you feel you have fully explored your topic.

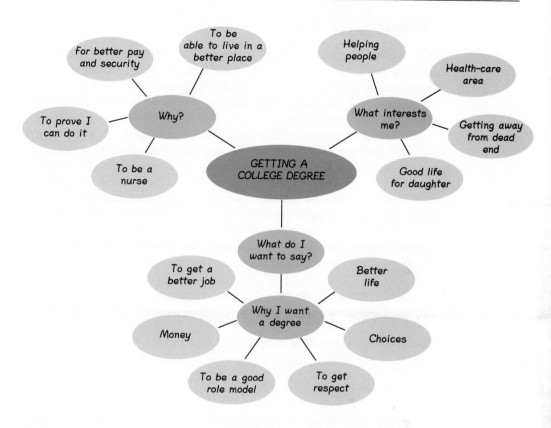

Keeping a Journal

Setting aside a few minutes on a regular schedule to write in a journal will give you a great source of ideas when you need them. What you write does not need to be long or formal. You can use a journal in several ways:

- to record and explore your personal thoughts and feelings;
- to comment on things that happen, to you personally or in politics, in your neighborhood, at work, in college, and so on;
- and to explore situations you do not understand (as you write, you may figure them out).

Research Your Topic Further

For some assignments, you may need to do some research, either on the internet or in your library. For more information on research, see Chapter 14. If you do choose to do some basic research, be sure to take careful notes so that you can document where you found the information and avoid plagiarism.

Avoid Plagiarism

In all the writing you do, it is important to avoid plagiarism—using other people's words or information as your own. Your instructors are aware of plagiarism and know how to look for it. Writers who plagiarize, either on purpose or by accident, risk failing a course or losing their jobs and damaging their reputations.

To avoid accidental plagiarism, take careful notes on every source (books, interviews, television shows, websites, and so on) you might use in your writing. When recording information from sources, take notes in your own words, unless you plan to use direct quotations. In that case, make sure to record the quotation word for word. Also, include quotation marks around it, both in your notes and in your paper. When you use material from other sources—whether you directly quote or put information in your own words (paraphrase or summary)—you must name and give citation information about these sources.

· ·

PRACTICE 2–3   Exploring Your Narrowed Topic

Use two or three prewriting techniques to explore your narrowed topic.

· ·

· ·

PRACTICE 2–4   Writing Assignment

Review your narrowed topic (recorded in Practice 2–2) and ideas from your prewriting. Use the checklist that follows to make sure your topic and ideas about it are clear. If necessary, spend some more time clarifying your topic or generating ideas before moving on to Chapter 3.

· ·

CHECKLIST: Evaluating Your Narrowed Topic

☐   This topic interests me.

☐   My narrowed topic is specific.

☐   I can write about it in a paragraph or an essay (whichever you have been assigned).

☐   I have generated some things to say about this topic.

3

Organizing Your Main Point and Support

Once you have settled on a topic to write about (see Chapter 2), you need to determine what your main point will be and how you will support that point.

Third Basic: Topic Sentences and Thesis Statements

Every good piece of writing has a **main point**—what the writer wants to get across to readers about the topic or the writer's position on that topic. A **topic sentence** (for a paragraph) and a **thesis statement** (for an essay) express the writer's main point. To see the relationship between the thesis statement of an essay and the topic sentences of paragraphs that support a thesis statement, see the diagram on page 24.

In many paragraphs, the main point is expressed in either the first or last sentence. In essays, the thesis statement is usually one sentence (often the first or last) in an introductory paragraph that contains several other sentences related to the main point.

One way to write a topic sentence for a paragraph or a thesis statement for an essay is to use this basic formula as a start:

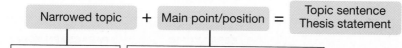

The tutoring center has helped me improve my writing.

A good topic sentence or thesis statement has several basic features.

BASICS OF A GOOD TOPIC SENTENCE OR THESIS STATEMENT

- It fits the size of the assignment.
- It states a single main point or position about a topic.
- It is specific.
- It is something you can show, explain, or prove.

The explanations and practices in the following four sections, organized according to the "basics" described above, will help you write good topic sentences and thesis statements.

Consider the Size of the Assignment

As you develop a topic sentence or thesis statement, think carefully about the length of the assignment.

Sometimes, a main-point statement can be the same for a paragraph or essay.

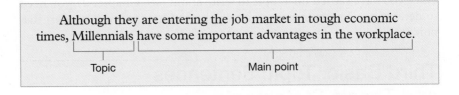

Although they are entering the job market in tough economic times, Millennials have some important advantages in the workplace.

Topic   Main point

If the writer had been assigned a paragraph, she might follow the main point with support sentences and a concluding sentence like those in the "paragraph" diagram on page 24. If the writer had been assigned an essay, she might develop the same support, but instead of writing single sentences to support her main idea, she would develop each support point into a paragraph. The support sentences she wrote in a paragraph might be topic sentences for support paragraphs. (For more on providing support, see pages 40–44.)

Often, however, a topic sentence for a paragraph is much narrower than a thesis statement for an essay, simply because a paragraph is shorter and allows less development of ideas.

Consider how one general topic could be narrowed into an essay topic and into an even more specific paragraph topic.

GENERAL TOPIC	NARROWED ESSAY TOPIC	NARROWED PARAGRAPH TOPIC
Internships →	How internships can help you get a job →	One or two important things you can learn from an internship
POSSIBLE THESIS STATEMENT (ESSAY)	The skills and connections you gain through a summer internship can help you get a good job after graduation.	
POSSIBLE TOPIC SENTENCE (PARAGRAPH)	A summer internship is a good way to test whether a particular career is right for you.	

PRACTICE 3-1 Writing Sentences to Fit the Assignment

For each of the topics below, write a thesis statement for the narrowed essay topic and a topic sentence for the narrowed paragraph topic.

EXAMPLE

GENERAL TOPIC: Sports

NARROWED TOPIC FOR AN ESSAY: Competition in school sports

POSSIBLE THESIS STATEMENT: Competition in school sports has reached dangerous levels.

NARROWED TOPIC FOR A PARAGRAPH: User fees for school sports

POSSIBLE TOPIC SENTENCE: This year's user fees for participation in school sports are too high.

1. **GENERAL TOPIC:** Public service opportunities

   NARROWED FOR AN ESSAY: Volunteering at a homeless shelter

   NARROWED FOR A PARAGRAPH: My first impression of the homeless shelter

2. **GENERAL TOPIC:** A personal goal

   NARROWED FOR AN ESSAY: Getting healthy

   NARROWED FOR A PARAGRAPH: Eating the right foods

3. **GENERAL TOPIC:** A great vacation

   NARROWED FOR AN ESSAY: A family camping trip

   NARROWED FOR A PARAGRAPH: A lesson I learned on our family camping trip

Some topic sentences or thesis statements are too broad for either a short essay or a paragraph. A main idea that is too broad is impossible to show, explain, or prove within the space of a paragraph or short essay.

TOO BROAD	Art is important.
	[How could a writer possibly support such a broad concept in a paragraph or essay?]
NARROWER	Art instruction for young children has surprising benefits.

A topic sentence or thesis statement that is too narrow leaves the writer with little to write about. There is little to show, explain, or prove.

TOO NARROW	Buy rechargeable batteries. *[OK, so now what?]*
BROADER	Choosing rechargeable batteries over conventional batteries is one action you can take to reduce your effect on the environment.

PRACTICE 3-2 Writing Topic Sentences That Are Neither Too Broad Nor Too Narrow

In the following five practice items, three of the topic sentences are either too broad or too narrow, and two of them are OK. Rewrite the three weak sentences to make them broader or narrower as needed.

EXAMPLE: Life can be tough for soldiers when they come home.

NARROWER: We are not providing our returning soldiers with enough help in readjusting to civilian life.

1. I take public transportation to work.

2. Because of state and national education budget cuts, schools are having to lay off teachers and cut important programs.

3. College is challenging.

4. I would like to be successful in life.

5. Having a positive attitude improves people's ability to function, improves their interactions with others, and reduces stress.

State a Single Main Point

Your topic sentence or thesis statement should focus on only one main point. Two main points can split and weaken the focus of the writing.

Main Idea with Two Main Points

High schools should sell healthy food instead of junk food, and they should start later in the morning.

The two main points are underlined. Although both are good main points, together they split both the writer's and the readers' focus. The writer would need to give reasons to support each point, and the ideas are completely different. The two main points that were combined in this example are separated below into statements that each have one main idea.

Main Idea with a Single Main Point

High schools should sell healthy food instead of junk food.

OR

High schools should start later in the morning.

PRACTICE 3-3   Writing Sentences with a Single Main Point

Determine which of the following sentences have more than one main point.

> **EXAMPLE:**   Shopping at secondhand stores is a fun way to save money, and you can meet all kinds of interesting people as you shop. Two main points underlined.

1. My younger sister, the baby of the family, is the most adventurous of my four siblings.

2. Servicing hybrid cars is a growing part of automotive technology education, and dealers cannot keep enough hybrids in stock.

3. My brother, Bobby, is incredibly creative, and he takes in stray animals.

4. Pets can actually bring families together, and they require lots of care.

5. Unless people conserve voluntarily, we will deplete our water supply.

Be Specific

A good topic sentence or thesis statement gives readers specific information so that they know exactly what the writer's main point is.

GENERAL	Students are often overwhelmed.
	[How are students overwhelmed?]
SPECIFIC	Working college students have to learn how to juggle many responsibilities.

One way to make sure your topic sentence or thesis statement is specific is to make it a preview of what you are planning to say in the rest of the paragraph or essay. Just be certain that every point you preview is closely related to your main idea.

PREVIEW	Working college students have to learn how to juggle many responsibilities: doing a good job at work, getting to class regularly and on time, being alert in class, and doing the homework assignments.

PREVIEW	I have a set routine every Saturday morning that includes sleeping late, going to the gym, and shopping for food.

PRACTICE 3–4   Writing Sentences That Are Specific

Revise each of the sentences below to make it more specific. There is no one correct answer. As you read the sentences, think about what would make them more understandable to you if you were about to read a paragraph or essay on the topic.

EXAMPLE: Marriage can be a wonderful thing.

Marriage to the right person can add love, companionship, and support to life.

1. My job is horrible.
2. Working with others is rewarding.
3. I am a good worker.
4. This place could use a lot of improvement.
5. Getting my driver's license was challenging.

Choose a Point You Can Show, Explain, or Prove

If a main point is so obvious that it does not need support or if it states a simple fact, you will not have much to say about it.

OBVIOUS	Many people like to take vacations in the summer.
REVISED	The vast and incredible beauty of the Grand Canyon draws crowds of visitors each summer.
FACT	Three hundred cities worldwide have bicycle-sharing programs.
REVISED	Bicycle-sharing programs are popular, but funding them long-term can be challenging for cities with tight budgets.

PRACTICE 3–5   Writing Sentences with Ideas You Can Show, Explain, or Prove

Revise the following sentences so that they contain an idea you could show, explain, or prove.

> **EXAMPLE:**   Leasing a car is popular.
>
> Leasing a car has many advantages over buying one.

1. Texting while driving is dangerous.

2. My monthly rent is $750.

3. Health insurance rates rise every year.

4. Many people in this country work for minimum wage.

5. Technology is becoming increasingly important.

WRITING ASSIGNMENT

Write a topic sentence or thesis statement using the narrowed topic you developed in Chapter 2 or one of the following topics (which you will have to narrow).

Community service	Voting
A controversial issue	Hate speech/speech codes
Dressing for success	Snitching

After writing your topic sentence or thesis statement, complete the checklist that follows.

CHECKLIST: Evaluating Your Main Point

- ☐ It is a complete sentence.
- ☐ It includes my topic and the main point I want to make about it.
- ☐ It fits the assignment.
- ☐ It states a single main point.
- ☐ It is specific.
- ☐ It is something I can show, explain, or prove.

Fourth Basic: Support for Your Main Point

Support is the collection of examples, facts, or evidence that shows, explains, or proves your main point. **Primary support points** are the major ideas that back up your main point, and **secondary support** gives details to back up your primary support.

Key Features of Good Support

Without support, you *state* the main point, but you do not *make* the main point. Consider these unsupported statements:

> The amount shown on my bill is incorrect.
> I deserve a raise.
> I am innocent of the crime.

The statements may be true, but without good support, they are not convincing. If you sometimes get papers back with the comment "You need to support /develop your ideas," the suggestions in this chapter will help you.

Also, keep in mind that the same point repeated several times is not support. It is just repetition.

REPETITION, NOT SUPPORT	The amount shown on my bill is incorrect. You over-charged me. It didn't cost that much. The total is wrong.
SUPPORT	The amount shown on my bill is incorrect. I ordered the bacon-cheeseburger plate, which is $6.99 on the menu. On the bill, the order is correct, but the amount is $16.99.

As you develop support for your main point, make sure it has these three features.

BASICS OF GOOD SUPPORT

- The details directly relate to the main point. The purpose of support is to show, explain, or prove your main point.

- The details take your audience into account and address what they will need to know.

- The details give readers enough primary support and specific secondary support, particularly through examples, so that your readers understand what you mean.

Support in Paragraphs versus Essays

In paragraphs, your main point is expressed in a topic sentence. In both paragraphs and essays, it is important to add enough details (secondary support) about the primary support to make the main point clear to readers.

In the following paragraph, the topic sentence is underlined twice, the primary support is underlined once, and the details for each primary support point are in italics.

When I first enrolled in college, I thought that studying history was a waste of time. But after taking two world history classes, I have come to the conclusion that these courses count for far more than some credit hours in my college record. First, learning about historical events has helped me put important current events in perspective. *For instance, by studying the history of migration around the world, I have learned that immigration has been going on for hundreds of years. In addition, it is common in many countries, not just the United States. I have also learned about ways in which various societies have debated immigration, just as Americans are doing today.* Second, history courses have taught me about the power that individual people can have, even under very challenging circumstances. *I was especially inspired by the story of Toussaint L'Ouverture, a former slave who, in the 1790s, led uprisings in the French colony of Saint-Domingue, transforming it into the independent nation of Haiti. Although L'Ouverture faced difficult odds, he persisted and achieved great things.* The biggest benefit of taking history courses is that they have encouraged me to dig more deeply into subjects than I ever have before. *For a paper about the lasting influence of **Anne Frank**, I drew on quotations from her famous diary, on biographies about her, and on essays written by noted historians. The research was fascinating, and I loved piecing together the various facts and insights to come to my own conclusions.* To sum up, I have become hooked on history, and I have a feeling that the lessons it teaches me will be relevant far beyond college.

Anne Frank (1929–1945): a German Jewish girl who fled to the Netherlands with her family after Adolf Hitler, leader of the Nazi Party, became chancellor of Germany. In 1944, Anne and her family were arrested by the Nazis, and she died in a concentration camp the following year.

In an essay, each primary support point, along with its supporting details, is developed into a separate paragraph. (See the diagram on page 24.) Specifically, each underlined point in the previous paragraph could be turned into a topic sentence that would be supported by the italicized details. However, in preparing an essay on the preceding topic, the writer would want to add more details and examples for each primary support point.

Generating Support

To generate support for the main point of a paragraph or essay, try one or more of the following strategies.

THREE QUICK STRATEGIES FOR GENERATING SUPPORT

1. *Circle an important word or phrase* in your topic sentence (for a paragraph) or thesis statement (for an essay), and write about it for a few minutes. As you work, refer back to your main point to make sure you're on the right track.

2. *Reread your topic sentence or thesis statement, and write down the first thought you have.* Then, write down your next thought. Keep going.

3. *Use an invention strategy* (see pages 29–31) (freewriting, listing, discussing, clustering, and so on) while thinking about your main point and your audience. Write for three to five minutes without stopping.

PRACTICE 3-6 Generating Supporting Ideas

Choose one of the following sentences, or your own topic sentence or thesis statement, and use one of the preceding three strategies to generate at least twelve supporting points. Keep your answers for use in later practices in this chapter.

1. Some television shows stir my mind instead of numbing it.

2. Today there is no such thing as a "typical" college student.

3. Learning happens not only in school but throughout a person's life.

4. Practical intelligence can't be measured by grades.

5. I deserve a raise.

Selecting the Best Primary Support

After you have generated possible support, review your ideas; then, select the best ones to use as primary support. Here you take control of your topic, shaping the way readers will see it and the main point you are making about it. The following steps can help.

1. Carefully read the ideas you have generated.
2. Select three to five primary support points that will be the clearest and most convincing to your readers, providing the best examples, facts, and observations to support your main point. If you are writing a paragraph, these points will become the primary support for your topic sentence. If you are writing an essay, they will become topic sentences of the individual paragraphs that support your thesis statement.
3. Cross out ideas that are not closely related to your main point.
4. If you find that you have crossed out most of your ideas and do not have enough left to support your main point, use one of the three strategies from page 42 to find more.

PRACTICE 3–7 Selecting the Best Support

Refer to your response to Practice 3–6. Of your possible primary support points, choose three to five that you think will best show, explain, or prove your main point to your readers.

Adding Secondary Support

Once you have selected your best primary support points, you need to flesh them out for your readers. Do this by adding **secondary support**, specific examples, facts, and observations to back up your primary support points.

PRACTICE 3–8 Adding Secondary Support

Using your answers to Practice 3–7, choose three primary support points, and write them down. Then, read each of them carefully, and write down at least three supporting details (secondary support) for each one. For examples of secondary support, see the example paragraph on page 41.

WRITING ASSIGNMENT

Develop primary support points and supporting details using the topic sentence or thesis statement you developed at the beginning of this chapter or one of the following topic sentences / thesis statements.

Same-sex marriages should / should not be legal in all fifty states.

The drinking age should / should not be lowered.

Work experience helps high school students develop essential skills.

People who do not speak "proper" English are discriminated against.

Many movies have important messages for viewers.

After developing your support, complete the following checklist.

> **CHECKLIST: Evaluating Your Support**
>
> ☐ It is directly related to my main point.
> ☐ It uses examples, facts, and observations that will make sense to my readers.
> ☐ It includes enough specific details to show my readers exactly what I mean.

Once you have pulled together your primary support points and secondary supporting details, you are ready to put your ideas in order.

Arrange Your Ideas

In writing, **order** means the sequence in which you present your ideas: What comes first, what comes next, and so on. There are three common ways of ordering—arranging—your ideas: time order (also called chronological order), space order, and order of importance.

Read the paragraph examples that follow. In each paragraph, the topic sentences are underlined twice, the primary support points are underlined once, and the secondary support is in italics.

Use Time Order to Write about Events

Use **time order** (chronological order) to arrange points according to when they happened. Time order works best when you are writing about events.

EXAMPLE USING TIME ORDER

Officer Meredith Pavlovic's traffic stop of August 23, 2011, was fairly typical of an investigation and arrest for drunk driving. First, at around 12:15 a.m. that day, she noticed that the driver of a blue Honda Civic was acting suspiciously. *The car was weaving between the fast and center lanes of Interstate 93 North near exit 12. In addition, it was proceeding at approximately 45 mph in a 55 mph zone.* Therefore, Officer Pavlovic took the second step of pulling the driver over for a closer investigation. *The driver's license told Officer Pavlovic that the driver was twenty-six-year-old Paul Brownwell. Brownwell's red eyes, slurred speech, and alcohol-tainted breath told Officer Pavlovic that Brownwell was very drunk.* But she had to be absolutely sure. Thus, as a next step, she tested his balance and blood alcohol level. *The results were that Brownwell could barely get out of the car, let alone stand on one foot. Also, a breathalyzer test showed that his blood alcohol level was 0.13, well over the legal limit of 0.08.* These results meant an arrest for Brownwell, an unfortunate outcome for him, but a lucky one for other people on the road at that time.

Use Space Order to Describe Objects, Places, or People

Use **space order** to arrange ideas so that your readers picture your topic the way you see it. Space order usually works best when you are writing about a physical object or place, or a person's appearance.

EXAMPLE USING SPACE ORDER

Donna looked professional for her interview. Her long, dark, curly hair was held back with a gold clip. *No stray wisps escaped. Normally wild and unruly, her hair was smooth, shiny, and neat.* She wore a white silk blouse *with just the top button open at her throat. Donna had made sure to leave time to iron it so that it wouldn't be wrinkled. The blouse was neatly tucked into her* black A-line skirt,

→

> *which came just to the top of her knee.* <u>She wore black stockings</u> *that she had checked for runs* and <u>black low-heeled shoes.</u> Altogether, her appearance marked her as serious and professional, and she was sure to make a good first impression.

Use Order of Importance to Emphasize a Particular Point

Use **order of importance** to arrange points according to their significance, interest, or surprise value. Usually, save the most important point for last.

EXAMPLE USING ORDER OF IMPORTANCE

> <u>People who keep guns in their homes risk endangering both themselves and others.</u> <u>Many accidental injuries occur when a weapon is improperly stored or handled.</u> *For example, someone cleaning a closet where a loaded gun is stored may handle the gun in a way that causes it to go off and injure him or her.* <u>Guns also feature in many reports of "crimes of passion."</u> *A couple with a violent history has a fight, and, in a fit of rage, one gets the gun and shoots the other, wounding or killing the other person.* <u>Most common and most tragic are incidents in which children find loaded guns and play with them, accidentally killing themselves or their playmates.</u> Considering these factors, the risks of keeping guns in the home outweigh the advantages, for many people.

Planning Your Draft

When you have decided how to order your primary support points, it is time to make a more detailed plan for your paragraph or essay. A good, visual way to plan a draft is to arrange your ideas in an outline. An **outline** lists the topic sentence (for a paragraph) or thesis statement (for an essay), the primary support points for the topic sentence or thesis statement, and secondary supporting details for each of the primary support points. It provides a map of your ideas that you can follow as you write.

The examples below are in "formal" outline form, which uses letters and numbers to distinguish between primary supporting and secondary supporting details. Some instructors require this format. If you are making an outline just for yourself, you might choose to write a less formal outline, simply indenting the secondary supporting details under the primary support rather than using numbers and letters.

SAMPLE OUTLINE FOR A PARAGRAPH

> **Topic sentence**
> - **A.   Primary support sentence 1**
>   - 1.   Supporting detail sentence 1
>   - 2.   Supporting detail sentence 2 (optional)
> - **B.   Primary support sentence 2**
>   - 1.   Supporting detail sentence 1
>   - 2.   Supporting detail sentence 2 (optional)
> - **C.   Primary support sentence 3**
>   - 1.   Supporting detail sentence 1
>   - 2.   Supporting detail sentence 2 (optional)
>
> **Concluding sentence**

SAMPLE OUTLINE FOR A FIVE-PARAGRAPH ESSAY

> **Thesis statement** (part of introductory paragraph 1)
> - **A.   Topic sentence for support point 1** (paragraph 2)
>   - 1.   Supporting detail 1 for support point 1
>   - 2.   Supporting detail 2 for support point 1 (and so on)
> - **B.   Topic sentence for support point 2** (paragraph 3)
>   - 1.   Supporting detail 1 for support point 2
>   - 2.   Supporting detail 2 for support point 2 (and so on)
> - **C.   Topic sentence for support point 3** (paragraph 4)
>   - 1.   Supporting detail 1 for support point 3
>   - 2.   Supporting detail 2 for support point 3 (and so on)
>
> **Concluding paragraph** (paragraph 5)

NOTE: Many essays will include more body paragraphs, depending on the topic, purpose, and audience.

PRACTICE 3-9   Making an Outline

Reread the paragraph on page 45 that illustrates time order of organization. Then, make an outline for it.

WRITING ASSIGNMENT

Create an outline using your topic sentence or thesis statement along with the primary support points and supporting details you have developed in this chapter. Arrange your ideas according to time order, space order, or order of importance. After creating your outline, complete the following checklist.

CHECKLIST: Evaluating Your Outline

- ☐ It includes my topic sentence or thesis statement.
- ☐ It includes at least three supporting points.
- ☐ Each supporting point has at least one supporting detail.
- ☐ It is organized according to time order, space order, or order of importance.
- ☐ If required by my instructor, it is prepared in formal outline format.

You now have a clear main point with support, organized in a logical way. In the next chapter, you will begin drafting your paragraph or essay.

4

Drafting and Revising Paragraphs and Essays

A **draft** is the first whole version of all your ideas put together in a piece of writing. Do the best job you can in drafting, but know that you can make changes later.

BASICS OF A GOOD DRAFT

- It has a topic sentence (for a paragraph) and a thesis statement (for an essay) that makes a clear main point.
- It has a logical organization of ideas.
- It has primary and secondary support that shows, explains, or proves the main point.
- It has a conclusion that makes an observation about the main point.
- It follows standard paragraph form (see p. 22) or standard essay form (see p. 23).

Drafting Paragraphs

Here are some useful guidelines for writing paragraphs.

Use Complete Sentences

Write your draft with your outline in front of you. Be sure to include your topic sentence and express each point in a complete sentence. As you write, you may want to add support or change the order. It is OK to make changes from your outline as you write.

Consider Introductory Techniques

Although paragraphs typically begin with topic sentences, they may also begin with a quote, an example, or a surprising fact or idea. The topic sentence is then presented later in the paragraph. For examples of various introductory techniques, see pages 52–53. For more on topic sentences, see pages 33–39.

End with a Concluding Sentence

A **concluding sentence** refers back to the main point and makes an observation based on what you have written. The concluding sentence does not just repeat the topic sentence. Concluding paragraphs for essays are discussed on page 53.

Title Your Paragraph

The title is the first thing readers see, so it should give them a good idea of what your paragraph is about. Decide on a title by rereading your draft, especially your topic sentence. A paragraph title should not repeat your topic sentence. Titles for essays are discussed on page 53.

NOTE: Center your title at the top of the page before the first paragraph. Do not put quotation marks around it or underline or bold it.

Sample Student Paragraph

Identifying information

Title identifies main point

Topic sentence (indented first line)

Support point 1

Supporting details

Support point 2

Supporting details

Support point 3

Chelsea Wilson
Professor Holmes
EN 099
September 7, 2017

My Career Goal

My career goal is to become a nurse because it offers so much that I value. Being a nurse is a good and practical job. Licensed practical nurses make an average of $40,000 per year. That amount is much more than I make now working long hours at a minimum-wage job in a restaurant. Working as a nurse, I could be a better provider for my daughter. I could also spend more time with her. Also, nursing is more than just a job; it is a profession. As a nurse, I will help people who are sick, and helping people is important to me. With time, I will be able to grow within the profession, like becoming a registered nurse who makes more money and has more responsibility. Because nursing is a profession, nurses are respected. When I become a nurse, I will respect myself and be proud of myself for reaching my goal, even though I know it will take a lot

→

of hard work. The most important thing about becoming a nurse is that it will be good for my young daughter. I will be a good role model for her. For all of these reasons, my goal is to become a nurse. Reaching this goal is important to me and worth the work.

> Supporting details
>
> Concluding sentence (refers back to main point)

WRITING ASSIGNMENT   Paragraph

Write a draft paragraph, using the material you have developed up to this point or working with one of the following topic sentences. If you use one of the topic sentences below, you may want to revise it to fit what you want to say.

Being a good _____ requires _____.

I can find any number of ways to waste my time.

People tell me I am _____, and I guess I have to agree.

So many decisions are involved in going to college.

The most important thing to me in life is _____.

After writing your draft paragraph, complete the following checklist.

CHECKLIST: Evaluating Your Draft Paragraph

- ☐ It has a clear, confident topic sentence that states my main point.
- ☐ Each primary support point is backed up with supporting details, examples, or facts.
- ☐ The support is arranged in a logical order.
- ☐ The concluding sentence reminds readers of my main point and makes an observation.
- ☐ The title reinforces the main point.
- ☐ All the sentences are complete, consisting of a subject and verb, and expressing a complete thought.
- ☐ The draft is properly formatted:
  - My name, my instructor's name, the course, and the date appear in the upper left corner.
  - The first sentence of the paragraph is indented, and the text is double-spaced (for easier revision).
- ☐ I have followed any other formatting guidelines provided by my instructor.

Drafting Essays

The draft of an essay has all the basics listed on page 49. In addition,

- The essay should include an introductory paragraph that draws readers in and includes the thesis statement.
- The topic sentences for the paragraphs that follow the introduction should directly support the thesis statement. In turn, each topic sentence should be backed by enough support.
- The conclusion should be a full paragraph rather than a single sentence.

Write Topic Sentences, and Draft the Body of the Essay

When you start to draft your essay, use your outline to write complete sentences for your primary support points. These sentences will serve as the topic sentences for the body paragraphs of your essay.

As you write support for your topic sentences, refer back to your outline, where you listed supporting details. Turn these supporting details into complete sentences, and add more support if necessary. (Invention strategies can help here; see Chapter 2.) Don't let yourself get stalled if you are having trouble with one word or sentence. Just keep writing. Remember that a draft is a first try; you will have time later to improve it.

Write an Introduction

The introduction to your essay captures your readers' interest and presents the main point. Ask yourself: How can I sell my essay to readers? You need to market your main point.

BASICS OF A GOOD INTRODUCTION

- It should catch readers' attention.
- It should present the thesis statement of the essay, usually in the first or the last sentence of an introductory paragraph.
- It should give readers a clear idea of what the essay will cover.

Here are some common kinds of introductions that spark readers' interest.

1. **Open with a quotation.** A good, short quotation definitely gets people interested. It must lead naturally into your main point, however, and not be there just for effect. If you start with a quotation, make sure you tell the reader who the speaker is.

2. **Give an example, or tell a story.** People like stories, so opening an essay with a brief story or example often draws readers in.

3. **Start with a surprising fact or idea.** Surprises capture people's interest. The more unexpected and surprising something is, the more likely people are to notice it.

4. **Offer a strong opinion or position.** The stronger the opinion, the more likely it is that your readers will pay attention. Don't write wimpy introductions. Make your point and shout it!

5. **Ask a question.** A question needs an answer, so if you start your introduction with a question, your readers will need to read on to get the answer.

Write a Conclusion

When they have finished the body of their essay, some writers believe their work is done—but it isn't *quite* finished. Remember that people usually remember best what they see, hear, or read last. Use your concluding paragraph to drive your main point home one final time. Make sure your conclusion has the same energy as the rest of the essay, if not more.

BASICS OF A GOOD ESSAY CONCLUSION

- It refers back to the main point.
- It sums up what has been covered in the essay.
- It makes a further observation or point.
- It answers the question, "So what?"

In general, a good conclusion creates a sense of completion. It brings readers back to where they started, but it also shows them how far they have come. One of the best ways to end an essay is to refer directly to something in the introduction. If you asked a question, re-ask and answer it. If you started a story, finish it. If you used a quote, use another one—maybe a quote by the same person or maybe one by another person on the same topic. Or, use some of the same words you used in your introduction.

Title Your Essay

Even if your title is the *last* part of the essay you write, it is the *first* thing readers read. Use your title to get your readers' attention and to tell them, in a brief way, what your paper is about. Use vivid, strong, specific words.

BASICS OF A GOOD ESSAY TITLE

- It makes people want to read the essay.
- It hints at the main point (thesis statement), but it does not repeat it.
- It is usually a not a complete sentence.

One way to find a good title is to consider the type of essay you are writing. If you are writing an argument, state your position in your title. If you are telling your readers how to do something, try using the term *steps* or *how to* in the title. This way, your readers will know immediately not only what you are writing about but how you will discuss it.

NOTE: Center your title at the top of the page before the first paragraph. Do not put quotation marks around it or underline or bold it.

Sample Student Essay

Identifying information

Chelsea Wilson
Professor Holmes
EN 099
September 14, 2017

Title indicates main point

The Benefits of Getting a College Degree

Introduction

My goal is to get a college degree. I have been taking college courses for two years, and it has been difficult for me. Many times I have wondered if getting a college degree is really worth the

Thesis statement

struggle. However, there are many benefits of getting a college degree.

Topic sentence/ Support point 1

I can work as a nurse, something I have always wanted to do. As a nurse, I can make decent money: The average salary for a licensed practical nurse is $40,000 per year. That amount is sub-

Supporting details

stantially more than I make now working at a restaurant job that pays minimum wage and tips. With the economy so bad, people are tipping less. It has been hard to pay my bills, even though I work more than forty hours a week. Without a degree, I don't see how that situation will change. I have almost no time to see my daughter, who is in preschool.

→

I didn't get serious about getting a degree until I became a mother. Then, I realized I wanted more for my daughter than I had growing up. I also wanted to have time to raise her properly and keep her safe. She is a good girl, but she sees crime and violence around her. I want to get her away from danger, and I want to show her that there are better ways to live. Getting a college degree will help me do that.

(Topic sentence/Support point 2)

(Supporting details)

The most important benefit of getting a college degree is that it will show me that I can achieve something hard. My life is moving in a good direction, and I am proud of myself. My daughter will be proud of me, too. I want to be a good role model for her as she grows up.

(Topic sentence/Support point 3)

(Supporting details)

Because of these benefits, I want to get a college degree. It pays well, it will give my daughter and me a better life, and I will be proud of myself.

(Conclusion)

WRITING ASSIGNMENT   Essay

Write a draft essay using the material you have developed up to this point or working with one of the following thesis statements. If you choose one of the thesis statements below, you may want to modify it to fit what you want to say.

Taking care of a sick (child/parent/spouse/friend) can test even the most patient person.

Being a good _____ requires _____.

Doing _____ gave me a great deal of pride in myself.

A good long-term relationship involves flexibility and compromise.

Some of the differences between men and women create misunderstandings.

After you have finished writing your draft essay, complete the following checklist.

CHECKLIST: Evaluating Your Draft Essay

- ☐ A clear, confident thesis statement states my main point.
- ☐ The primary support points are now topic sentences that support the main point.
- ☐ Each topic sentence is part of a paragraph, and the other sentences in the paragraph support the topic sentence.
- ☐ The support is arranged in a logical order.
- ☐ The introduction will interest readers.
- ☐ The conclusion reinforces my main point and makes an additional observation.
- ☐ The title reinforces the main point.
- ☐ All the sentences are complete, consisting of a subject and verb, and expressing a complete thought.
- ☐ The draft is properly formatted:
  - My name, my instructor's name, the course, and the date appear in the upper left corner.
  - The first sentence of each paragraph is indented, and the text is double-spaced (for easier revision).
  - The pages are numbered.
- ☐ I have followed any other formatting guidelines provided by my instructor.

Do not think about your draft anymore—for the moment. Give yourself some time away from it, at least a few hours and preferably a day or two. Taking a break will allow you to return to your writing later with a fresher eye and more energy for revision, resulting in a better piece of writing—and a better grade. After your break, you will be ready to take the next step: revising your draft.

Revising Paragraphs and Essays

When you finish a draft, you probably wish that you were at the end: you don't want to have to look at it again. But a draft is just the first whole version, a rough cut; it is not the best you can do to represent yourself and your ideas. After taking a break, you need to look at the draft with fresh eyes to revise and edit it.

Revising is making your ideas clearer, stronger, and more convincing. When revising, you are evaluating how well you have made your point. **Editing** is finding and correcting problems with grammar, word usage, punctuation, and capitalization. When editing, you are evaluating the words, phrases, and sentences you have used.

Most writers find it difficult to revise and edit well if they try to do both at once. It is easier to solve idea-level problems first (by revising) and then to correct smaller, word-level ones (by editing).

TIPS FOR REVISING YOUR WRITING

- Wait a few hours or, if possible, a couple of days before starting to revise.

- Read your draft aloud, and listen for places where the writing seems weak or unclear.

- Read critically and ask yourself questions, as if you were reading through someone else's eyes. (For more on reading critically, see Chapter 1.)

- Write notes about changes to make. For small things, like adding a transition (p. 59), you can make the change on the draft. For other things, like adding or getting rid of an idea or reordering your support points, make a note in the margin.

- Get help from a tutor at the writing center, or get feedback from a friend (see p. 64 for information on peer review).

Even the best writers do not get everything right the first time. So, if you finish reading your draft and have not found anything that could be better, either you are not reading carefully enough or you are not asking the right questions. Use the following checklist to help you make your writing better.

CHECKLIST: Revising Your Writing

☐ If someone else just read my topic sentence or thesis statement, what would he or she think the paper is about? Would the main point make a lasting impression? What would I need to do to make it more interesting?

☐ Does each support point really relate to my main point? What more could I say about the topic so that someone else will see it my way? Is any of what I have written weak? If so, should I delete it?

☐ What about the way the ideas are arranged? Should I change the order so that the writing makes more sense or has more effect on a reader?

☐ What about the ending? Does it just droop and fade away? How could I make it better?

☐ If, before reading my paragraph or essay, someone knew nothing about the topic or disagreed with my position, would what I have written be enough for him or her to understand the material or be convinced by my argument?

You may need to read what you have written several times before deciding what changes would improve it. Remember to consider your audience and your purpose when you revise. You should also review your draft for unity, development, and coherence.

Revise for Unity

Unity in writing means that all the points you make are related to your main point; they are *unified* in support of it. As you draft a paragraph or an essay, you may detour from your main point without even being aware of it, as the writer of the following paragraph did with the underlined sentences. (The main point in the paragraph has been double-underlined.)

> <u>If you want to drive like an elderly person, use a cell phone while driving</u>. A group of researchers from the University of Utah tested the reaction times of two groups of people — those between the ages of sixty-five to seventy-four and those who were eighteen to twenty-five — in a variety of driving tasks. All tasks were done with hands-free cell phones. <u>That part of the study surprised me because I thought the main problem was using only one hand to drive. I hardly ever drive with two hands, even when I'm not talking to anyone</u>. Among other results, braking time for both groups slowed by 18 percent. A related result is that the number of rear-end collisions doubled. The study determined that the younger drivers were paying as much — or more — attention to their phone conversations as they were to what was going on around them on the road. The elderly drivers also experienced longer reaction times and more accidents, pushing most of them into the category of dangerous driver. This study makes a good case for turning off the phone when you buckle up.

Detours such as the underlined sentences in the example weaken your writing because readers' focus is shifted from your main point. As you revise, check to make sure your paragraph or essay has unity.

Revise for Development of Support

When you revise a paper, look carefully at the support you have developed. Will readers have enough information to understand and be convinced by the main point? In the margin or between the lines of your draft (which should be double-spaced), note ideas that seem weak or unclear. As you revise, build up your support by adding more details. Focus on being specific: do your details show your reader who, what, when, and where? Do they help the reader visualize or imagine the key point?

In the example below, the main point has been double-underlined and notes have been made in the margins to suggest revision ideas for improved support.

<u><u>Sports fans can turn from normal people into destructive</u></u> maniacs. After big wins, a team's fans sometimes riot. Police have to be brought in. Even in school sports, parents of the players can become violent. People get so involved watching the game that they lose control of themselves and are dangerous.

What makes them act this way?

Provide an example of a riot?

Why do parents turn violent? Example?

Revise for Coherence: Transitions and Key Words

Coherence in writing means that all your support connects to form a whole, and the supporting points flow logically from one to the next. In other words, you have provided enough "glue" for readers to see how one point leads to another.

A good way to improve coherence is to use **transitions**—words, phrases, and sentences that connect your ideas so that your writing moves smoothly from one point to the next. The table on page 60 shows some common transitions and what they are used for.

In the paragraph that follows, the transitions have been underlined. As you read, consider this question: What would happen if these transitions were removed from the paragraph?

It is not difficult to get organized—<u>even though</u> it takes discipline to stay organized. All you need to do is follow a few simple ideas. You must decide what your priorities are and do these tasks first. <u>For example</u>, you should ask yourself every day: What is the most important task I have to accomplish? <u>Then</u>, make the time to do it. To be organized, you <u>also</u> need a personal system for keeping track of things. Making lists, keeping records, and using a

→

schedule help you remember what tasks you need to do. <u>Finally</u>, it is a good idea not to let belongings and obligations stack up. Get rid of possessions you do not need, put items away every time you are done using them, and do not take on more responsibilities than you can handle. Getting organized is not a mystery; it is just good sense.

Common Transitional Words and Phrases

INDICATING SPACE			
above	below	near	to the right
across	beside	next to	to the side
at the bottom	beyond	opposite	under
at the top	farther/further	over	where
behind	inside	to the left	

INDICATING TIME			
after	eventually	meanwhile	soon
as	finally	next	then
at last	first	now	when
before	last	second	while
during	later	since	

INDICATING IMPORTANCE			
above all	in fact	more important	most important
best	in particular	most	worst
especially			

SIGNALING EXAMPLES			
for example	for instance	for one thing	one reason

SIGNALING ADDITIONS			
additionally	and	as well as	in addition
also	another	furthermore	moreover

SIGNALING CONTRAST			
although	however	nevertheless	still
but	in contrast	on the other hand	yet
even though	instead		

SIGNALING CAUSES OR RESULTS			
as a result	finally	so	therefore
because			

Another way to give your writing coherence is to repeat a **key word**—a word that is directly related to your main point. For example, in the paragraph on page 59, the writer repeats the word *organized* several times. Repetition of a key word is a good way to keep your readers focused on your main point, but make sure you don't overdo it. To avoid repeating the same word in every sentence, you can use synonyms (words with similar meanings), related words, or pronouns to replace the key word. What related words and pronouns are used in the paragraph at the bottom of page 59?

Sample Student Paragraph: Revised

Compare the revised paragraph below to the original draft on page 50.

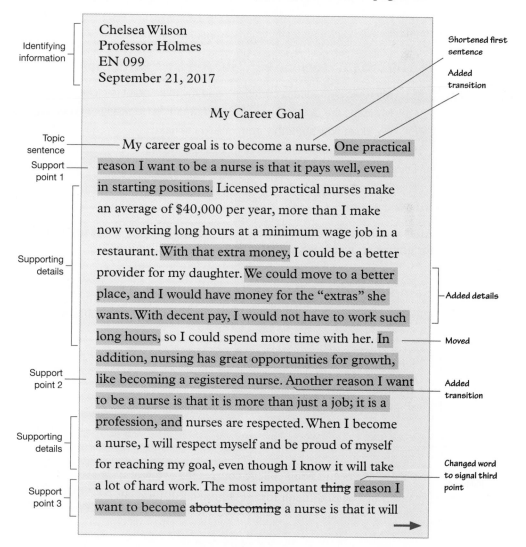

Identifying information

Chelsea Wilson
Professor Holmes
EN 099
September 21, 2017

Shortened first sentence

Added transition

My Career Goal

Topic sentence — My career goal is to become a nurse. One practical

Support point 1 — reason I want to be a nurse is that it pays well, even

in starting positions. Licensed practical nurses make

an average of $40,000 per year, more than I make

now working long hours at a minimum wage job in a

Supporting details — restaurant. With that extra money, I could be a better

provider for my daughter. We could move to a better

place, and I would have money for the "extras" she

wants. With decent pay, I would not have to work such

long hours, so I could spend more time with her. In

addition, nursing has great opportunities for growth,

Support point 2 — like becoming a registered nurse. Another reason I want

to be a nurse is that it is more than just a job; it is a

profession, and nurses are respected. When I become

Supporting details — a nurse, I will respect myself and be proud of myself

for reaching my goal, even though I know it will take

Support point 3 — a lot of hard work. The most important ~~thing~~ reason I

want to become ~~about becoming~~ a nurse is that it will

Added details

Moved

Added transition

Changed word to signal third point

Supporting details [be good for my daughter, not just because of the money, but because I will be a good role model for her. She will see that hard works pays off and that having a goal—and] Added details

Concluding sentence [achieving it—is important. I have always known I wanted to be a nurse: it is a goal worth working for.] Stronger last sentence

WRITING ASSIGNMENT   **Paragraph**

Revise the draft paragraph you wrote earlier in this chapter. After revising your draft, complete the following checklist.

CHECKLIST: Evaluating Your Revised Paragraph

☐ My topic sentence is confident, and my main point is clear.

☐ My ideas are detailed, specific, and organized logically.

☐ My ideas flow smoothly from one to the next.

☐ This paragraph fulfills the original assignment.

☐ I am ready to turn in this paragraph for a grade.

☐ This paragraph is the best I can do.

After you have finished revising your paragraph, you are ready to edit it for grammar, word use, punctuation, and capitalization.

Sample Student Essay: Revised

Compare the revised essay below to the original draft on pages 54–55.

Identifying information [Chelsea Wilson
Professor Holmes
EN 099
September 28, 2017]

Title, centered ——— The Benefits of Getting a College Degree

First line indented ——— I have been taking college courses for two years, and it has been difficult for me. I have a full-time job,

Details — a young daughter, and a car that breaks down often. Added details — Many times as I have sat, late at night, struggling to stay awake to do homework or to study, I have wondered if getting a college degree is really worth the struggle.

Thesis statement — That is when I remind myself why getting a degree is so important: it will benefit every aspect of my life.

Topic sentence/ Support point 1 — One benefit of getting a degree is that I can work Added transition — as a nurse, something I have always wanted to do. Even as a child, I enjoyed helping my mother care for my grandmother or take care of my younger brothers and sisters when they were sick. I enjoy helping others, Supporting details — and nursing will allow me to do so while making good money. The average salary for a licensed practical nurse is $40,000 per year, substantially more than I make now working at a restaurant. Without a degree, I don't see how that situation will change. Meanwhile, I have almost no time to spend with my daughter. Added transitions

Topic sentence/ Support point 2 — Another benefit of getting a college degree is that it will allow me to be a better mother. In fact, I didn't get serious about getting a degree until I became a mother. Then, I realized I wanted more for my daughter than I had had: a safer place to live, a bigger apartment, some nice clothes, and birthday presents. Supporting details — I also wanted to have time to raise her properly and keep her safe. She is a good girl, but she sees crime and violence around her. I want to get her away from danger, and I want to show her that there are better ways to live. The job opportunities I will have with a college degree will enable me to do those things.

Topic sentence/ Support point 3 — The most important benefit of getting a college degree is that it will show me that I can achieve something hard. In the past, I have often given up Added details — and taken the easy way, which has led to nothing

→

Supporting details

good. The easy way has led to a hard life. Now, however, working toward a goal has moved my life in a good direction. I have confidence and self-respect. I can honestly say that I am proud of myself, and my daughter will be proud of me, too. I will be a good role model as she grows up, not only for her but also for her friends. She will go to college, just like her mother.

Added details

Conclusion

So why am I working so hard to get a degree? I am doing it because I see in that degree the kind of life I want to live on this earth and the kind of human being I want to be. Achieving that vision is worth all the struggles.

Conclusion strengthened with an observation

Peer Reviewing

Peer review—when students exchange drafts and comment on one another's work—is one of the best ways to get help with revising. Other students can often see things that you might not—parts that are good and parts that need to be strengthened or clarified. Peer review is also the best way to determine how real readers will perceive what you have written.

BASICS OF USEFUL FEEDBACK

- It is given in a positive way.
- It asks specific questions and offers specific suggestions.
- It may be given in writing or orally.

If you are working with one other student, read each other's papers and write down a few comments. If you are working in a small group, you may want to have writers take turns reading their papers aloud. Group members can make notes while listening and then offer comments to the writer that will help improve the paper.

Learning to give and receive helpful feedback takes practice. If you are having trouble getting started, you might consider first just stating what you heard ("You seem to be saying …") and asking for confirmation ("Is that right?"). Then you can ask your questions or make comments. If, on the other hand, others are struggling to find comments for your paper, you might begin by asking them to focus on a few questions as they read or listen to your paper, such as those in the list below.

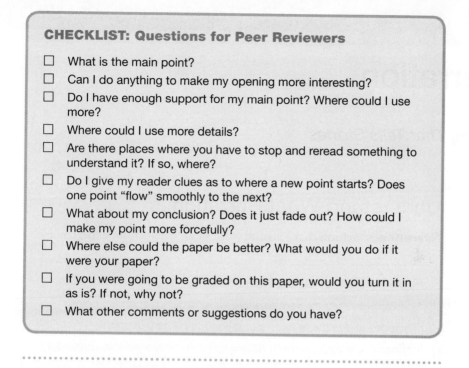

CHECKLIST: Questions for Peer Reviewers

☐ What is the main point?

☐ Can I do anything to make my opening more interesting?

☐ Do I have enough support for my main point? Where could I use more?

☐ Where could I use more details?

☐ Are there places where you have to stop and reread something to understand it? If so, where?

☐ Do I give my reader clues as to where a new point starts? Does one point "flow" smoothly to the next?

☐ What about my conclusion? Does it just fade out? How could I make my point more forcefully?

☐ Where else could the paper be better? What would you do if it were your paper?

☐ If you were going to be graded on this paper, would you turn it in as is? If not, why not?

☐ What other comments or suggestions do you have?

WRITING ASSIGNMENT   **Essay**

Revise the draft essay you wrote earlier in this chapter. After revising your draft, complete the following checklist.

CHECKLIST: Evaluating Your Revised Essay

☐ My thesis statement is confident, and my main point is clear.

☐ My ideas are detailed, specific, and organized logically.

☐ My ideas flow smoothly from one to the next.

☐ This essay fulfills the original assignment.

☐ I am ready to turn in this essay for a grade.

☐ This essay is the best I can do.

After you have revised your writing to make the ideas clear and strong, you need to edit it for grammar, word use, punctuation, and capitalization. The information in Part Three, Chapters 15–18, will help you edit your paragraphs and essays more effectively.

5

Narration

Writing That Tells Stories

Understand What Narration Is

Narration is writing that tells the story of an event or an experience.

> ### Four Basics of Good Narration
>
> **1** It has a message you want to share with readers (your main point).
>
> **2** It includes all the major events of the story (primary support).
>
> **3** It brings the story to life with details about the major events (secondary support).
>
> **4** It presents the events in a clear order, usually according to when they happened.

In the following paragraph, the numbers and colors correspond to the Four Basics of Good Narration.

1 Last year, a writing assignment that I hated produced the best writing I have done. **2** When my English teacher told us that our assignment would be to do a few hours of community service and write about it, I was furious. **3** I am a single mother, I work full-time, and I am going to school: Isn't that enough? **2** The next day, I spoke to my teacher during her office hours and told her that I was already so busy that I could hardly make time for homework, never mind housework. My own life was too full to help with anyone else's life. **3** She said that she understood perfectly and that the majority of her students had lives as full as mine. Then, she explained that the service assignment was just for four hours and that other students had enjoyed both doing the assignment and writing about

4 Events in time order.

their experiences. She said they were all surprised and that I would be, too. |2| After talking with her, I decided to accept my fate. The next week, I went to the Community Service Club, and was set up to spend a few hours at an adult day-care center near where I live. A few weeks later, I went to the Creative Care Center in Cocoa Beach, not knowing what to expect. |3| I found friendly, approachable people who had so many stories to tell about their long, full lives. |2| The next thing I knew, I was taking notes because I was interested in these people: |3| their marriages, life during the Depression, the wars they fought in, their children, their joys and sorrows. I felt as if I was experiencing everything they lived while they shared their history with me. |2| When it came time to write about my experience, I had more than enough to write about: |3| I wrote the stories of the many wonderful elderly people I had talked with. |2| I got an A on the paper, and beyond that accomplishment, I made friends whom I will visit on my own, not because of an assignment, but because I value them.

You may read and write narration in many practical situations.

COLLEGE	In a lab course, you tell what happened in an experiment.
WORK	Something goes wrong at work, and you are asked to explain to your boss—in writing—what happened.
EVERYDAY LIFE	In a letter of complaint about service you received, you need to tell what happened that upset you.

In college, the word *narration* probably will not appear in writing assignments. Instead, an assignment might ask you to *describe* the events, *report* what happened, or *retell* what happened. Words or phrases that call for an *account of events* are situations that require narration.

First Basic: Main Point in Narration

In narration, the **main point** is what is important about the story—to you and to your readers. The topic sentence (paragraph) or thesis statement (essay) usually includes the topic and the main point the writer wants to make about the topic. Let's look at a topic sentence first.

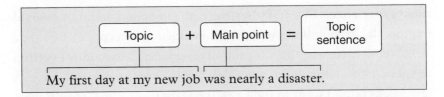

Remember that a topic for an essay can be a little broader than one for a paragraph.

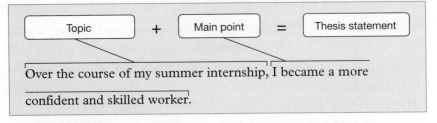

Whereas the topic sentence is focused on just one work day, the thesis statement considers a season-long internship.

Second and Third Basics: Support in Narration

In narration, primary **support** includes the major events that demonstrate the main point—what's important about the story. Secondary support gives details to bring the major events to life for the reader, details which appeal to the senses: sight, sound, smell, touch, or taste.

The paragraph and essay models on pages 70–71 use the topic sentence (paragraph) and thesis statement (essay) from the Main Point section of this chapter. (The thesis statement has been revised slightly.) Both models include the support used in all narration writing—major events backed up by details about the events. In the essay model, however, the major support points (events) are topic sentences for individual paragraphs.

Fourth Basic: Organization in Narration

Narration usually presents events in the order in which they happened, known as **time (chronological) order**. (For more on time order, see page 44.) As shown in the paragraph and essay models on pages 70–71, a narration starts at the beginning of the story and describes events as they unfolded.

Transitions move readers from one event to the next.

COMMON TRANSITIONS IN NARRATION						
after	before	finally	later	now	since	when
as	during	first	meanwhile	once	soon	while
at last	eventually	last	next	second	then	

Read and Analyze Narration

After you have read each of the selections below, answer the questions that follow.

Narration in the Real World

Anne Terreden, Registered Nurse

Nursing Note

Anne Terreden works per diem at a residential treatment facility for children 8 to 21 with significant mental health challenges. She earned her RN and BSN from the University of Massachusetts, Amherst in 1986. Her current position involves collaboration with the clinical team, treating acute health concerns, administering medications, and overall health management for the students. Below is an example of a narrative note on care delivered for a student's self-inflicted wound.

4/06/17 2:10 pm

Elena Martin, a 16-year-old female, came to my office after reporting self-harm to school staff. Elena presents as **A & O x 3**, with normal eye contact, flat affect, and irritable mood. She denies **SI**. Elena reports she was upset by news from her **DCF** worker that her visit with her sister was to be postponed. She reports scraping her arm with a plastic pen cap during class and that she turned the cap into staff. She has a 1/2 cm wide, 3 cm long, straight, shallow-depth abrasion to her left anterior forearm. Wound pink, surrounding skin intact, small amount of dried blood to proximal end of wound, and no foreign material seen in wound. Cleansed with soap and water, **TAO** and band-aid applied. Elena denies any pain. Instructed her to keep the abrasion clean and covered and to report any pain, swelling, discharge, or redness to staff or school nurse. Elena agreed. Email reporting above visit sent to her therapist and residential manager. Elena left to meet with her therapist.

1. For whom is this note written? How do you know?
2. What is the main point of the narrative note?
3. What specific details support the main idea?
4. The writer uses a few sentence fragments. Why?

A & O x 3:
Alert and oriented times 3 (aware of who she is, where she is, and what time it is)

SI:
suicidal ideation

DCF:
Department of Children and Families

TAO:
triple antibiotic ointment

PARAGRAPHS VS. ESSAYS IN NARRATION

For more on the important features of narration, see the Four Basics of Good Narration on page 66.

Paragraph Form

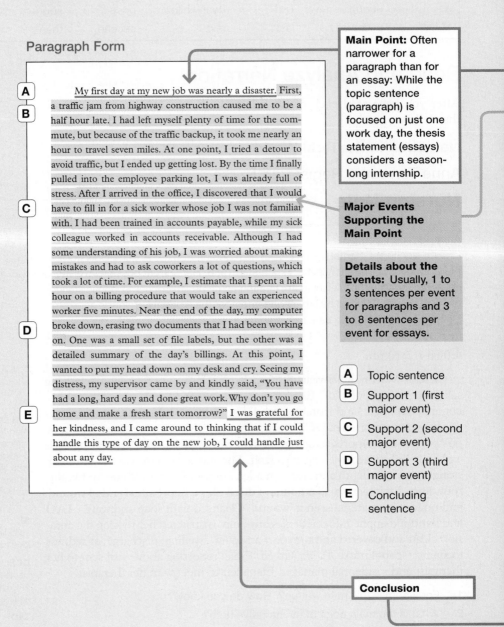

A My first day at my new job was nearly a disaster. First, **B** a traffic jam from highway construction caused me to be a half hour late. I had left myself plenty of time for the commute, but because of the traffic backup, it took me nearly an hour to travel seven miles. At one point, I tried a detour to avoid traffic, but I ended up getting lost. By the time I finally pulled into the employee parking lot, I was already full of stress. After I arrived in the office, I discovered that I would **C** have to fill in for a sick worker whose job I was not familiar with. I had been trained in accounts payable, while my sick colleague worked in accounts receivable. Although I had some understanding of his job, I was worried about making mistakes and had to ask coworkers a lot of questions, which took a lot of time. For example, I estimate that I spent a half hour on a billing procedure that would take an experienced worker five minutes. Near the end of the day, my computer **D** broke down, erasing two documents that I had been working on. One was a small set of file labels, but the other was a detailed summary of the day's billings. At this point, I wanted to put my head down on my desk and cry. Seeing my distress, my supervisor came by and kindly said, "You have had a long, hard day and done great work. Why don't you go **E** home and make a fresh start tomorrow?" I was grateful for her kindness, and I came around to thinking that if I could handle this type of day on the new job, I could handle just about any day.

Main Point: Often narrower for a paragraph than for an essay: While the topic sentence (paragraph) is focused on just one work day, the thesis statement (essays) considers a season-long internship.

Major Events Supporting the Main Point

Details about the Events: Usually, 1 to 3 sentences per event for paragraphs and 3 to 8 sentences per event for essays.

A Topic sentence

B Support 1 (first major event)

C Support 2 (second major event)

D Support 3 (third major event)

E Concluding sentence

Conclusion

Essay Form

Summer Internships: Are They Worth It? 1

Several of my friends question whether summer internships are really worthwhile, especially if the pay is low or nonexistent. However, the right internship definitely pays off professionally in the long run even if it doesn't financially in the short run. The proof is in my own summer marketing internship, which made me a far more confident and skilled worker. **[A]**

During the first two weeks of the internship, I received thorough training in every part of my job. For example, my immediate supervisor spent three full days going over everything I would need to do to help with email campaigns, online marketing efforts, and other promotions. She even had me draft a promotional email for a new product and gave me feedback about how to make the message clearer and more appealing. I also spent a lot of time with other staffers, who taught me everything from how to use the photocopier and printers to how to pull together marketing and sales materials for executive meetings. Most impressive, the president of the company took some time out of a busy afternoon **[B]**

2

to answer my questions about how he got started in his career and what he sees as the keys to success in the marketing field. As I explained to a friend, I got a real "insider's view" of the company and its leadership.

Next, I got hands-on experience with listening to customers and addressing their needs. **[C]** Specifically, I sat in on meetings with new clients and listened to them describe products and services they would like the company's help in promoting. They also discussed the message they would like to get across about their businesses. After the meetings, I sat in on brainstorming sessions with other staffers in which we came up with as many ideas as we could about campaigns to address the clients' needs. At first, I didn't think anyone would care about my ideas, but others listened to them respectfully and even ended up including some of them in the marketing plans that were sent back to the clients. Later, I learned that some of my ideas would be included in the actual promotional campaigns.

3

By summer's end, I had advanced my skills so much that I was asked to return next summer. My supervisor told me that she was pleased not only with all I had learned about marketing but also with the responsibility I took for every aspect of my job. I did not roll my eyes about having to make photocopies or help at the reception desk, nor did I seem intimidated by bigger, more meaningful tasks. Although I'm not guaranteed a full-time job at the company after graduation, I think my chances are good. Even if I don't end up working there long term, I am very grateful for how the job has helped me grow. **[D]**

In the end, the greatest benefit of the internship might be the confidence it gave me. I have learned that no matter how challenging the task before me—at work or in real life—I can succeed at it by getting the right information and input on anything unfamiliar, working effectively with others, and truly dedicating myself to doing my best. My time this past summer was definitely well spent. **[E]**

A Thesis statement
B Topic sentence 1 (first major event)
C Topic sentence 2 (second major event)
D Topic sentence 3 (third major event)
E Concluding paragraph

Student Narration Paragraph

Jelani Lynch

My Turnaround

Jelani Lynch graduated from Cambridge College / Year Up in 2009 with a degree in information technology. Now, he runs the video production company J / L visual media. As a writer, he says he is interested in exploring "issues that affect the community and the disparities that continue to affect the world." Reflecting on what motivated him to write this essay, Lynch said, "I wrote this after I had just begun to get my life on track. I felt that my struggles needed to be publicized so my mistakes are not repeated by the people who read it."

Before my big turnaround, my life was headed in the wrong direction. I grew up in the city and had a typical sad story: broken home, not much money, gangs, and drugs. In this world, few positive male role models are available. I played the game "Street Life": running the streets, stealing bikes, robbing people, carrying a gun, and selling drugs. The men in my neighborhood did not have regular jobs; they got their money outside the system. No one except my mother thought school was worth much. I had a history of poor school performance, a combination of not showing up and not doing any work when I did. My pattern of failure in that area was pretty strong. When I was seventeen, though, things got really bad. I was arrested for possession of crack cocaine. I was kicked out of school for good. During this time, I realized that my life was not going the way I wanted it to be. I was headed nowhere, except a life of crime, violence, and possibly early death. I knew that way of life, because I was surrounded by people who had chosen that direction. I did not want to go there anymore. When I made that decision, my life started to change. First, I met Shawn Brown, a man who had had the same kind of life I did. He got out of that life, though, by graduating from high school and college and getting a good job. He has a house, a wife, and children, along with great clothes. Shawn became my role model, showing me that with honesty, integrity, and hard work I could live a much better life. Since meeting Shawn, I have turned my life around. I started taking school seriously and graduated from high school, something I thought I would never do. Working with Shawn, I have read books and learned I enjoy writing. I have met the mayor of Boston and got a summer job at the State House. I have been part of an educational video and had many opportunities to meet and work with people who are successful. Now, I am a mentor with Diamond Educators, and I work with other young, urban males to give them a role model and help them make good choices. Now, I have a bright future with goals and plans. I have turned my life around and know I will be a success.

1. Double-underline the topic sentence.
2. Who is Jelani's audience? What is his purpose?
3. Underline the major events.
4. Circle the transitions.
5. Does Lynch's paragraph follow the Four Basics of Good Narration (p. 66)?

Professional Narration Essay

Amy Tan

Fish Cheeks

Amy Tierney/Getty Images

Amy Tan was born in Oakland, California, in 1952, several years after her mother and father emigrated from China. She studied at San Jose City College and later San Jose State University, receiving a B.A. with a double major in English and linguistics, and in 1973, an M.A. in linguistics. In 1989, Tan published her first novel, *The Joy Luck Club*, which was nominated for the National Book Award and the National Book Critics Circle Award. Tan's other books include *The Kitchen God's Wife* (1991), *Saving Fish from Drowning* (2005), and *The Valley of Amazement* (2013).

In the following essay, Tan uses narration to describe an experience that taught her an important lesson.

1   I fell in love with the minister's son the winter I turned fourteen. He was not Chinese, but as white as Mary in the manger. For Christmas I prayed for this blond-haired boy, Robert, and a slim new American nose.

2   When I found out that my parents had invited the minister's family over for Christmas dinner, I cried. What would Robert think of our shabby Chinese Christmas? What would he think of our noisy Chinese relatives who lacked proper American manners? What terrible disappointment would he feel upon seeing not a roasted turkey and sweet potatoes but Chinese food?

3   On Christmas Eve I saw that my mother had outdone herself in creating a strange menu. She was pulling black veins out of the backs of fleshy prawns. The kitchen was littered with appalling mounds of raw food: A slimy rock cod with bulging eyes that pleaded not to be thrown into a pan of hot oil. Tofu, which looked like stacked wedges of rubbery white sponges. A bowl soaking dried fungus back to life. A plate of squid, their backs crisscrossed with knife markings so they resembled bicycle tires.

4   And then they arrived—the minister's family and all my relatives in a clamor of doorbells and rumpled Christmas packages. Robert grunted hello, and I pretended he was not worthy of existence.

5   Dinner threw me into despair. My relatives licked the ends of their chopsticks and reached across the table, dipping them into the dozen or so plates of food. Robert and his family waited patiently for platters to be passed to them. My relatives murmured with pleasure when my mother brought out the whole steamed fish. Robert grimaced. Then my father poked his chopsticks just below the fish eye and plucked out the soft meat. "Amy, your favorite," he said, offering me the tender fish cheek. I wanted to disappear.

6   At the end of the meal my father leaned back and belched loudly, thanking my mother for her fine cooking. "It's a polite Chinese custom to show you are satisfied," explained my father to our astonished guests. Robert was looking down at his plate with a reddened face. The minister managed to muster up a quiet burp. I was stunned into silence for the rest of the night.

7   After everyone had gone, my mother said to me, "You want to be the same as American girls on the outside." She handed me an early gift. It was a miniskirt in beige tweed. "But inside you must always be Chinese. You must be proud you are different. Your only shame is to have shame."

8   And even though I didn't agree with her then, I knew that she understood how much I had suffered during the evening's dinner. It wasn't until many years later—long after I had gotten over my crush on Robert—that I was able to fully appreciate her lesson and the true purpose behind our particular menu. For Christmas Eve that year, she had chosen all my favorite foods.

1.   What is Tan's purpose for writing? Does she achieve it?

2.   Paraphrase Tan's main point (write it in your own words).

3.   How has Tan organized her essay? Circle the transitional words and phrases that indicate this order.

4.   Write a short summary of Tan's essay, following the guidelines in Chapter 1 (p. 14–15).

Write Your Own Narration

Write a narration paragraph or essay on one of the following topics or on one of your own choice. For help, refer to the How to Write Narration checklist on page 76.

College

- Interview a college graduate working in your field. Write a summary of that person's story, focusing on his or her journey to success.

- Consider the following question required for a transfer application: When have you achieved success or experienced a difficulty in school? Think about your purpose and audience as you write your response.

Work

Many prospective employers ask about previous work experiences, both good and bad. For the following questions, write for a potential employer.

- Write about a situation or incident that made you decide to leave a job.

- Imagine a successful day at your current or previous job. Then, tell the story of that day, including examples of successes.

Everyday Life

Write about an experience that triggered a strong emotion: happiness, sadness, fear, anger, regret. Choose an audience for your essay: a friend, coworker, fellow student, or teacher.

- Go to the student government office and find out if there is a community service club that offers short-term assignments. Take one of these assignments, and write about your experience.

CHECKLIST: How to Write Narration	
STEPS	**DETAILS**
☐ Narrow and explore your topic. See Chapter 2.	• Make the topic more specific. • Prewrite to get ideas about the narrowed topic.
☐ Write a topic sentence (paragraph) or thesis statement (essay). See Chapter 3.	• State what is most important to you about the topic and what you want your readers to understand.
☐ Support your point. See Chapter 3.	• Come up with examples and details to explain your main point to readers.
☐ Write a draft. See Chapter 4.	• Make a plan that puts events or examples in a logical order. • Include a topic sentence (paragraph) or thesis statement (essay) and all the supporting events, examples, and details.
☐ Revise your draft. See Chapter 4.	• Make sure it has *all* of the Four Basics of Good Narration. • Make sure you include transitions to move readers smoothly from one event or example to the next.
☐ Edit your revised draft. See Chapters 15–18.	• Correct errors in grammar, spelling, word use, and punctuation.

6

Illustration

Writing That Gives Examples

Understand What Illustration Is

Illustration is writing that uses examples to support a point.

> **Four Basics of Good Illustration**
>
> **1** It has a point to communicate to readers.
> **2** It gives specific examples that show, explain, or prove the point.
> **3** It gives details to support the examples.
> **4** It presents examples in a logical order: order of emphasis, order of importance, or chronological order.

In the following paragraph, the numbers and colors correspond to the Four Basics of Good Illustration.

1 Many people would like to serve their communities or help with causes that they believe in, but they do not have much time and do not know what to do. Now, the internet provides people with ways to help that do not take much time or money. **2** Websites now make it convenient to donate online. With a few clicks, an organization of your choice can receive your donation or money from a sponsoring advertiser. **3** Some examples of click-to-give sites are www.thechildhealthsite.com, www.theliteracysite.com, and www.breastcancersite.com. These sites have click-to-give links, online stores that direct a percentage of sales income to charity, and links to help you learn about causes you are interested in. One hundred percent of the sponsors' donations go to the charities, and you can give with a click every single day. **2** Similarly, if you are interested

4 Examples are organized by order of importance.

77

in helping rescue unwanted and abandoned animals, you can go to www.theanimalrescuesite.com. 3 When you click as instructed, a sponsoring advertiser will make a donation to help provide food and care for the 27 million animals in shelters. Also, a portion of any money you spend in the site's online store will go to providing animal care. 2 Finally, if your goal is much bigger, such as fighting world hunger, you can go to www.thehungersite.com 3 and click daily to have sponsor fees directed to hungry people in more than seventy countries via the Mercy Corps, Feeding America, and Millennium Promise. Each year, hundreds of millions of cups of food are distributed to one billion hungry people around the world. Since I have found out about sites like these, I go to at least one of them every day. I have learned a lot about various problems, and every day I feel as if I have helped a little.

It is hard to explain anything without using examples, so you read and write illustration in many academic, professional, and everyday situations.

COLLEGE	An exam question asks you to explain and give examples of a concept.
WORK	Your boss asks you to tell her what office equipment needs to be replaced and why.
EVERYDAY LIFE	You complain to your landlord and provide examples that the building superintendent is not doing his job.

In college, the words *illustration* and *illustrate* may not appear in writing assignments. Instead, you might be asked to *give examples of* _____ or to *be specific about* _____. Regardless of an assignment's wording, to be clear and effective, most types of writing require specific examples. Include them whenever they help you make your point.

First Basic: Main Point in Illustration

In illustration, the **main point** is the message you want your readers to receive and understand. The topic sentence (in a paragraph) or thesis statement (in an essay) usually includes the topic and the main point the writer wants to make about the topic. Let's look at a topic sentence first.

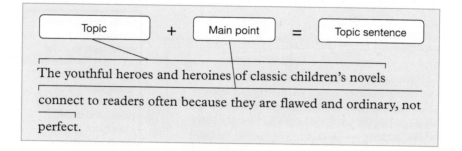

Remember that a thesis statement for an essay can be a little broader than a paragraph topic.

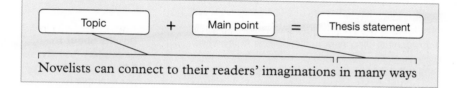

Whereas the topic sentence focuses on just one novel, the thesis statement for the essay considers novels in general.

Second and Third Basics: Support in Illustration

The paragraph and essay models on pages 80–81 use the topic sentence (paragraph) and thesis statement (essay) from the Main Point section of this chapter. Both models include the primary and secondary support used in all illustration writing: examples backed up by details about the examples. In the essay model, however, the major support points (examples) are topic sentences for individual paragraphs.

To generate good detailed examples, use one or more of the prewriting techniques discussed in Chapter 2. First, write down all the examples that come into your mind. Then, review your examples, and choose the ones that will best communicate your point to your readers. Support your examples with specific details that will help your reader visualize each one.

PARAGRAPHS VS. ESSAYS IN ILLUSTRATION

For more on the important features of narration, see the Four Basics of Good Illustration on page 77.

Paragraph Form

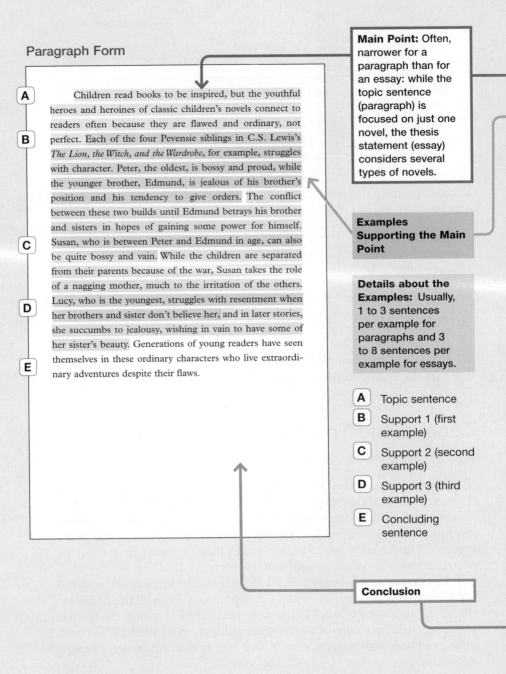

A   Children read books to be inspired, but the youthful heroes and heroines of classic children's novels connect to readers often because they are flawed and ordinary, not perfect. **B** Each of the four Pevensie siblings in C.S. Lewis's *The Lion, the Witch, and the Wardrobe,* for example, struggles with character. Peter, the oldest, is bossy and proud, while the younger brother, Edmund, is jealous of his brother's position and his tendency to give orders. The conflict between these two builds until Edmund betrays his brother and sisters in hopes of gaining some power for himself. **C** Susan, who is between Peter and Edmund in age, can also be quite bossy and vain. While the children are separated from their parents because of the war, Susan takes the role of a nagging mother, much to the irritation of the others. **D** Lucy, who is the youngest, struggles with resentment when her brothers and sister don't believe her, and in later stories, she succumbs to jealousy, wishing in vain to have some of her sister's beauty. **E** Generations of young readers have seen themselves in these ordinary characters who live extraordinary adventures despite their flaws.

Main Point: Often, narrower for a paragraph than for an essay: while the topic sentence (paragraph) is focused on just one novel, the thesis statement (essay) considers several types of novels.

Examples Supporting the Main Point

Details about the Examples: Usually, 1 to 3 sentences per example for paragraphs and 3 to 8 sentences per example for essays.

A   Topic sentence

B   Support 1 (first example)

C   Support 2 (second example)

D   Support 3 (third example)

E   Concluding sentence

Conclusion

Essay Form

Novel Love, by Katie Horn   1

Reading provides great joy; from newspapers to cereal boxes to blogs about physics, people seek to satisfy their craving for words, stories, and escape from everyday worries. This is why, of all the forms of reading material available to us, we often choose novels. Novels unravel tales filled with suspense, heroism, romance, and adventure. In penning fiction, every novelist's goal is to captivate readers; there are many ways that novelists can connect to their readers' imaginations. **[A]**

For example, mystery novelists engage readers' thinking skills. As characters uncover clues, the writer challenges the reader to assemble the puzzle pieces and solve the mystery before the characters do. In this way, the readers become the world-class detectives and unassuming gumshoes they admire on the page. The most talented mystery novelists often withhold a tidbit of truth from readers, waiting until the last moment to reveal the pivotal detail. Agatha Christie does this in *And Then There Were None*, in which the murderer is not revealed until a telltale manuscript is discovered in the epilogue. Because of such challenges, readers **[B]**

2

continue to seek new mystery titles, hungry for fresh plots to hone their armchair detective skills.

Novelists also rely on readers' insatiable curiosity: They tease readers to press through "just one more page" to find out what happens. Writers design stories with gaps that readers must fill. In horror fiction, for example, a reader's speculations can be more terrifying than the words on the page. Stephen King relies on this tactic in his novel *It*. What makes "It" terrifying is that It's identity is unknown; it could be nothing, or it could be something grotesque. By leaving readers to their own devices, writers like Stephen King allow each reader's psyche to conjure that which he or she fears most. **[C]**

In contrast to blood-chilling possibilities offered by horror writers, romance and fantasy writers invite readers to escape. The romance novelist, for example, allows the reader to admit inner yearnings and experience them through prose. Successful romance novelists sweep readers off their feet, much as their heroes charm the heroines. Taking escape to another level, fantasy novelists never tell their readers to "be realistic"; **[D]**

3

instead, they encourage people to embrace wonderment. But reading for escape is more than entertainment; many fantasy writers use their stories to reveal truth about what it means to be human. One of the most famous examples of this is C. S. Lewis's children's novel *The Lion, the Witch, and the Wardrobe*, a whimsical tale about siblings who travel to a snowy kingdom inside a closet. However, careful readers will recognize a battle between good and evil and a wealth of Christian symbolism. By grappling with topics, such as loyalty, purpose, betrayal, and faith in the context of an alternate universe, fantasy writers allow readers to deal with these issues at their own pace. Readers revisit fantasy for the opportunity to explore new worlds and to consider human experience.

Finally, novelists engage readers by exploring answers to the question "what if?" For example, science fiction writers take readers to an augmented reality. Beginning with a familiar reality, the author introduces a new scientific advancement that changes the very state of that reality. For example, what begins as a commonplace dinner party in H. G. Wells' novel *The Time Machine* quickly becomes an adventure in **[E]**

4

a futuristic Earth with the addition of a technological contraption. Sci-fi novelists appeal to budding scientists and dreamers alike, both of whom are spellbound by speculations on the future of technology and the people who use it. In today's technological age, readers are fascinated by the notion that the dreams of the sci-fi novelists may become the realities of tomorrow.

Novelists connect with their readers by presenting stories that enchant, enrich, and enthrall. Whether through intellectual stimulation, startling speculations, imaginative world-building, or the allure of romance, novelists provide entertainment and enjoyment. Storytelling has captivated humanity for thousands of years, and thanks to the skill of novelists, generations to come will be able to lose themselves in a good book. **[F]**

A Thesis statement

B Topic sentence 1 (first example)

C Topic sentence 2 (second example)

D Topic sentence 3 (third example)

E Topic sentence 4 (fourth example)

F Concluding paragraph

Fourth Basic: Organization in Illustration

Illustration often uses **order of importance**, saving the most powerful example for last. (For more on order of importance and time order, see pages 44 and 46.) This strategy is used in the paragraph and essay models on pages 80–81. Writers may also use order of emphasis, choosing which examples to emphasize based on the purpose of the essay. Or, if the examples are given according to when they happened, it might be organized by time order.

Transitions in illustration let readers know that you are introducing an example or moving from one example to another.

COMMON TRANSITIONS IN ILLUSTRATION			
also	first, second, and	for instance	in addition
another	so on	for one thing / for	the most / the least
finally	for example	another	one example / another example

Read and Analyze Illustration

After you read each of the selections below, answer the questions that follow.

Illustration in the Real World

Karen Upright, Systems Manager

Memo

After graduating from Florida Community College with an associate's degree, Karen Upright went on to earn her B.S. from Florida State University, her M.B.A. from Purdue University, and a B. A. in Modern Languages with a concentration in French at the University of Louisiana at Monroe in 2015. As a systems manager at Procter & Gamble, Upright writes memos, systems development plans, speeches for presentations, talk sheets to provide background at meetings, and technical design documents, and email. Below is an example of one of Upright's memos.

From: Upright, Karen
Subject: Women's Network: Assignment Planning Matrix

As you know, we have an enrollment goal for 30 percent of our employees to be women, but we are currently at 20 percent. We need to grow our enrollment, but we also need to retain the women currently in the organization. Greg and I met a few weeks ago to determine how to improve assignment planning for the women in our organization. We agreed to use the Assignment Planning Matrix as a starting point. The matrix is a good career-planning tool, with a section on career interests, rated from "highly desirable" to "undesirable." It also contains a section on specific P&G career interests, with sections to describe aspects that make a particular choice desirable or undesirable and a place to give weight to the various career choices. Completing the matrix requires thought as to what course an individual wants to pursue and why. I have reviewed a sample with and provided training to the women in our organization. Each of them has been asked to complete the matrix, meet with her manager to align on content, and submit a final version to her manager. This information can be shared at the next Leadership Team meeting.

This initiative has several objectives:

- Have each member of the network start a long-term plan for her career.
- Use the long-term plan to develop a short-term plan for assignments and competency development.
- Share this information in written form with the immediate manager and section manager of each member of the network, enabling the manager to speak for each woman's career interests and providing a reference point for each member's career goals.
- Enable the Leadership Team to plan assignments within the organization for each member of the network, matching individual goals and interests to organizational goals and needs.

I encourage you to support the women on your teams as they work through the Assignment Planning Matrix over the next few weeks. Please let me know if you have any questions.

1. Double-underline the main point of the memo.
2. Karen gives examples about two topics. What are the two topics?
3. What is the purpose of the memo? How does the purpose of the memo affect Karen's choice of examples and details?

Student Illustration Paragraph

Casandra Palmer

Gifts from the Heart

Casandra Palmer graduated from the University of Akron / Wayne College in 2009. After completing her essay "Gifts from the Heart," Palmer submitted it for publication in her campus paper at the encouragement of her instructor. She spent a few days revising the essay and looked to feedback from others to strengthen her points. Palmer enjoys reading inspirational novels and offers this advice to other student writers: "Learn all you can and never give up. Follow your dreams!"

In our home, gift exchanges have always been meaningful items to us. We do not just give things so that everyone has lots of presents. Each item has a purpose, such as a need or something that someone has desired for a long time. Some things have been given that may have made the other person laugh or cry. I remember one Christmas, our daughter Hannah had her boyfriend, who looked a lot like Harry Potter, join us. We wanted to include him, but we did not know him well, so it was hard to know what to give him. We decided to get Hannah a Harry Potter poster and crossed out the name Harry Potter. In place of Harry Potter, we put her boyfriend's name. Everyone thought it was funny, and we were all laughing, including Hannah's boyfriend. It was a personal gift that he knew we had thought about. For some reason, Hannah did not think it was so funny, but she will still remember it. Another meaningful gift came from watching the movie *Titanic* with my other daughter, Tabitha. We both cried hard and hugged each other. She surprised me by getting a necklace that resembled the gem known as "Heart of the Ocean." I was so touched that she gave me something to remind me of the experience we shared. These special moments have left lasting impressions on my heart.

1.   Double-underline the topic sentence.
2.   Underline the examples that support the main point.
3.   Circle the transitions.
4.   Does the paragraph have the Four Basics of Good Illustration (p. 77)? Why or why not?
5.   How is the paragraph organized? How does the organization relate to the purpose of the paragraph? Could Palmer have organized differently and still achieved her purpose?

Professional Illustration Essay

Susan Adams

The Weirdest Job Interview Questions and How to Handle Them

Seth David Cohen

Susan Adams is a senior editor at Forbes, a major publisher of business news. Previously, she was a reporter for the *MacNeil/Lehrer NewsHour*. Adams holds a B.A. from Brown University and a J.D. from Yale University Law School.

   Every week, Adams writes an advice column for Forbes.com. In the column reprinted below, she gives examples of some of the stranger questions that come up in job interviews.

1   I once interviewed for a job with a documentary producer who made boring if well-meaning films for public TV. By way of preparation, I studied up on the producer's projects and gave a lot of thought to how my interests and experience dovetailed with his. Our chat went swimmingly until he asked me a question that caught me completely off guard: "Who is your favorite comedian?"

2   Wait a second, I thought. Comedy is the opposite of what this guy does. My mind did back flips while I desperately searched for a comedian who might be a favorite of a tweedy, bearded liberal Democrat. After maybe 30 seconds too long, I blurted out my personal favorite: David Alan Grier, an African-American funnyman on the weekly Fox TV show *In Living Color*. My potential boss looked at me blankly as I babbled about how much I liked Grier's characters, especially Antoine Merriweather, one of the two gay reviewers in the brilliantly hilarious sketch "Men on Film."

3   Wrong answer. I had derailed the interview. My potential employer asked me a few more **perfunctory** questions and then saw me to the door.

perfunctory: quick

4   We all prepare studiously for job interviews, doing our homework about our potential employers and compiling short but detailed stories to illustrate our accomplishments, but how in the world do we prep for an off-the-wall interview question?

5   Glassdoor.com, a three-year-old Sausalito, California, website that bills itself as "the TripAdvisor for careers," has compiled a list of "top oddball interview questions" for two years running. Glassdoor gets its information directly from employees who work at 120,000 companies.

6   Crazy as it sounds, an interviewer at Schlumberger, the giant Houston oilfield services provider, once asked some poor job applicant, "What was your best MacGyver moment?," referring to a 1980s action-adventure TV show. At Goldman Sachs, the question was, "If you were shrunk to the size of a pencil and put in a blender, how would you get out?" At Deloitte, "How many ridges [are there] around a quarter?" At AT&T, "If you were a superhero, which superhero would you be?" And at Boston Consulting: "How many hair salons are there in Japan?"

7   No matter where you apply for work, there is a chance you could get a question from left field. According to Rusty Rueff—a consultant at Glassdoor who is the author of *Talent Force: A New Manifesto for the Human Side of Business* and former head of human resources at PepsiCo and Electronic Arts—most job applicants are woefully unprepared for off-the-wall questions. "Ninety percent of people don't know how to deal with them," he says. Like me, they freeze and their minds go blank.

8   To deal with that, Rueff advises, first you have to realize that the interviewer isn't trying to make you look stupid, as stupid as the question may seem. For instance, the MacGyver question is meant as an invitation to talk about how you got out of a tough jam. "They're not looking for you to tell about the time you took out your ballpoint and did a tracheotomy," Rueff notes. Rather, you can probably extract an answer from one of the achievement stories you prepared in advance.

9   With a question like "How many hair salons are there in Japan," the interviewer is giving you an opportunity to demonstrate your thought processes. Rueff says you should think out loud, like the contestants on *Who Wants to Be a Millionaire?* You might start by saying, We'd have to know the population of Japan, and then we'd have to figure out what percentage of them get their hair done and how often. Rueff says it's fine to pull out a pen and paper and start doing some calculations right there in the interview.

10   Connie Thanasoulis-Cerrachio, a career services consultant at Vault.com, agrees with Rueff. "These are called case interview questions," she says. Another example, which may seem equally impossible to answer: Why are manhole covers round?

11   In fact the manhole cover question, and "How would you move Mt. Fuji?," were brought to light in a 2003 book, *How Would You Move Mount Fuji? Microsoft's Cult of the Puzzle: How the World's Smartest Company Selects the Most Creative Thinkers*. Microsoft's grueling interview process often includes such problem-solving and logic questions. Just start thinking through the question, out loud, Thanasoulis-Cerrachio advises. "I would say, a round manhole cover could keep the framework of the tunnel stronger, because a round frame is much stronger than a square frame," she suggests. In fact, there are several reasons, including the fact that a round lid can't fall into the hole the way a square one can and the fact that it can be rolled.

12 Business schools teach students how to deal with case interview questions, and Vault has even put out a book on the subject, *Vault Guide to the Case Interview.*

13 Other weird-seeming questions, like "If you were a brick in a wall, which brick would you be and why," or "If you could be any animal, what would you be and why," are really just invitations to show a side of your personality. Thanasoulis-Cerrachio says a friend who is chief executive of a market research company used to ask applicants what kind of car they would be. "She wanted someone fast, who thought quickly," Thanasoulis-Cerrachio says. "She wanted someone who wanted to be a **Maserati**, not a **Bentley**." For the brick question, Thanasoulis-Cerrachio advises saying something like, "I would want to be a foundational brick because I'm a solid person. You can build on my experience and I will never let you down."

14 According to Rueff and Thanasoulis-Cerrachio, my comedian question was also a behavioral question, a test of my personality. "You gave a fine answer," says Rueff. Maybe. But I didn't get the job.

Maserati: a fast Italian sports car

Bentley: a British luxury car known more for elegance than speed

1. In your own words, state Adams's main point.
2. Underline the examples of weird interview questions.
3. Circle the transitional words in paragraph 8. Can you find more places to add transitions?
4. Who is Adams's intended audience? How does that audience influence her choice of examples to use? What assumptions does Adams make about her audience?
5. What is Adams's purpose? Do you think she accomplishes that purpose? Explain.

Write Your Own Illustration

Write an illustration paragraph, essay, or other document (as described below) on one of the following topics or on one of your own choice. For help, refer to the How to Write Illustration checklist on page 89.

College

■ Describe your goals for this course, making sure to explain the benefits of achieving each goal.

■ Produce a one- or two-page newsletter for other students in your class on one of the following topics. Make sure to describe each club, opportunity, and event in enough detail for readers. Also, include contact information, as well as hours and locations for events and club meetings.

- Student clubs
- Volunteer opportunities
- Upcoming campus events (such as lectures, movies, and sports events)
- Upcoming events in the larger community

Work

- What is the best or worst job you have ever had? Give examples of what made it the best or worst job.

- Think of the job you would most like to have after graduation. Then, write a list of your skills—both current ones and ones you will be building in college—that are relevant to the job. To identify skills you will be building through your degree program, you might refer to a course catalog. To identify relevant work skills, consider your past or present jobs as well as internships or other work experiences you would like to have before graduation. Finally, write a cover letter explaining why you are the best candidate for your ideal job. Be sure to provide several examples of your skills, referring to the list that you prepared.

Everyday Life

- Write a letter to your future grandchildren or great grandchildren. Describe the stresses in your life or things that you like about your life. Give plenty of details for each example.

- Imagine an exchange student is coming to your area for a few months. How would you characterize your city (county or region)? Is it fast-paced and busy? Relaxing? Artistic? Give examples to support your characterization.

CHECKLIST: How to Write Illustration	
STEPS	**DETAILS**
☐ **Narrow and explore your topic.** See Chapter 2.	• Make the topic more specific. • Prewrite to get ideas about the narrowed topic.
☐ **Write a topic sentence (paragraph) or thesis statement (essay).** See Chapter 3.	• State what you want your readers to understand about your topic.
☐ **Support your point.** See Chapter 3.	• Come up with examples and details to show, explain, or prove your main point to readers.
☐ **Write a draft.** See Chapter 4.	• Make a plan that puts examples in a logical order. • Include a topic sentence (paragraph) or thesis statement (essay) and all the supporting examples and details.
☐ **Revise your draft.** See Chapter 4.	• Make sure it has *all* of the Four Basics of Good Illustration. • Make sure you include transitions to move readers smoothly from one example to the next.
☐ **Edit your revised draft.** See Chapters 15 through 18.	• Correct errors in grammar, spelling, word use, and punctuation.

7

Description

Writing That Creates Pictures with Words

Understand What Description Is

Description is writing that creates a clear and vivid impression of a person, place, or thing, often by appealing to the physical senses.

> **Four Basics of Good Description**
>
> **1** It creates a main impression — an overall effect, feeling, or image — about the topic.
>
> **2** It uses specific examples to support the main impression.
>
> **3** It supports those examples with details that appeal to the five senses: sight, hearing, smell, taste, and touch.
>
> **4** It is organized logically by space, time, or order of importance or emphasis, according to the purpose of the essay.

In the following student paragraph, the numbers and colors correspond to the Four Basics of Good Description.

4 Details presented in chronological order.

Scars are stories written on a person's skin and sometimes on his heart. **1** My scar is not very big or very visible. **2** It is only about three inches long and an inch wide. It is on my knee, so it is usually covered, unseen. **3** It puckers the skin around it, and the texture of the scar itself is smoother than my real skin. It is flesh-colored, almost like a raggedy bandage. The story on my skin is a small one. **1** The story on my heart, though, is much deeper. **2** It was night, very cold, **3** my breath pluming into the frigid air. I took deep breaths that smelled like winter, piercing through my nasal passages and into my lungs as I walked to my car. I saw a couple making out against the wall of a building I was nearing. 2 I smiled and thought about them making their own heat. 3 I thought I saw steam coming from them, but maybe I imagined that. As I got near, I heard a familiar giggle: my girlfriend's. Then I saw her scarlet scarf, one I had given her, along with soft red leather gloves. I turned and ran, before they could see me. There was loud pounding in my ears, from the inside, sounding and feeling as if my brain had just become the loudest bass I had ever heard. My head throbbed, and slipping on some ice, I crashed to the ground, landing on my hands and knees, ripping my pants. I knew my knee was bleeding, even in the dark. I didn't care: that scar would heal. The other one would take a lot longer.

We read and write with description in many situations.

COLLEGE	On a physical therapy test, you describe the symptoms you observed in a patient.
WORK	You write a memo to your boss describing how the office could be arranged for increased efficiency.
EVERYDAY LIFE	You describe something you lost to the lost-and-found clerk at a store.

In college assignments, the word *describe* may mean *tell about* or *report*. When an assignment asks you to actually describe a person, place, or thing, however, you will need to use the kinds of specific descriptive details discussed later in this chapter.

First Basic: Main Point in Description

In description, the **main point** is the main impression you want to create for your readers. If you do not have a main impression about your topic, think about how it smells, sounds, looks, tastes, or feels.

The topic sentence (paragraph) or thesis statement (essay) in description usually contains both your narrowed topic and your main impression. Here is a topic sentence for a description paragraph:

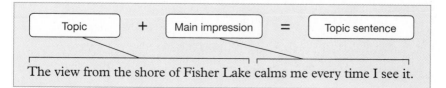

Topic + Main impression = Topic sentence

The view from the shore of Fisher Lake calms me every time I see it.

PARAGRAPHS VS. ESSAYS IN DESCRIPTION

For more on the important features of description, see the Four Basics of Good Description on page 90.

Paragraph Form

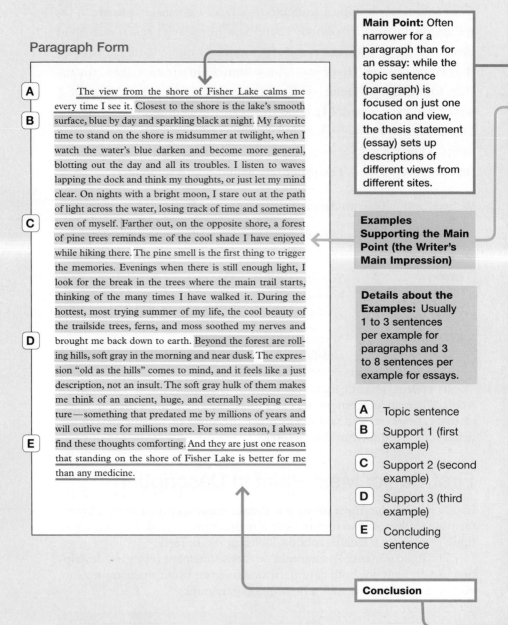

A The view from the shore of Fisher Lake calms me every time I see it. **B** Closest to the shore is the lake's smooth surface, blue by day and sparkling black at night. My favorite time to stand on the shore is midsummer at twilight, when I watch the water's blue darken and become more general, blotting out the day and all its troubles. I listen to waves lapping the dock and think my thoughts, or just let my mind clear. On nights with a bright moon, I stare out at the path of light across the water, losing track of time and sometimes even of myself. **C** Farther out, on the opposite shore, a forest of pine trees reminds me of the cool shade I have enjoyed while hiking there. The pine smell is the first thing to trigger the memories. Evenings when there is still enough light, I look for the break in the trees where the main trail starts, thinking of the many times I have walked it. During the hottest, most trying summer of my life, the cool beauty of the trailside trees, ferns, and moss soothed my nerves and brought me back down to earth. **D** Beyond the forest are rolling hills, soft gray in the morning and near dusk. The expression "old as the hills" comes to mind, and it feels like a just description, not an insult. The soft gray hulk of them makes me think of an ancient, huge, and eternally sleeping creature—something that predated me by millions of years and will outlive me for millions more. For some reason, I always find these thoughts comforting. **E** And they are just one reason that standing on the shore of Fisher Lake is better for me than any medicine.

Main Point: Often narrower for a paragraph than for an essay: while the topic sentence (paragraph) is focused on just one location and view, the thesis statement (essay) sets up descriptions of different views from different sites.

Examples Supporting the Main Point (the Writer's Main Impression)

Details about the Examples: Usually 1 to 3 sentences per example for paragraphs and 3 to 8 sentences per example for essays.

A Topic sentence

B Support 1 (first example)

C Support 2 (second example)

D Support 3 (third example)

E Concluding sentence

Conclusion

Essay Form

1

I have worked in many places, from a basement-level machine shop to a cubicle in a tenth-floor insurance office. Now that I am in the construction industry, I want to sing the praises of one employment benefit that does not get enough attention: The views from my sky-high welding jobs have been more stunning than any seen through an office window. **[A]**

From a platform at my latest job, on a high-rise, the streets below look like scenes from a miniature village. **[B]** The cars and trucks—even the rushing people—remind me of my nephews' motorized toys. Sometimes, the breeze carries up to me one of the few reminders that what I see is real: the smell of sausage or roasting chestnuts from street vendors, the honking of taxis or the scream of sirens, the dizzying clouds of diesel smoke. Once, the streets below me were taken over for a fair, and during my lunch break, I sat on a beam and watched the scene below. I spotted the usual things—packs of people strolling by concession stands or game tents, and bands playing to crowds at different ends of the fair. As I finished my lunch, I saw two small flames near

2

the edge of one band stage, nothing burning, nothing to fear. It was, I soon realized, an acrobat carrying two torches. I watched her climb high and walk a rope, juggling the torches as the crowd looked up and I looked down, fascinated.

Even more impressive are the sights from an oil rig. **[C]** Two years ago, I worked on a rig in Prudhoe Bay, Alaska, right at the water's edge. In the long days of summer, I loved to watch the changing light in the sky and on the water: bright to darker blue as the hours passed, and at day's end, a dying gold. At the greatest heights I could see white dots of ships far out at sea, and looking inland, I might spot musk ox or bears roaming in the distance. In the long winter dark, we worked by spotlights, which blotted the views below. But I still remember one time near nightfall when the spotlights suddenly flashed off. As my eyes adjusted, a crowd of caribou emerged below like ghosts. They snuffled the snow for food, oblivious to us.

To me, the most amazing views are those from bridges high over rivers. **[D]** In 2006, I had the privilege of briefly working on one of the tallest

3

bridge-observatories in the world, over the Penobscot River in Maine. As many tourists now do, I reached the height of the observatory's top deck, 437 feet. Unlike them, however, my visits were routine and labor-intensive, giving me little time to appreciate the beauty all around me. But on clear days, during breaks and at the end of our shift, my coworkers and I would admire the wide, sapphire-colored river as it flowed to Penobscot Bay. Looking south, we would track the Maine coast's winding to the Camden Hills. Looking east, we would spot Acadia National Park, the famous Mount Desert Island offshore in the mist. Each sight made up a panoramic view that I will never forget.

My line of work roots me in no one place, and it has a generous share of discomforts and dangers. But there are many reasons I would never trade it for another, and one of the biggest is the height from which it lets me see the world. For stretches of time, I feel nearly super human. **[E]**

[A] Thesis statement
[B] Topic sentence 1 (first example)
[C] Topic sentence 2 (second example)
[D] Topic sentence 3 (third example)
[E] Concluding paragraph

A topic for an essay can be a little broader than one for a paragraph.

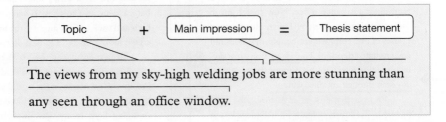

Whereas the topic sentence is focused on just one location and view, the thesis statement sets up descriptions of different views from different sites.

To be effective, your topic sentence or thesis statement should be specific. You can make it specific by adding details that appeal to the senses.

Second and Third Basics: Support in Description

In description, primary support consists of the specific examples and details that show readers the main idea or dominant impression of the essay. Secondary support includes details that help readers experience the sights, sounds, smells, tastes, and textures of your topic. With strong support in description, writers do more than tell their readers a main idea—they show it.

The paragraph and essay models on pages 92–93 use the topic sentence (paragraph) and thesis statement (essay) from the Main Point section of this chapter. Both models include the support used in all descriptive writing—examples that communicate the writer's main impression, backed up by specific sensory details. In the essay model, however, the major support points (examples) are topic sentences for individual paragraphs.

Fourth Basic: Organization in Description

Description can use any of the orders of organization—**time, space,** emphasis, or **importance**—depending on your purpose. (For more on these orders of organization, see pp. 44–46.) If you are writing to create a main impression of an event (for example, a description of fireworks), you might use time order. If you are describing what someone or something looks like, you might use space order, the strategy used in the paragraph model on page 92. If one detail about your topic is stronger than the others, you could use order of importance and leave that detail for last. This approach is taken in the essay model on page 93.

Use **transitions** that match your order of organization to move your readers from one sensory detail to the next (see p. 60 for a list of transitions).

Read and Analyze Description

After you read each of the selections below, answer the questions that follow.

Description in the Real World

James C. Roy

Incident Report: Malicious Wounding

James C. Roy is the Chief of Police for Lord Fairfax Community College in Middletown, Virginia. As a police officer, he writes reports daily. In these reports, he must document what he observes, what he says, and what he does. Because these reports can be used in court, it is important to be accurate and thorough. As Roy explains, "In police reports, if you don't write it down, it didn't happen."

At 03:20 a.m. I responded to a call for a fight and gunshots. When I arrived in the area, several people in the roadway pointed across a field to a mobile home on Yancey Drive. A woman, Ginny Pyle, was walking around a car in front of the mobile home and shouting. Two men, later identified as Jerry Smythe and his father Willie Smythe, were sitting on the porch of the mobile home, and two other men were on the ground. I approached them and saw Gary Pyle Sr. on top of his son, Gary Pyle Jr., holding him down on the ground. Pyle Sr. yelled, "Arrest him! He's drunk and out of control." Pyle Jr. was bleeding from his nose and had small bloody scrapes on his arms. A strong odor of alcohol was on his breath, and he exhibited bloodshot eyes, slurred speech, and unsteady balance. Deputy White arrested Pyle Jr. for being drunk in public.

When I walked back to the mobile home, Jerry Smythe said, "I've been shot." I noticed two bloody wounds above and below his right knee. Smythe claimed he was sleeping on his couch when Pyle Jr. shot him through the window of the front door of his mobile home. The front door window was approximately ten inches by ten inches and was broken, with most of the broken glass lying on the inside of the doorway. Blood was mingled with broken glass on the porch.

I spoke with Pyle Jr., who was handcuffed and sitting in the back of Deputy White's patrol vehicle. I read him his Miranda Rights and then asked, "Where is the gun?" Pyle Jr. laughed and said, "You'll never find it." Deputy White transported Pyle Jr. to the county jail, and Jerry Smythe was transported to the hospital at 03:30 a.m. Detective Gomez arrived on location at 04:14 a.m. to process the scene.

1. What is your main impression of the scene?
2. Underline the details that support the main impression. How does Roy's purpose affect his choice of details?
3. What senses do the details appeal to?
4. How is the description organized?

Student Description Paragraph

Alessandra Cepeda

Bird Rescue

Alessandra Cepeda became deeply involved in animal welfare during her time at Bunker Hill Community College (BHCC), from which she received associate's degrees in education and early childhood education. While at BHCC, Cepeda assisted the Humane Society with animal-rescue efforts. In the following paragraph, Cepeda describes the scene at a storage unit containing abandoned birds.

When the owner opened the empty storage unit, we could not believe that any living creature could have survived under such horrible conditions. The inside was complete darkness, with no windows and no ventilation. The air hit us with the smell of rot and decay. A flashlight revealed three birds, quiet and huddled in the back corner. They were quivering and looked sickly. Two of the birds had injured wings, hanging from them uselessly at odd angles, obviously broken. They were exotic birds who should have had bright and colorful feathers, but the floor of the unit was covered in the feathers they had molted. We entered slowly and retrieved the abused birds. I cried at how such beautiful and helpless creatures had been mistreated. We adopted two of them, and our Samantha is now eight years old, with beautiful green feathers topped off with a brilliant blue and red head. She talks, flies, and is a wonderful pet who is dearly loved and, I admit, very spoiled. She deserves it after such a rough start to her life.

1. Double-underline the topic sentence.
2. What main impression does the writer create?
3. Underline the sensory details (sight, sound, smell, taste, texture) that create the main impression.
4. Does the paragraph have the Four Basics of Good Description (p. 90)? Why or why not?

Professional Description Essay

Oscar Hijuelos

Memories of New York City Snow

Taylor Hill/Getty Images

Oscar Hijuelos, the son of Cuban immigrants, was born in New York City in 1951. After receiving undergraduate and master's degrees from the City University of New York, he took a job at an advertising firm and wrote fiction at night. His first novel, *The Mambo Kings Play Songs of Love* (1989), was awarded the Pulitzer Prize for fiction, making Hijuelos the first Latino writer to receive this honor. His most recent novels include *Dark Dude* (2008) and *Beautiful Maria of My Soul* (2010).

The following essay was taken from the anthology *Metropolis Found* (2003). In it, Hijuelos describes a New York City winter from the perspective of new immigrants.

1   For immigrants of my parents' generation, who had first come to New York City from the much warmer climate of Cuba in the mid-1940s, the very existence of snow was a source of fascination. A black-and-white photograph that I have always loved, circa 1948, its surface cracked like that of a thawing ice-covered pond, features my father, Pascual, and my godfather, Horacio, fresh up from **Oriente Province**, posing in a snow-covered meadow in Central Park. Decked out in long coats, scarves, and black-rimmed hats, they are holding, in their be-gloved hands, a huge chunk of hardened snow. Trees and their straggly witch's hair branches, glimmering with ice and frost, recede into the distance behind them. They stand on a field of whiteness, the two men seemingly afloat in midair, as if they were being held aloft by the magical substance itself.

> **Oriente Province:** a former province of Cuba, in the eastern part of the country

2   That they bothered to have this photograph taken—I suppose to send back to family in Cuba—has always been a source of enchantment for me. That something so common to winters in New York would strike them as an object of exotic admiration has always spoken volumes about the newness—and innocence—of their immigrants' experience. How thrilling it all must have seemed to them, for their New York was so very different from the small town surrounded by farms in eastern Cuba that they hailed from. Their New York was a fanciful and bustling city of endless sidewalks and unimaginably high buildings; of great bridges and twisting outdoor elevated train trestles; of walkup **tenement houses** with mysteriously dark basements, and subways that burrowed through

> **tenement houses:** apartment buildings, often crowded and in poor shape

burlesque houses: theaters that offer live, often humorous, performances and/or striptease acts

an underworld of girded tunnels; of dance halls, **burlesque houses,** and palatial department stores with their complement of Christmas Salvation Army Santa Clauses on every street corner. Delightful and perilous, their New York was a city of incredibly loud noises, of police and air raid sirens and factory whistles and subway rumble; a city where people sometimes shushed you for speaking Spanish in a public place, or could be unforgiving if you did not speak English well or seemed to be of a different ethnic background. (My father was once nearly hit by a garbage can that had been thrown off the rooftop of a building as he was walking along La Salle Street in upper Manhattan.)

3   Even so, New York represented the future. The city meant jobs and money. Newly arrived, an aunt of mine went to work for Pan Am; another aunt, as a Macy's saleslady. My own mother, speaking nary a word of English, did a stint in the garment district as a seamstress. During the war some family friends, like my godfather, were eventually drafted, while others ended up as factory laborers. Landing a job at the Biltmore Men's Bar, my father joined the hotel and restaurant workers' union, paid his first weekly dues, and came home one day with a brand new white chef's

toque: a hat worn by chefs or kitchen staff

toque in hand. Just about everybody found work, often for low pay and ridiculously long hours. And while the men of that generation worked a lot of overtime, or a second job, they always had their day or two off. Dressed

to the hilt: [dressed] in the fanciest clothing

to the hilt, they'd leave their uptown neighborhoods and make an excursion to another part of the city—perhaps to one of the grand movie palaces of Times Square or to beautiful Central Park, as my father and godfather, and their ladies, had once done, in the aftermath of a snowfall.

4   Snow, such as it can only fall in New York City, was not just about the cold and wintry differences that mark the weather of the north. It was about a purity that would descend upon the grayness of its streets like a heaven of silence, the city's complexity and bustle abruptly subdued. But as beautiful as it could be, it was also something that provoked nostalgia; I am certain that my father would miss Cuba on some bitterly cold days. I remember that whenever we were out on a walk and it began to snow,

connotation: meaning or association

my father would stop and look up at the sky, with wonderment—what he was seeing I don't know. Perhaps that's why to this day my own as-sociations with a New York City snowfall have a mystical **connotation,**

inaccessible divinity: unreachable god

as if the presence of snow really meant that some kind of **inaccessible divinity** had settled his breath upon us.

1. Double-underline the thesis statement.
2. Underline the sensory details (sight, sound, smell, taste, texture).
3. Circle the transitions.
4. Does the essay create a clear picture of New York City in the winter? Why or why not?
5. What is Hijuelos's purpose? For whom is the author writing?

Write Your Own Description

Write a description paragraph or essay on one of the following topics or on one of your own choice. For help, refer to the How to Write Description checklist on page 100.

College

Many college writing assignments require careful observation and description, especially in the sciences and social sciences. The following two assignments help you to practice these skills.

- Describe the sights, sounds, smells, and tastes in the cafeteria or another dining spot on campus.

- Find a place where you can get a good view of your campus (for instance, a window on an upper floor of one of the buildings). Then, describe the scene using space order (pp. 44–46). Consider how your location influences the details of your description.

Work

- Describe your workplace, including as many sensory details as you can. Before you begin, choose an audience: a friend considering a job at your workplace, an inspector or auditor, or a family member who has never visited your workplace.

- Describe your boss or a colleague you work with closely. First, think of the main impression you get from this person. Then, choose details that would make your impression clear to readers.

Everyday Life

- Describe a holiday celebration from your past, including as many sensory details as possible. Think back on the people who attended, the food served, the decorations, and so on.

- Visit an organization that serves your community, such as an animal shelter or a food pantry. During your visit, take notes about what you see. Later, write a detailed description of the scene.

CHECKLIST: How to Write Description	
STEPS	**DETAILS**
☐ Narrow and explore your topic. See Chapter 2.	• Make the topic more specific. • Prewrite to get ideas about the narrowed topic.
☐ Write a topic sentence (paragraph) or thesis statement (essay). See Chapter 3.	• State what is most interesting, vivid, and important about your topic.
☐ Support your point. See Chapter 3.	• Come up with examples and details that create a main impression about your topic.
☐ Write a draft. See Chapter 4.	• Make a plan that puts examples in a logical order. • Include a topic sentence (paragraph) or thesis statement (essay) and all the supporting examples and details.
☐ Revise your draft. See Chapter 4.	• Make sure it has *all* the Four Basics of Good Description. • Make sure you include transitions to move readers smoothly from one detail to the next.
☐ Edit your revised draft. See Chapters 15 through 18.	• Correct errors in grammar, spelling, word use, and punctuation.

Process Analysis

Writing That Explains How Things Happen

Understand What Process Analysis Is

Process analysis either explains how to do something (so that your readers can do it) or explains how something works (so that your readers can understand it).

> **Four Basics** of Good Process Analysis
>
> **1** It tells readers what process the writer wants them to know about and makes a point about it.
>
> **2** It presents the essential steps in the process.
>
> **3** It explains the steps in detail.
>
> **4** It presents the steps in a logical order (usually time order).

In the following paragraph, the numbers and colors correspond to the Four Basics of Good Process Analysis.

The poet Dana Gioia once said, "Art delights, instructs, consoles. It educates our emotions." **1** Closely observing paintings, sculpture, and other forms of visual art is a great way to have the type of experience that Gioia describes, and following a few basic steps will help you get the most from the experience. **2** First, choose an art exhibit that interests you. **3** You can find listings for exhibits on local museums' websites or in the arts section of a newspaper. Links on the websites or articles in a newspaper may give you more information about the exhibits, the artists featured in them, and the types of work to be displayed. **2** Second, go to the museum with an open mind and, ideally, with a friend. **3** While moving through the exhibit, take time to examine each work

4 Time order is used.

101

carefully. As you do so, ask yourself questions: What is my eye most drawn to, and why? What questions does this work raise for me, and how does it make me feel? How would I describe it to someone over the phone? Ask your friend the same questions, and consider the responses. You might also consult an exhibit brochure for information about the featured artists and their works. **2** Finally, keep your exploration going after you have left the museum. **3** Go out for coffee or a meal with your friend. Trade more of your thoughts and ideas about the artwork, and discuss your overall impressions. If you are especially interested in any of the artists or their works, you might look for additional information or images on the internet, or you might consult books at the library. Throughout the whole experience, put aside the common belief that only artists or cultural experts "get" art. The artist Eugène Delacroix described paintings as "a bridge between the soul of the artist and that of the spectator." Trust your ability to cross that bridge and come to new understandings.

You read and write process analysis in many situations:

COLLEGE	In a science course, you read and follow instructions for a lab experiment, or you explain photosynthesis for a written exam.
WORK	You write instructions to explain how to operate something (the copier, the fax machine).
EVERYDAY LIFE	You read and follow directions for cleaning up your PC, or you write out a recipe for an aunt.

In college, a writing assignment may ask you to *describe the process of,* but you might be also be asked to *describe the stages of* _____ or *explain how* _____ *works.* Whenever you need to identify and explain the steps or stages of anything, you will use process analysis.

First Basic: Main Point in Process Analysis

In process analysis, your **purpose** is to explain how to do something or how something works. Your **main point** should tell readers what process you are describing and what you want readers to know about it. Here is an example of a topic sentence for a paragraph:

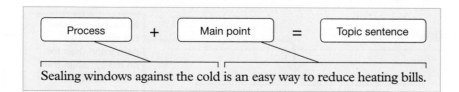

Remember that the topic for an essay can be a little broader than one for a paragraph.

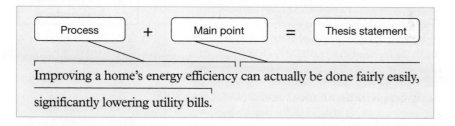

Whereas the topic sentence focuses on just one method to improve energy efficiency, the thesis statement sets up a discussion of multiple methods.

Second and Third Basics: Support in Process Analysis

The paragraph and essay models on pages 104–105 use the topic sentence (paragraph) and thesis statement (essay) from the Main Point section of this chapter. Both models include the primary and secondary support used in all writing about processes: the steps in the process backed up by descriptive details that allow readers to understand the process or follow the steps for themselves. In the essay model, however, the major support points (steps) are topic sentences for individual paragraphs.

Fourth Basic: Organization in Process Analysis

Process analysis is usually organized by **time order** because it explains the steps of the process in the order in which they occur, starting with the first step. (For more on time order, see p. 44.) This is the strategy used in the paragraph and essay models on pages 104–105.

PARAGRAPHS VS. ESSAYS IN PROCESS ANALYSIS

For more on the important features of process analysis, see the Four Basics of Good Process Analysis on page 101.

Paragraph Form

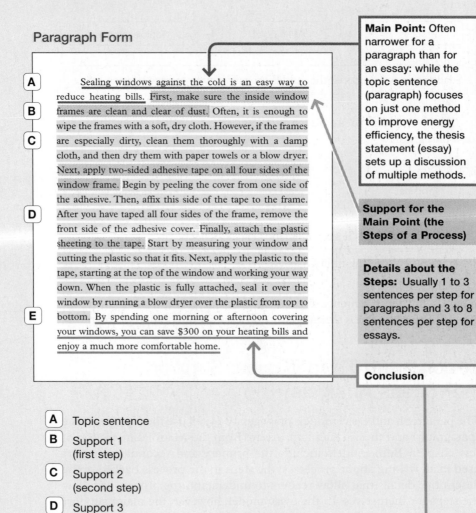

A   Sealing windows against the cold is an easy way to reduce heating bills. **B** First, make sure the inside window frames are clean and clear of dust. Often, it is enough to wipe the frames with a soft, dry cloth. However, if the frames **C** are especially dirty, clean them thoroughly with a damp cloth, and then dry them with paper towels or a blow dryer. Next, apply two-sided adhesive tape on all four sides of the window frame. Begin by peeling the cover from one side of the adhesive. Then, affix this side of the tape to the frame. **D** After you have taped all four sides of the frame, remove the front side of the adhesive cover. Finally, attach the plastic sheeting to the tape. Start by measuring your window and cutting the plastic so that it fits. Next, apply the plastic to the tape, starting at the top of the window and working your way down. When the plastic is fully attached, seal it over the window by running a blow dryer over the plastic from top to **E** bottom. By spending one morning or afternoon covering your windows, you can save $300 on your heating bills and enjoy a much more comfortable home.

Main Point: Often narrower for a paragraph than for an essay: while the topic sentence (paragraph) focuses on just one method to improve energy efficiency, the thesis statement (essay) sets up a discussion of multiple methods.

Support for the Main Point (the Steps of a Process)

Details about the Steps: Usually 1 to 3 sentences per step for paragraphs and 3 to 8 sentences per step for essays.

Conclusion

A Topic sentence

B Support 1 (first step)

C Support 2 (second step)

D Support 3 (third step)

E Concluding sentence

Essay Form

1

Many people are intimidated by the work necessary to make their homes more energy efficient, and they do not see it as a do-it-yourself job. However, improving a home's energy efficiency can actually be done fairly easily, significantly lowering utility bills.

First, seal air leaks around windows and doors. To seal air leaks around windows, apply caulk between window frames and walls. Also, if you have old-fashioned windows that are not weather-proof, cover them with plastic before the cold temperatures set in. This process involves affixing two-sided adhesive tape to the window frames and then attaching plastic sheeting, which is sealed with the use of a blow dryer. Next, look for drafty spots around doors. Many air leaks at the top or sides of doors can be sealed with adhesive-backed foam strips. Leaks under doors can be stopped with foam draft guards. Alternatively, a rolled-up blanket, rug, or towel can keep the cold from coming in. All of these measures can save up to $600 per season on heating bills.

2

Second, install water-saving shower heads and faucet aerators. These fixtures are inexpensive and are available in most hardware stores. Also, they are easy to install. First, unscrew the old shower or faucet head. Then, follow the package instructions for affixing the new shower head or aerator. In some cases, you might have to use pipe tape or a rubber washer to ensure a good seal. After this step, run the water to make sure there are no leaks. If you find any leaks, use pliers to tighten the seal. In time, you will discover that the new shower heads and aerators will cut your water usage and the cost of water heating by up to 50 percent.

Finally, look for other places where energy efficiency could be increased. One simple improvement is to replace traditional light bulbs with LED bulbs, which use up to 80 percent less energy. Also, make sure your insulation is as good as it can be. Many utilities now offer free assessments of home insulation, identifying places where it is missing or inadequate. In some cases, any necessary insulation improvements

3

may be subsidized by the utilities or by government agencies. It is well worth considering such improvements, which, in the case of poorly insulated homes, can save thousands of dollars a year, quickly covering any costs. Although some people prefer to have professionals blow insulating foam into their walls, it is not difficult to add insulation to attics, where a large amount of heat can be lost during cold months.

Taking even one of these steps can make a significant financial difference in your life and also reduce your impact on the environment. My advice, though, is to improve your home's energy efficiency as much as possible, even if it means doing just a little at a time. The long-term payoff is too big to pass up.

A Thesis statement
B Topic sentence 1 (first step)
C Topic sentence 2 (second step)
D Topic sentence 3 (third step)
E Concluding paragraph

Transitions move readers smoothly from one step to the next.

COMMON TRANSITIONS IN PROCESS ANALYSIS			
after	eventually	meanwhile	since
as	finally	next	soon
at last	first	now	then
before	last	once	when
during	later	second	while

Read and Analyze Process Analysis

After you read each of the selections below, answer the questions that follow.

Process Analysis in the Real World

Stephen Martin, Musician

How to Practice Simple Meditation

Stephen Martin is a musician and graphic artist, who, like many people in the workplace, deals with daily stresses and anxieties. After learning about meditation, he started practicing it regularly and found that it helped him to relax and cope better with the pressures of life both personally and professionally. Here he writes about the steps in a simple meditation practice.

Meditation is a general term for mental exercises used for focusing one's awareness on the present moment. There is a growing literature on the many psychological benefits of meditative practice including the reduction of stress, anxiety, and depression. There are many techniques, and what follows is a step-by-step process for a basic practice you can do at home or at the office. First, set aside time to meditate. You can meditate for as long as or as short a time as you feel comfortable, but it's important to designate a regular daily time for your practice. This will help you stay focused and free from distraction. Next, sit or lie down comfortably with your back straight. You can sit in a chair with your feet flat on the ground or on a cushion with your legs crossed, or you can lie on the floor with your head on a pillow. Find what works best for you and make sure to keep your spine straight. Once you are situated, close your eyes and breathe through your nose, becoming aware of the sensation of breathing. Notice where you feel the breath most clearly, perhaps on your upper lip or in your diaphragm as it expands and contracts, and focus your attention on this place. When you notice your mind wandering, gently and determinedly move your attention back to the sensation of the breath. Continue this process of observing your breathing for the duration of time you set aside. This is a basic way to train and quiet your mind.

1. What are the steps in this process?
2. How does Martin show transitions from one step to the next?
3. What is Martin's purpose?
4. Does this paragraph have the Four Basics of Good Process Analysis (p. 101)?

Student Process Analysis Paragraph

Charlton Brown

Buying a Car at an Auction

Buying a car at an auction is a good way to get a cheap car, but buyers need to be prepared. First, decide what kind of vehicle you want to buy. Then, find a local auction. Scams are common, though, so be careful. Three top sites that are legitimate are www.gov-auctions.org, www .carauctioninc.com, and www.seizecars.com. When you have found an auction and a vehicle you are interested in, become a savvy buyer. Make sure you know the car's actual market value. You can find this out from Edmunds.com, Kellybluebook.com, or NADA (the National Automobile Dealers Association). Because bidding can become like a competition, decide on the highest bid you will make, and stick to that. Do not get drawn into the competition. On the day of the auction, get to the auction early so that you can look at the actual cars. If you do not know about cars yourself, bring someone who does with you to the auction so that he or she can examine the car. Next, begin your thorough examination. Check the exterior; especially look for any signs that the car has been in an accident. Also, check the windshield because many states will not give an inspection sticker to cars with any damage to the windshield. Check the interior and try the brakes. Start the engine and listen to how it sounds. Check the heat and air conditioning, the CD player, and all other functions. As a final check before the bidding, look at the car's engine and transmission. Finally, get ready to place your bid, and remember, do not go beyond the amount you settled on earlier. Good luck!

1. Double-underline the topic sentence.

2. What are Brown's main point, audience, and purpose?

3. Underline the major steps. Are all the major steps included? Will readers have any unanswered questions?

4. Circle the transition words that signal when Brown moves from one step to the next.

5. Does Brown's paragraph follow the Four Basics of Good Process Analysis (p. 101)? Why or why not?

Professional Process Analysis Essay

Eric Rosenberg

How to Start Your Service Based Side Hustle

Eric Rosenberg is a finance, travel, and technology writer in Ventura, California. When away from the keyboard, Eric enjoys exploring the world, flying small airplanes, discovering new craft beers, and spending time with his wife and daughters. You can connect with him at PersonalProfitability.com or EricRosenberg.com.

1   Many people think their income is capped at what they make at their day job, but that is far from the case. Over the last few years, people of all ages, though most notably Millennials, have jumped on the side hustle bandwagon looking to earn more outside of their "9 to 5" income source. Starting a new side business is not always easy, but it can be fun, educational, and lead to a great payoff.

Identify Your Strongest Skills

2   Before you start a side hustle, you should take some time to list out your skills and favorite hobbies, as those are the best places to look when starting a new, service-based side hustle. If you are already good at something or enjoy doing it, you might as well make money at the same time!

3   Some popular side hustles today include home and lawn care and maintenance, website and application design and development, and

gig-based income from apps like Uber, Lyft, TaskRabbit, and Fiverr. There is no right or wrong choice, just what works best for you.

Register Your Business, Maybe

4   Any time you earn money outside of a job, you are considered by the government to be running a business. However, that doesn't mean you have to register your business with the state right away. If you are not worried about legal issues and earn less than $40,000 per year, you are likely safe operating as a sole proprietorship, a legal term for a business run under your own name.

5   If you are serious about building something long-term, or even turning your side hustle into a full-time income at some point in the future, you may be best off registering as a limited liability corporation, or LLC. Registering offers some legal benefits in the event of a lawsuit and may help you save on taxes, but it also comes with additional paperwork and some costs. If in doubt, speak to a local attorney or tax professional for additional information and advice.

Build a Website and Promote Your Business

6   Depending on the service you choose, you have multiple options to sell your services to potential clients. In the new Millennium, the first place you should look is the internet. Nearly everyone in the developed world has internet access, so a website gives you a wide reach. It also shows that your business is serious and professional, and gives you an opportunity to show off why someone should hire you instead of a competitor.

7   Next, get offline and promote your business in your local community. Post flyers at local businesses and tell anyone who will listen about your new business. You might find friends and family make the best first customers, even if you give them a discount, as they can help you build a client base and give feedback to improve as you bring on additional customers.

Refine Processes and Grow Your Income

8   Pay attention to every little detail in your business as it begins to bring in revenue. As a business owner, you may find regular opportunities to improve your customer's experience and business processes to save you time and money.

9   For example, it should be very easy on your customers to pay you. Whether they want to pay by check, credit card, or online at your website, you should have the ability to turn on those features. By focusing on your customer's pain points, you are working to turn one-time customers into valuable, repeat customers.

10   No detail is too small to overlook. Business leader Jeff Bezos founded a company in his garage with a core value that leaders "obsess over customers." That little company turned into Amazon.com and made Bezos

the wealthiest person alive. Never underestimate the value of customer loyalty when building a new business, even if it is just a small side hustle.

The Bottom Line

11   The business climate is always changing. Starting a new business is easier than ever, and if you can draw on your skills to earn more outside of work, there is no limit to what you can earn. Side hustlers use their added income to pay off debt, buy homes, and reach new levels of financial stability. You can do the same, but you can't earn a dollar until you make the effort to get started.

1.   The first paragraph contains Rosenberg's thesis statement. Double underline it.

2.   Rosenberg uses both subtitles and transitions to show the steps in the process. Circle the transitions that introduce the steps.

3.   Does this essay follow the Four Basics of Good Process Analysis (p. 101)? Why or why not?

4.   Look at the supporting details that Rosenberg uses to illustrate each step. What does his choice of details (especially his use of proper nouns) tell you about his target audience?

Write Your Own Process Analysis

Write a process analysis paragraph or essay on one of the following topics or on one of your own choice. For help, refer to the How to Write Process Analysis checklist on page 111.

College

■   Think about the last time you prepared for a major test. Describe your process using as many details as possible. Were you successful on the test? Review your process in light of the results, and consider any changes you might need to make.

■   Attend a tutoring session at your college's writing center. Afterward, describe the process: what specific things did the tutor do to help you? Also, explain what you learned from the process.

Work

■   Interview at least three people who have recently been interviewed for a job. Use that information to describe how to make a positive impression at a job interview.

- Think of a challenging task you had to accomplish at work. What steps did you go through to complete it?

Everyday Life

- Consider a hobby or talent that you can share. Describe the process of making something, such as a favorite meal, a set of shelves, or a sweater.

- Take part in a community activity, such as a fund-raising event for a charity, a neighborhood cleanup, or food preparation at a homeless shelter. Then, describe the process you went through.

CHECKLIST: How to Write Process Analysis	
STEPS	**DETAILS**
☐ Narrow and explore your topic. See Chapter 2.	• Make the topic more specific. • Prewrite to get ideas about the narrowed topic.
☐ Write a topic sentence (paragraph) or thesis statement (essay). See Chapter 3.	• Decide what you want readers to know about the process you are describing.
☐ Support your point. See Chapter 3.	• Include the steps in the process, and explain the steps in detail.
☐ Write a draft. See Chapter 4.	• Make a plan that puts examples in a logical order. • Include a topic sentence (paragraph) or thesis statement (essay) and all the supporting details about each step.
☐ Revise your draft. See Chapter 4.	• Make sure it has *all* the Four Basics of Good Process Analysis. • Make sure you include transitions to move readers smoothly from one step to the next.
☐ Edit your revised draft. See Chapters 15 through 18.	• Correct errors in grammar, spelling, word use, and punctuation.

9

Classification

Writing That Sorts Things into Groups

Understand What Classification Is

Classification is writing that organizes, or sorts, people or items into categories. It uses an **organizing principle**: *how* the people or items are sorted. The organizing principle is directly related to the purpose for classifying. For example, you might sort clean laundry (your purpose) using one of the following organizing principles: by ownership (yours, your roommate's) or by where it goes (the bedroom, the bathroom).

Four Basics of Good Classification

1 It makes sense of a group of people or items by organizing them into categories according to a single organizing principle.

2 It sets up logical and comprehensive categories.

3 It gives detailed explanations or examples with details of what fits into each category.

4 It organizes information by time, space, emphasis, or importance depending on its purpose.

In the following paragraph, the numbers and colors correspond to the Four Basics of Good Classification.

4
Categories arranged by order of emphasis.

1 In researching careers I might pursue, I have learned that there are three major types of workers, each having different strengths and preferences. **2** The first type of worker is a big-picture person, who likes to look toward the future and think of new businesses, products, and services. **3** Big-picture people might also identify ways to make their workplaces more successful and productive. Often, they hold

112

leadership positions, achieving their goals by assigning specific projects and tasks to others. Big-picture people may be drawn to starting their own businesses. Or they might manage or become a consultant for an existing business. **2** The second type of worker is a detail person, who focuses on the smaller picture, whether it be a floor plan in a construction project, a spreadsheet showing a business's revenue and expenses, or data from a scientific experiment. **3** Detail people take pride in understanding all the ins and outs of a task and doing everything carefully and well. Some detail people prefer to work with their hands, doing such things as carpentry or electrical wiring. Others prefer office jobs, such as accounting or clerical work. Detail people may also be drawn to technical careers, such as scientific research or engineering. **2** The third type of worker is a people person, who gets a lot of satisfaction from reaching out to others and helping meet their needs. **3** A people person has good social skills and likes to get out in the world to use them. Therefore, this type of worker is unlikely to be happy sitting behind a desk. A successful people person often shares qualities of the other types of workers; for example, he or she may show leadership potential. In addition, his or her job may require careful attention to detail. Good jobs for a people person include teaching, sales, nursing, and other health-care positions. Having evaluated my own strengths and preferences, I believe that I am equal parts big-picture person and people person. I am happy to see that I have many career options.

You read and write classification anytime you work with organized groups of people or things.

COLLEGE	In a criminal justice course, you are asked to discuss the most common types of chronic offenders.
WORK	For a sales presentation, you classify the kinds of products your company produces.
EVERYDAY LIFE	You explore types of budgeting systems, and then you classify your typical monthly expenses to make a budget.

In college, writing assignments probably will not use the word *classification*. Instead, you might be asked to *describe the types of* _____ or *explain the types or kinds of* _____. You might also be asked, *How is* _____ *organized?* or *How is* _____ *divided into groups?* These are words and phrases that signal that you need to use classification to sort things into categories.

First Basic: Main Point in Classification

The **main point** in classification uses a single **organizing principle** to sort items in a way that serves your purpose. The categories should help you achieve your purpose. The main point may or may not state the organizing principle directly. Look at the following examples:

TOPIC SENTENCE

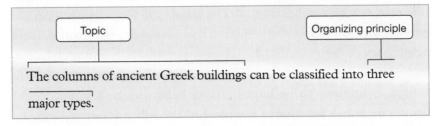

THESIS STATEMENT

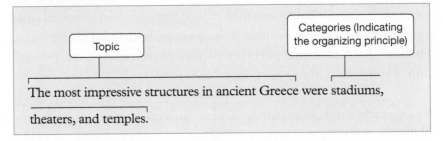

In the first example, the organizing principle is the type of column as determined by the date of development and the major structural features. While the words "date" and "features" are not mentioned directly, each category is defined by these principles. In the second example, the structures of ancient Greece are divided into types according to the purpose of the structure (sports, performances, or worship). The words "type of building" and "purpose" are not stated directly. Instead, the categories themselves—stadiums, theaters, and temples—and the details given about each one make the organizing principle clear.

Also, notice that the topic for the essay is broader than the one for the paragraph, which is often the case. Whether you are writing a paragraph or an essay, make sure that you use only one organizing principle; two organizing principles can confuse readers. Consider the following categories of professors: *demanding, monotonous,* and *fashionable.* There are three principles at work here: difficulty, way of speaking, and way of dressing. A professor could logically fit into all three categories, or none at all. Use only one organizing principle in your classification.

Second and Third Basics: Support in Classification

The paragraph and essay models on pages 116–117 use the topic sentence (paragraph) and thesis statement (essay) from the Main Point section of this chapter. Both models include the primary and secondary support used in all classification writing: categories backed up by descriptions, explanations, or examples of each category. In the essay model, however, the major support points (categories) are topic sentences for individual paragraphs.

Fourth Basic: Organization in Classification

Classification can be organized in different ways (time order, space order, order of emphasis, or order of importance) depending on its purpose. (For more on the orders of organization, see pp. 44–46.)

PURPOSE	LIKELY ORGANIZATION
to explain changes or development over time	time
to describe the arrangement of groups in physical space	space
to analyze parts of an issue or problem	importance
to focus on a specific feature of groups	emphasis

In the essay model on page 117, order of emphasis is used to highlight the beauty of the structures.

As you write your classification, use **transitions** to move your readers smoothly from one category to another.

COMMON TRANSITIONS IN CLASSIFICATION	
another	for example
another kind	for instance
first, second, third, and so on	last
	one example / another example

PARAGRAPHS VS. ESSAYS IN CLASSIFICATION

For more on the important features of classification, see the Four Basics of Good Classification on page 112.

Paragraph Form

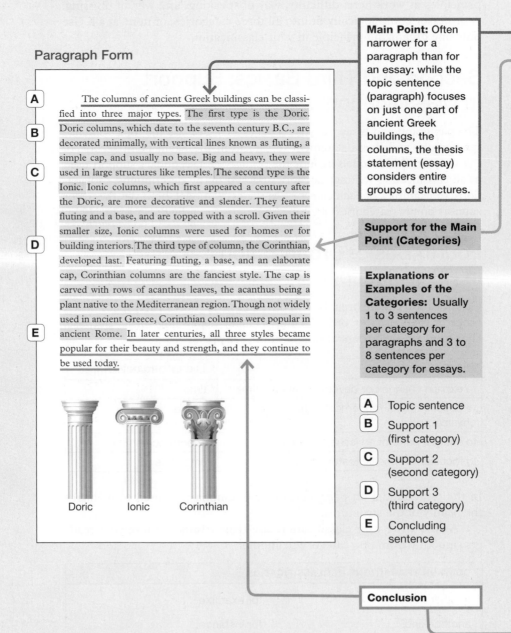

A The columns of ancient Greek buildings can be classified into three major types. **B** The first type is the Doric. Doric columns, which date to the seventh century B.C., are decorated minimally, with vertical lines known as fluting, a simple cap, and usually no base. Big and heavy, they were used in large structures like temples. **C** The second type is the Ionic. Ionic columns, which first appeared a century after the Doric, are more decorative and slender. They feature fluting and a base, and are topped with a scroll. Given their smaller size, Ionic columns were used for homes or for building interiors. **D** The third type of column, the Corinthian, developed last. Featuring fluting, a base, and an elaborate cap, Corinthian columns are the fanciest style. The cap is carved with rows of acanthus leaves, the acanthus being a plant native to the Mediterranean region. Though not widely used in ancient Greece, Corinthian columns were popular in ancient Rome. **E** In later centuries, all three styles became popular for their beauty and strength, and they continue to be used today.

Doric   Ionic   Corinthian

Main Point: Often narrower for a paragraph than for an essay: while the topic sentence (paragraph) focuses on just one part of ancient Greek buildings, the columns, the thesis statement (essay) considers entire groups of structures.

Support for the Main Point (Categories)

Explanations or Examples of the Categories: Usually 1 to 3 sentences per category for paragraphs and 3 to 8 sentences per category for essays.

A Topic sentence

B Support 1 (first category)

C Support 2 (second category)

D Support 3 (third category)

E Concluding sentence

Conclusion

Essay Form

1

Ancient Greek civilization produced a wealth of architectural wonders that were both beautiful and lasting. **The most impressive structures were stadiums, theaters, and temples.** **(A)**

The stadiums were designed to hold thousands of spectators. **(B)** These open-air spaces were set into hillsides so that the seating, often stone benches, would rise up from the central space, giving all spectators a decent view. One of the most famous stadiums, built in Delphi in the fifth century B.C., seated audiences of about 7,000 people. Many stadiums featured ornamental details such as dramatic arches, and some of the more sophisticated examples included heated bathhouses with heated floors. Most often, the stadiums hosted sporting events, such as foot races. A common racing distance was the "stade," equaling one length of the stadium.

Another type of structure, the theater, was also a popular public gathering place. **(C)** Like stadiums, the theaters were open-air sites that were set into hillsides. But instead of sports, they

2

featured plays, musical performances, poetry readings, and other cultural events. In the typical Greek theater, a central performance area was surrounded by semicircular seating, which was often broken into different sections. Wooden, and later stone, stages were set up in the central area, and in front of the stage was a space used for singing and dancing. This space was known as the "orchestra." Among the most famous ancient Greek theaters is the one at Epidaurus, built in the fourth century B.C. and seating up to 14,000 people. Performances still take place there.

The most beautiful structures were the temples, with their grand entrances and large open spaces. **(D)** Temples were rectangular in shape, and their outer walls as well as some interior spaces were supported by columns. Their main structures were typically made of limestone or marble, while their roofs might be constructed of terra-cotta or marble tiles. Temples were created to serve as "homes" for particular gods or

3

goddesses, who were represented by statues. People left food or other offerings to these gods or goddesses to stay in their good graces, and communities often held festivals and other celebrations in their honor. Temples tended to be built in either the Doric or Ionic style, with Doric temples featuring simple, heavy columns and Ionic temples featuring slightly more ornate columns. The most famous temple, in the Doric style, is the Parthenon in Athens.

Turning to the present day, many modern stadiums, theaters, and columned civic buildings show the influence of ancient Greek buildings. Recognizing the lasting strength and beauty of these old structures, architects and designers continue to return to them for inspiration. I predict that this inspiration will last at least a thousand more years. **(E)**

A Thesis statement
B Topic sentence 1 (first category)
C Topic sentence 2 (second category)
D Topic sentence 3 (third category)
E Concluding paragraph

Read and Analyze Classification

After you read each of the selections below, answer the questions that follow.

Classification in the Real World

Leigh King, Fashion Writer/Blogger

Prom Fashions

When she was a student at the Fashion Institute of Design & Merchandising (FIDM), Leigh King used the skills she learned in her introduction-to-writing course to start a fashion blog. Blogging helped King get noticed in the competitive world of New York City fashion, where she got an internship at *Teen Vogue* magazine. King is now a self-employed fashion writer and blogger. Below is part of an email that King sent to colleagues about upcoming blog posts.

Now that we're on the eve of prom season, I am going to be writing about some of the most eye-catching prom fashions:

- **Dresses:** The newest looks range from classic and romantic, to glittery and modern, to vintage. And the new styles come in a variety of colors, from understated cream, to striking black and white, to candy colors or pastels.

- **Clutch purses:** There are plenty of new looks to choose from, including purses made of bold-patterned fabrics or accented with stylish beading.

- **Shoes:** No matter what style of dress a prom-goer chooses, there are beautiful shoes to go with it: ballet flats, chunky wooden heels, heels with jewels or bows, and more.

1. Double-underline the main point of the email.
2. What categories does Leigh break the fashions into? Are there additional categories she could also include?
3. Does the email have the Four Basics of Good Classification (p. 112)?

Student Classification Paragraph

Lorenza Mattazi

All My Music

From the time I was young, I have always loved music, all kinds of music. My first experience of music was the opera that both of my parents always had playing in our house. I learned to understand the drama and emotion of operas. My parents both spoke Italian, and they told me the stories of the operas and translated the words sung in Italian to English so that I could understand. Because hearing opera made my parents happy, and they taught me about it, I loved it, too. Many of my friends think I am weird when I say I love opera, but to me it is very emotional and beautiful. When I was in my early teens, I found rock music and listened to it no matter what I was doing. I like the music with words that tell a story that I can relate to. In that way, rock can be like opera, with stories that everyone can relate to, about love, heartbreak, happiness, and pain. The best rock has powerful guitars and bass, and a good, strong drumbeat. I love it when I can feel the bass in my chest. Rock has good energy and power. Now, I love rap music, too, not the rap with words that are violent or disrespectful of women, but the rest. The words are poetry, and the energy is so high that I feel as if I just have to move my body to the beat. That rhythm is so steady. I have even written some good rap, which my friends say is really good. Maybe I will try to get it published, even on something like Helium, or I could start a blog. I will always love music because it is a good way to communicate feelings and stories, and it makes people feel good.

1. Double-underline the topic sentence.
2. What categories of music does Mattazi write about?
3. Circle the transitions.
4. Does the paragraph have the Four Basics of Good Classification (p. 112)? Why or why not?
5. What kind of organization does Mattazi use? How does this choice relate to the purpose of the paragraph?

Professional Classification Essay

Frances Cole Jones

Don't Work in a Goat's Stomach

Cosimo Scianna

Frances Cole Jones, who holds a B.A. in English/ creative writing from Connecticut College and an M.A. in liberal studies from New York University, is founder and president of Cole Media Management, a firm that focuses on improving clients' communication skills. Jones has also published her own books: *How to Wow: Proven Strategies for Presenting Your Ideas, Persuading Your Audience, and Perfecting Your Image* (2008) and *The Wow Factor: The 33 Things You Must (and Must Not) Do to Guarantee Your Edge in Today's Business World* (2010).

In the following excerpt from *The Wow Factor,* Jones discusses the types of workplace clutter that can get in the way of success on the job.

Magic 8 Ball: a fortune-telling toy that when shaken provides answers to questions

hazmat: short for *hazardous materials*

1   When I was working in the nine-to-five world, there was a gentleman down the hall whose office inevitably looked like it had been stirred up with a stick: a desk loaded with piles of paper, dirty cups, takeout containers, a **Magic 8 Ball**, and a keyboard that looked like you'd be better off wearing a **hazmat** suit when you touched it, more piles of papers on the desk, on the floor, on the chairs; shelving that was loaded with books, photos, and (bizarrely) pieces of sporting equipment, various items of clothing tossed hither and yon: jackets, sweaters, socks, shoes, hats. . . . One day, our boss walked by and said, "That office looks like the inside of a goat's stomach."

2   Not surprisingly, the occupant of the messy office wasn't with the company much longer.

3   What I've learned since then is that my colleague had created a petri dish of the three kinds of recognized office clutter. As identified by psychologist Sam Gosling, they are "identity clutter": photos of family, friends, pets, etc. that are designed to remind us we have a life outside the office; "thought and feeling regulators," which are chosen to change our mood: squeezable stress balls, miniature **Zen gardens**, daily **affirmation calendars**, and "behavior residues"—old coffee cups, food wrappers, Post-its stuck to the keyboard, etc.

Zen gardens: miniature (in this case) gardens meant to create a peaceful setting

affirmation calendars: calendars that include encouraging sayings

4   The trouble with having a disproportionate number of these items in and around your office is that it sends a message to those around you that you are out of control. As one of my CEO clients said to me after we'd walked past his junior report's disastrously messy office on the way to his company's conference room, "Doesn't she realize I notice—and care?"

5   Now I'm not saying you can't have a few personal items. And I am certainly not going to mandate, as one of my clients has done, what kinds of flowers you are allowed to receive. In that office, your loved ones can send you a white orchid. That's it. But I am saying it's important to choose carefully, **cull** frequently, and clean daily.

6   In an effort to help you decide what stays and what goes, I have put together two lists: Remove Immediately and Keep Selectively. Given its urgency, let's first look at those items I'd prefer you remove immediately.

cull: to reduce (in this case, cluttering items)

Remove Immediately:

■   Leftover food: food wrappers; dirty cups, plates, or silverware. While this may seem self-evident, I imagine that more than a few of you have found yourself at five o'clock speaking to your coworkers from amid a small forest of half-empty coffee cups. (And I am hoping there are at least one or two of you who—like me—are still drinking absentmindedly from your 8 a.m. coffee at 5 p.m., a practice I'm prone to if not carefully supervised, which always makes my assistant exclaim with disgust.) All of these must go—again, if you're like me, for your own sake if no one else's. When you do remove them, please don't simply dump them in the sink of the shared kitchen down the hall. I know of one office that based its recent decision as to which of two equally qualified and experienced people was laid off on who was more prone to leaving their dirty dishes in the communal kitchen; deciding factors these days are, indeed, this small.

■   Dead flowers/plants. The roses your ex gave you last Valentine's Day shouldn't become a dried flower arrangement on the shelf. That shedding ficus tree will be much happier if given to a friend with a green thumb.

■   Stuffed animals/"**whimsical**" toys (such as the aforementioned Magic 8 Ball). While these can be helpful should your—or your boss's—kids come to the office, day to day they have the potential to undermine others' perceptions of the professionalism you bring to your work.

whimsical: cute

Keep Selectively:

■   Grooming products. Hairbrushes, toothbrushes/paste, shaving and nail **paraphernalia** can all be handy to have on hand. Please don't, however, leave them in plain sight—or perform any personal maintenance in front of others.

paraphernalia: personal belongings

■   Extra pairs of shoes/a shirt. Again, both are useful on days when you have an unexpectedly important meeting, or uncooperative weather. They should, however, be stowed out of others' sight lines.

■   Photos of family/friends. While these are lovely reminders of your life outside the office and can be great conversation starters, please do make sure everyone in each photo is fully clothed and behaving appropriately. . . .

All this said, I do know that an office has to be worked in—and that worrying about keeping it pristine can, ultimately, detract from focusing on what you need to accomplish. For this reason, it can help to set aside fifteen minutes at the middle and end of each day to clear your desk/ chairs/floor of any accumulated clutter. A principle applied by airlines and luxury bus lines, these intermittent sweeps help keep things from piling up.

1. Double-underline the thesis statement.

2. Within the categories "Remove Immediately" and "Keep Selectively," Jones presents six subcategories of things. Underline them. What secondary support does she include? Are there enough examples for the reader to understand the categories?

3. Circle the transitions. How is the essay organized?

4. Write a summary of Jones's essay.

5. Do you agree with Jones's categorizations? For instance, do you see value in keeping any of the things Jones thinks should be removed immediately? Why or why not?

Write Your Own Classification

Write a classification paragraph or essay on one of the following topics or on one of your own choice. For help, refer to the How to Write Classification checklist on page 123.

College

- Classify the types of resources available in your college's library, giving examples of things in each category. If you don't have time to visit the library, spend time looking at its website. (Some library websites include virtual tours.)

- Classify the course requirements for your program into different categories, such as easy, challenging, and very challenging. Your purpose could be to help a future student in the program understand what to expect. Be sure to define your categories clearly, using both description and examples.

Work

- Classify the different types of bosses, giving explanations and examples for each category.

- Look back at the paragraph on page 112 that illustrates the Four Basics of Classification. Based on your own experience, think of another logical way to classify types of workers. As you develop your categories, think about the types of jobs each type of worker would like or dislike, or how each worker would respond to different kinds of bosses.

Everyday Life

- Using Lorenza Mattazi's paragraph as a guide (see p. 119), classify the types of music you enjoy or the types of music currently on your phone or streaming service, such as Spotify.

- Write about types of service organizations in your community and the opportunities for community members to be involved. For your audience, think of people who might be moving into your community.

CHECKLIST: How to Write Classification	
STEPS	**DETAILS**
☐ **Narrow and explore your topic.** See Chapter 2.	• Make the topic more specific. • Prewrite to get ideas about the narrowed topic.
☐ **Write a topic sentence (paragraph) or thesis statement (essay).** See Chapter 3.	• State your topic and your organizing principle or categories.
☐ **Support your point.** See Chapter 3.	• Come up with explanations/examples to support each category.
☐ **Write a draft.** See Chapter 4.	• Make a plan that puts the categories in a logical order. • Include a topic sentence (paragraph) or thesis statement (essay) and all the supporting categories with explanations and examples.
☐ **Revise your draft.** See Chapter 4.	• Make sure it has *all* the Four Basics of Good Classification. • Make sure you include transitions to move readers smoothly from one category to the next.
☐ **Edit your revised draft.** See Chapters 15 through 18.	• Correct errors in grammar, spelling, word use, and punctuation.

10

Definition

Writing That Tells What Something Means

Understand What Definition Is

Definition is writing that explains what a term or concept means.

Four Basics of Good Definition

1 It presents a term, clear boundaries for defining the term, and a purpose for the definition.

2 It provides examples or characteristics that show the meaning of the term.

3 It uses details to make the examples clear.

4 It is organized logically by order of emphasis or order of importance.

In the following paragraph, the numbers and colors correspond to the Four Basics of Good Definition.

4 Examples and details presented in order of importance.

1 A stereotype is a conventional idea or image that is simplistic — and often wrong, particularly when it is applied to people or groups of people. Stereotypes can prevent us from seeing people as they really are because stereotypes blind us with preconceived notions about what a certain type of person is like. **2** For example, I had a stereotyped notion of Native Americans until I met my friend Daniel, a Chippewa Indian. **3** I thought all Indians wore feathers and beads, had long black hair, and avoided all contact with non–Native Americans because they resented their land being taken away. Daniel, however, wears jeans and T-shirts, and we talk about everything — even our different ancestries. After meeting him, I understood that my stereotype of Native Americans was completely wrong. 2 Not only was it wrong, but it set up an us–them concept in my mind that made me feel that I, as a non–Native American, would never have anything in common with Native Americans. My stereotype would not have allowed me to see any Native American as an individual: I would have seen him or her as part of a group that I thought was all alike, and all different from me. From now on, I won't assume that any individual fits my stereotype; I will try to see that person as I would like them to see me: as myself, not a stereotyped image.

You will read and write definition in many practical situations.

COLLEGE	You study the meaning of *social democrat* for a political science course, or you define *exponential notation* for a math exam.
WORK	You study the definition of *harassment* in the employee manual before filing a complaint, or you choose one word that describes you and explain why on a job application.
EVERYDAY LIFE	You read definitions online to help you understand a rental agreement, or you define for your partner what you mean by *commitment* or *communication* in a relationship.

In college, writing assignments may include the word *define*, but they might also use phrases such as *explain the meaning of* _____ and *discuss the meaning of* _____. In these cases, use the strategies discussed in this chapter to complete the assignment.

First Basic: Main Point in Definition

In definition, the **main point** usually relates to defining a term or concept. The main point is related to your purpose: to help your readers understand the term or concept as you are using it. Good definitions are like boundaries: they help us understand what something is, and what it is not. An example is not a definition, although we can use examples to illustrate a definition.

When you write your definition, do not just copy a dictionary definition; write it in your own words as you want your readers to understand it. Your topic sentence (paragraph) or thesis statement (essay) can take the forms shown on page 128.

PARAGRAPHS VS. ESSAYS IN DEFINITION

For more on the important features of definition, see the Four Basics of Good Definition on page 124.

Paragraph Form

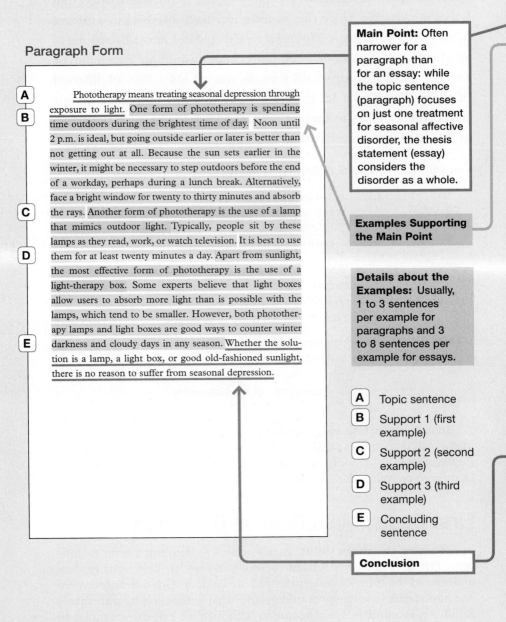

A   Phototherapy means treating seasonal depression through exposure to light. **B** One form of phototherapy is spending time outdoors during the brightest time of day. Noon until 2 p.m. is ideal, but going outside earlier or later is better than not getting out at all. Because the sun sets earlier in the winter, it might be necessary to step outdoors before the end of a workday, perhaps during a lunch break. Alternatively, face a bright window for twenty to thirty minutes and absorb the rays. **C** Another form of phototherapy is the use of a lamp that mimics outdoor light. Typically, people sit by these lamps as they read, work, or watch television. It is best to use them for at least twenty minutes a day. **D** Apart from sunlight, the most effective form of phototherapy is the use of a light-therapy box. Some experts believe that light boxes allow users to absorb more light than is possible with the lamps, which tend to be smaller. However, both phototherapy lamps and light boxes are good ways to counter winter darkness and cloudy days in any season. **E** Whether the solution is a lamp, a light box, or good old-fashioned sunlight, there is no reason to suffer from seasonal depression.

Main Point: Often narrower for a paragraph than for an essay: while the topic sentence (paragraph) focuses on just one treatment for seasonal affective disorder, the thesis statement (essay) considers the disorder as a whole.

Examples Supporting the Main Point

Details about the Examples: Usually, 1 to 3 sentences per example for paragraphs and 3 to 8 sentences per example for essays.

A Topic sentence

B Support 1 (first example)

C Support 2 (second example)

D Support 3 (third example)

E Concluding sentence

Conclusion

Essay Form

1

Seasonal affective disorder (SAD) is a form of depression caused by inadequate exposure to sunlight in fall or winter. It can seriously affect the daily life of those who suffer from it. **[A]**

One consequence of SAD is sleepiness and a lack of energy. SAD sufferers may find that they are sleeping longer yet are still drowsy during the day, especially during the afternoon. Connected to the drowsiness may be moodiness and an inability to concentrate. The latter effect can result in poorer performance at work and at other tasks. Those affected by SAD may also find that they move more slowly than usual and that all types of physical activity are more challenging than they used to be. All these difficulties can be a source of frustration, sometimes worsening the depression. **[B]**

Another consequence of SAD is loss of interest in work, hobbies, and other activities. To some extent, these symptoms may be connected to a lack of energy. Often, however, the feelings run deeper than that. Activities that once lifted one's spirits may have the opposite **[C]**

2

effect. For instance, a mother who at one time never missed her child's soccer games might now see attending them as a burden. Someone who was once a top performer at work may find that it is all he or she can do to show up in the morning. Such changes in one's outlook can contribute to a feeling of hopelessness.

The most serious consequence of SAD is withdrawal from interactions with others. SAD sufferers may find that they are no longer interested in going out with friends, and they may turn down requests to get together for movies, meals, or social events. They may even withdraw from family members, engaging less frequently in conversation or even spending time alone in their rooms. Furthermore, they may postpone or cancel activities, such as vacation trips, that might require them to interact with family for hours at a time. Withdrawal symptoms may also extend to the workplace, with SAD sufferers becoming less vocal at meetings or avoiding lunches or conversations with colleagues. Concern that family members or coworkers may be **[D]**

3

noticing such personality changes can cause or worsen anxiety in those with SAD.

Because the effects of SAD can be so significant, it is important to address them as soon as possible. Fortunately, there are many good therapies for the condition, from drug treatment to greater exposure to sunlight, whether real or simulated through special lamps or light boxes. Often, such treatments have SAD sufferers feeling better quickly. **[E]**

A Thesis statement
B Topic sentence 1 (first example)
C Topic sentence 2 (second example)
D Topic sentence 3 (third example)
E Concluding paragraph

TOPIC SENTENCE

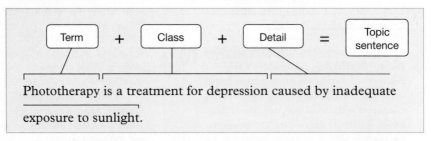

In this example, "Class" is the larger group the term belongs to. Main-point statements do not have to include a class, however. For example:

TOPIC SENTENCE

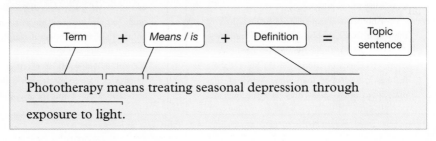

THESIS STATEMENT

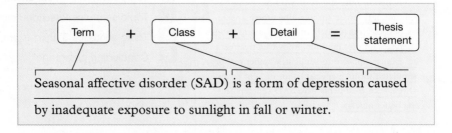

The thesis statement is broader in scope than the topic sentences because it sets up a discussion of the larger subject of seasonal affective disorder. In contrast, the topic sentences consider one particular treatment for this disorder (phototherapy).

Second and Third Basics: Support in Definition

The paragraph and essay models on pages 126–127 use the topic sentence (paragraph) and the thesis statement (essay) from the Main Point section in this chapter. Both models include the primary and secondary support used in all definition writing: examples or characteristics that explain what a term or concept is, as well as details about these examples or characteristics. In the essay model, however, the major support points (examples) are topic sentences for individual paragraphs.

Fourth Basic: Organization in Definition

The examples in definition are often organized by **order of importance**, meaning that the example that will have the most effect on readers is saved for last. (For more on order of importance, see p. 46.) This strategy is used in the paragraph and essay models on pages 126–127.

   Transitions in definition move readers from one example to the next. Here are some transitions you might use in definition, although many others are possible, too.

COMMON TRANSITIONS IN DEFINITION	
another; one/another	for example
another kind	for instance
first, second, third, and so on	

Read and Analyze Definition

After you read each of the selections below, answer the questions that follow.

Definition in the Real World

Walter Scanlon, Program and Workplace Consultant

Employee Assistance Program

Walter Scanlon got hooked early on drugs and alcohol and spent a decade on the streets and in and out of hospitals and prisons. He turned his life around after joining Alcoholics Anonymous and earned a GED, a B.A. from Pace University, an M.B.A. from New York Institute of Technology, and finally a Ph.D. from Columbus University. As the owner of a successful consulting business, Scanlon does all kinds of writing: letters, proposals, presentations, emails, and memos. He has also published two books and numerous professional articles. In the paragraph below, Scanlon defines "employee assistance program" for a client.

The "employee assistance program" (EAP) is a confidential, early-intervention workplace counseling service designed to help employees who are experiencing personal problems. It is a social service within a work environment that can be found in most major corporations, associations, and government organizations. EAP services are always free to the employee and benefit the organization as much as the employee. Employees who are free of emotional problems are far more productive than those who are not. An employee whose productivity is negatively affected by a drinking problem, for example, might seek help through the EAP. He/she would be assessed by a counselor and then referred to an appropriate community resource for additional services. The *employee* is helped through the EAP while the *employer* is rewarded with improved productivity. An EAP is a win-win program for all involved.

1. Double-underline the topic sentence.
2. Identify the term defined in the paragraph and define it in your own words.
3. Underline an example of what an EAP might do.
4. Double-underline the sentence that makes a final observation about the topic. What does this observation tell you about the purpose for Scanlon's definition?

Student Definition Paragraph

Corin Costas

What Community Involvement Means to Me

While at Bunker Hill Community College (BHCC), Corin Costas helped start a business club on campus. Later, he took on the leadership of SHOCWAVES and initiated several projects, including Light One Little Candle, which raised money for the Dana-Farber Cancer Institute to buy books for children with cancer. In the following paragraph, Costas defines SHOCWAVES and what it does.

SHOCWAVES is a student organization at Bunker Hill Community College. SHOCWAVES stands for Students Helping Our Community with Activities, and its mission is to get students involved with the community—to become part of it by actively working in it in positive ways. Each year, SHOCWAVES is assigned a budget by the Student Activities Office, and it spends that budget in activities that help the community in a variety of ways. Some of the money is spent, for example, in fund-raising events for community causes. We have money to plan and launch a fund-raiser, which raises far more than we spend. In the process, other students and members of the community also become involved in the helping effort. We get to know lots of people, and we usually have a lot of fun—all while helping others. Recently, we have worked as part of the Charles River Cleanup, the Walk for Hunger, collecting toys for sick and needy children, and Light One Little Candle. While SHOCWAVES's mission is to help the community, it also benefits its members. Working in the community, I have learned so many valuable skills, and I always have something I care about to write about for my classes. I have learned about budgeting, advertising, organizing, and managing. I have also developed my creativity by coming up with new ways to do things. I have networked with many people, including people who are important in the business world. SHOCWAVES has greatly improved my life, and my chances for future success.

1. Double-underline the topic sentence.
2. Underline the examples of what SHOCWAVES does for the community. What does the choice of examples suggest about Costas's purpose?
3. Double-underline the sentence that makes a final observation about the topic.
4. Does this paragraph follow the Four Basics of Good Definition (p. 124)? Why or why not?

Professional Definition Essay

Janice E. Castro with Dan Cook and Cristina Garcia

Spanglish

Janice E. Castro is an assistant professor in the Medill New Media Program at Northwestern University. She worked as a reporter for *Time* for more than twenty years and started the magazine's health policy beat. After the publication of her book, *The American Way of Health* (1994), she became the managing editor of *Time*'s online division.

Castro wrote "Spanglish" while at *Time* with the help of Dan Cook and Cristina Garcia. In the essay, she defines the language created when Spanish and English speakers come together.

TIME
From the Pages of TIME

1   In Manhattan a first-grader greets her visiting grandparents, happily exclaiming, "Come here, *siéntate*!" Her bemused grandfather, who does

not speak Spanish, nevertheless knows she is asking him to sit down. A Miami personnel officer understands what a job applicant means when he says, "*Quiero un* part time." Nor do drivers miss a beat reading a billboard alongside a Los Angeles street advertising CERVEZA — SIX-PACK!

2   This free-form blend of Spanish and English, known as Spanglish, is common **linguistic currency** wherever concentrations of Hispanic Americans are found in the U.S. In Los Angeles, where 55 percent of the city's 3 million inhabitants speak Spanish, Spanglish is as much a part of daily life as sunglasses. Unlike the broken-English efforts of earlier immigrants from Europe, Asia, and other regions, Spanglish has become a widely accepted conversational mode used casually — even playfully — by Spanish-speaking immigrants and native-born Americans alike.

3   Consisting of one part Hispanicized English, one part Americanized Spanish, and more than a little **fractured syntax**, Spanglish is a bit like a Robin Williams comedy routine: a crackling line of cross-cultural patter straight from the melting pot. Often it enters Anglo homes and families through the children, who pick it up at school or at play with their young Hispanic contemporaries. In other cases, it comes from watching TV; many an Anglo child watching *Sesame Street* has learned *uno dos tres* almost as quickly as one two three.

4   Spanglish takes a variety of forms, from the Southern California Anglos who bid farewell with the utterly silly "*hasta la* bye-bye" to the Cuban American drivers in Miami who *parquean* their *carros*. Some Spanglish sentences are mostly Spanish, with a quick detour for an English word or two. A Latino friend may cut short a conversation by glancing at his watch and excusing himself with the explanation that he must "*ir al* supermarket."

5   Many of the English words transplanted in this way are simply hardier than their Spanish counterparts. No matter how distasteful the subject, for example, it is still easier to say "income tax" than *impuesto sobre la renta*. At the same time, many Spanish-speaking immigrants have adopted such terms as *VCR*, *microwave*, and *dishwasher* for what they view as largely American **phenomena**. Still other English words convey a cultural context that is not **implicit** in the Spanish. A friend who invites you to *lonche* most likely has in mind the brisk American custom of "doing lunch" rather than the **languorous** afternoon break traditionally implied by *almuerzo*.

6   Mainstream Americans exposed to similar hybrids of German, Chinese, or Hindi might be mystified. But even Anglos who speak little or no Spanish are somewhat familiar with Spanglish. Living among them, for one thing, are 19 million Hispanics. In addition, more American high school and university students sign up for Spanish than for any other foreign language.

7   Only in the past ten years [in 1978–1988], though, has Spanglish begun to turn into a national slang. Its popularity has grown with the explosive increases in U.S. immigration from Latin American countries. English has increasingly collided with Spanish in retail stores, offices and classrooms, in pop music, and on street corners. Anglos whose ancestors picked up such Spanish words as *rancho*, *bronco*, *tornado*, and *incommunicado*, for instance, now freely use such Spanish words as *gracias*, *bueno*, *amigo*, and *por favor*.

---

linguistic currency: typical speech

fractured syntax: language that breaks grammatical rules

phenomena: strange experiences or things

implicit: not expressed directly

languorous: long and relaxing

8   Among Latinos, Spanglish conversations often flow easily from Spanish into several sentences of English and back.

9   Spanglish is a sort of code for Latinos: the speakers know Spanish, but their hybrid language reflects the American culture in which they live. Many lean to shorter, clipped phrases in place of the longer, more graceful expressions their parents used. Says Leonel de la Cuesta, an assistant professor of modern languages at Florida International University in Miami: "In the U.S., time is money, and that is showing up in Spanglish as an economy of language." Conversational examples: *taipiar* (type) and *winshiwiper* (windshield wiper) replace *escribir a máquina* and *limpiaparabrisas*.

10   Major advertisers, eager to tap the estimated $134 billion in spending power wielded by Spanish-speaking Americans, have ventured into Spanglish to promote their products. In some cases, attempts to sprinkle Spanish through commercials have produced embarrassing **gaffes**.   **gaffes:** mistakes
A Braniff Airlines ad that sought to tell Spanish-speaking audiences they could settle back *en* (in) luxuriant *cuero* (leather) seats, for example, inadvertently said they could fly without clothes (*encuero*). A fractured translation of the Miller Lite slogan told readers the beer was "Filling, and less delicious." Similar blunders are often made by Anglos trying to impress Spanish-speaking pals. But if Latinos are amused by mangled Spanglish, they also recognize these goofs as a sort of friendly acceptance. As they might put it, *no problema*.

TIME and the TIME logo are registered trademarks of Time Inc. used Under License.

1.   Double-underline the thesis statement and then paraphrase it.
2.   Circle the transitions used to introduce examples.
3.   Do the writers provide enough examples of what they mean by *Spanglish*? If not, where could more examples be added?
4.   For whom are the authors writing? What is their purpose?
5.   Look back at the final paragraph. Why do you suppose the authors chose to conclude in that way?

Write Your Own Definition

Write a definition paragraph or essay on one of the following topics or on one of your own choice. For help, refer to the How to Write Definition checklist on page 135.

College

■   Talk to several classmates. How would you as students define a good student or a bad student? As you develop examples for your definition, consider whether your instructors would agree with your definition.

■   Identify a difficult or technical term from a class you are taking. Then, define the term for a student who is not in the same course, and give examples of different ways in which it might be used.

Work

■   How would you define a satisfying job? Write about your definition for a potential employer, giving explanations and examples.

■   If you have ever held a job that used unusual or interesting terminology, write about some of the terms used, what they meant, and their function on the job.

Everyday Life

■   What does it mean to be a good citizen? Is good citizenship more a matter of what you believe or what you do? Provide a definition, giving explanations and examples.

■   What does it mean to be a good parent? Provide a definition, giving explanations and examples.

CHECKLIST: How to Write Definition	
STEPS	**DETAILS**
☐ **Narrow and explore your topic.** See Chapter 2.	• Make the topic more specific. • Prewrite to get ideas about the narrowed topic.
☐ **Write a topic sentence (paragraph) or thesis statement (essay).** See Chapter 3.	• State the term that you are focusing on, and provide a definition for it.
☐ **Support your point.** See Chapter 3.	• Come up with examples and details to explain your definition.
☐ **Write a draft.** See Chapter 4.	• Make a plan that puts the examples in a logical order. • Include a topic sentence (paragraph) or thesis statement (essay) and all the supporting examples and details.
☐ **Revise your draft.** See Chapter 4.	• Make sure it has *all* the Four Basics of Good Definition. • Make sure you include transitions to move readers smoothly from one example to the next.
☐ **Edit your revised draft.** See Chapters 15 through 18.	• Correct errors in grammar, spelling, word use, and punctuation.

11

Comparison and Contrast

Writing That Shows Similarities and Differences

Understand What Comparison and Contrast Are

Comparison is writing that shows the similarities among subjects—people, ideas, situations, or items; **contrast** shows the differences. In conversation, people often use the word *compare* to mean either compare or contrast, but as you work through this chapter, the terms will be separated.

| Compare | = | Similarities |
| Contrast | = | Differences |

> #### Four Basics of Good Comparison and Contrast
>
> **1** It compares and contrasts for a purpose — to help readers make a decision, to help them understand the subjects, or to show your understanding of the subjects.
>
> **2** It presents several important, parallel points of comparison/contrast.
>
> **3** It develops supporting points fairly, with supporting details for both subjects.
>
> **4** It arranges points in a logical order.

In the following paragraph, written for a biology course, the numbers and colors correspond to the Four Basics of Good Comparison and Contrast.

1 Although frogs and toads are closely related, they differ in appearance, in habitat, and in behavior. **2** The first major difference is in the creatures' physical characteristics. **3** Whereas most frogs have smooth, slimy skin that helps them move through water, toads tend to have rough, bumpy skin suited to drier surroundings. Also, whereas frogs have long, muscular hind legs that help them leap away from predators or toward food, most toads have shorter legs and, therefore, less ability to move quickly. Another physical characteristic of frogs and toads is their bulging eyes, which help them see in different directions. This ability is important, because neither creature can turn its head to look for food or spot a predator. However, frogs' eyes may protrude more than toads'. **2** The second major difference between frogs and toads is their choice of habitat. **3** Frogs tend to live in or near ponds, lakes, or other sources of water. In contrast, toads live mostly in drier areas, such as gardens, forests, and fields. But, like frogs, they lay their eggs in water. **2** The third major difference between frogs and toads concerns their behavior. **3** Whereas frogs may be active during the day or at night, most toads keep a low profile until nighttime. Some biologists believe that it is nature's way of making up for toads' inability to escape from danger as quickly as frogs can. At night, toads are less likely to be spotted by predators. Finally, although both frogs and toads tend to live by themselves, toads, unlike frogs, may form groups while they are hibernating. Both creatures can teach us a lot about how animals adapt to their environments, and studying them is a lot of fun.

4 Points arranged in a logical order.

Many situations require you to understand and write about similarities and differences.

COLLEGE	In a pharmacy course, you read about the side effects of two drugs prescribed for the same illness, and then you compare and contrast these side effects for a class report.
WORK	You compare this year's sales with last year's and present a report highlighting the most important contrasts you discovered.
EVERYDAY LIFE	You read about organic and nonorganic produce online, sample both at a local grocery store, and write a review of your findings for a community website.

In college, writing assignments may include the words *compare and contrast*, but they might also use phrases such as *discuss similarities and differences, how is* X *like* (or *unlike*) Y?, or *what do* X *and* Y *have in common?* Also, assignments may use only the word *compare*.

First Basic: Main Point in Comparison and Contrast

The **main point** should state the subjects you want to compare or contrast and help you achieve your purpose. Your topic sentence (paragraph) or thesis statement (essay) identifies the subjects and states the main point you want to make about them. Here is an example of a topic sentence for a paragraph:

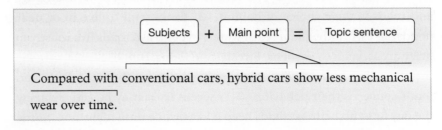

Remember that the topic for an essay can be a little broader than one for a paragraph.

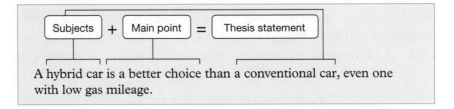

Whereas the topic sentence focuses on the mechanical advantages of hybrid cars, the thesis statement sets up a broader discussion of these cars' benefits.

Second and Third Basics: Support in Comparison and Contrast

The paragraph and essay models on pages 140–141 use the topic sentence (paragraph) and thesis statement (essay) from the Main Point section in this chapter. Both models include the primary and secondary support used in all comparison and contrast writing: points of comparison/contrast supported by details about both subjects. In the essay model, however, the points of comparison/contrast are topic sentences for individual paragraphs.

The support in comparison/contrast should show how your subjects are the same or different. To find support, many people make a list with two columns, one for each subject, with parallel points of comparison or contrast. Make sure you have details about both subjects so that you can support the points of comparison or contrast fairly.

Topic Sentence/Thesis Statement: The two credit cards I am considering offer different financial terms.

BIG CARD	MEGA CARD
no annual fee	$35 annual fee
$1 fee per cash advance	$1.50 fee per cash advance
30 days before interest charges begin	25 days before interest charges begin
15.5% finance charge	17.9% finance charge

Choose points that will be convincing and understandable to your readers. Explain your points with facts, details, or examples.

Fourth Basic: Organization in Comparison and Contrast

Comparison/contrast can be organized in one of two ways. A **point-by-point** organization presents one point of comparison or contrast between the subjects and then moves to the next point. (See the essay model on p. 141.) A **whole-to-whole** organization presents all the points of comparison or contrast for one subject and then all the points for the next subject. (See the paragraph model on p. 140.) Consider which organization will best explain the similarities or differences to your readers. Whichever organization you choose, stay with it throughout your writing.

Comparison/contrast is often organized by **order of importance**, meaning that the most important point is saved for last. (For more on order of importance, see p. 46.) This strategy is used in the essay model on page 141.

PARAGRAPHS VS. ESSAYS IN COMPARISON AND CONTRAST

For more on the important features of comparison and contrast, see the Four Basics of Good Comparison and Contrast on page 136.

Paragraph Form

A   Compared with conventional cars, hybrid cars show less mechanical wear over time. **B** In conventional vehicles, braking and idling place continual stress on the engine and brakes. When braking, drivers of such vehicles rely completely on the friction of the brake pads to come to a stop. As a result, brakes wear down over time, sometimes rather quickly. Additionally, these vehicles burn gas even while idling, making the engine use unnecessary energy and fuel. **C** In contrast, hybrid cars are designed to reduce brake and engine wear. Say that a hybrid driver is moving from a sixty-mile-per-hour stretch of highway to a twenty-five-mile-per-hour off-ramp. When he or she brakes, the hybrid's motor goes into reverse, slowing the car and allowing the driver to place less strain on the brakes. Then, as the driver enters stop-and-start traffic in town, the electric motor takes over from the gas engine, improving energy efficiency during idling and reducing engine wear. **D** These mechanical benefits of hybrids can lead to lower maintenance costs, a significant improvement over conventional cars.

Main Point: Often narrower for a paragraph than for an essay: while the topic sentence (paragraph) focuses on the mechanical advantages of hybrid cars, the thesis statement (essay) sets up a broader discussion of these cars' benefits.

Support for the Main Point (Points of Comparison / Contrast)

Details about Each Point of Comparison / Contrast: Usually, 1 to 3 sentences per point for paragraphs and 3 to 8 sentences per point for essays.

A   Topic sentence

B   Support 1 (first point of comparison / contrast)

C   Support 2 (second point of comparison / contrast)

D   Concluding sentence

Conclusion

Essay Form

1

They are too expensive. For the last two years, while trying to keep my dying 1999 Chevy on the road, these words have popped into my head every time I have thought about a purchasing a hybrid car. But now that I have done some research, I am finally convinced: hybrid car is a better choice than a conventional car, even one with low gas mileage.

[A]

The first advantage of hybrid cars over conventional cars is that buyers can get tax breaks and other hybrid-specific benefits. Although federal tax credits for hybrid purchasers expired in 2010, several states, including Colorado, Louisiana, Maryland, and New Mexico, continue to offer such credits. Also, in Arizona, Florida, and several other states, hybrid drivers are allowed to use the less congested high-occupancy vehicle (HOV) lanes even if the driver is the only person on board. Additional benefits for hybrid drivers include longer warranties than those offered for conventional cars and, in some states and cities, rebates, reduced licensing fees, and free

[B]

2

parking. None of these benefits are offered to drivers of conventional cars.

The second advantage of hybrid cars over conventional cars is that they save money over the long term. In addition to using less fuel, hybrids show less mechanical wear over time, reducing maintenance costs. When braking, drivers of conventional cars rely completely on the friction of the brake pads to come to a stop. As a result, brakes wear down over time, sometimes rather quickly. Additionally, these vehicles burn gas even while idling, making the engine use unnecessary energy and fuel. In contrast, when hybrid drivers hit the brakes, the car's motor goes into reverse, slowing the car and allowing the driver to place less strain on the brakes. Then, as the driver enters stop-and-start traffic in town, the electric motor takes over from the gas engine, improving energy efficiency during idling and reducing engine wear.

[C]

The most important benefit of hybrid cars over conventional cars is that they have a lower impact on the environment. Experts estimate

[D]

3

that each gallon of gas burned by conventional motor vehicles produces 28 pounds of carbon dioxide (CO_2), a greenhouse gas that is a major contributor to global warming. Because hybrid cars use about half as much gas as conventional vehicles, they reduce pollution and greenhouse gases by at least 50 percent. Some experts estimate that they reduce such emissions by as much as 80 percent. The National Resources Defense Council says that if hybrid vehicles are widely adopted, annual reductions in emissions could reach 450 million metric tons by the year 2050. This reduction would be equal to taking 82.5 million cars off the road.

Although hybrid cars are more expensive than conventional cars, they are well worth it. From an economic standpoint, they save on fuel and maintenance costs. But, to me, the best reasons for buying a hybrid are ethical: by switching to such a vehicle, I will help reduce my toll on the environment. So goodbye, 1999 Chevy, and hello, Toyota Prius!

[E]

[A] Thesis statement

[B] Topic sentence 1 (first point of comparison/contrast)

[C] Topic sentence 2 (second point of comparison/contrast)

[D] Topic sentence 3 (third point of comparison/contrast)

[E] Concluding paragraph

Transitions in comparison/contrast move readers from one subject to another and from one point of comparison or contrast to the next.

Common Transitions in Comparison and Contrast

COMPARISON	CONTRAST
both	in contrast
like/unlike	most important difference
most important similarity	now/then
one similarity/another similarity	one difference/another difference
similarly	unlike
	while

Read and Analyze Comparison and Contrast

After you read each of the selections below, answer the questions that follow.

Comparison and Contrast in the Real World

Brad Leibov, President, New Chicago Fund, Inc.

Who We Are

Although he entered a community college with little motivation, Brad Leibov was inspired to succeed with the help of a school instructor. Leibov earned a bachelor's degree from a four-year university and eventually got his master's degree in urban planning and policy. He now owns his own company that helps to revitalize inner-city commercial areas. The following paragraph describes how Leibov's company restored a special service area (SSA), a declining community targeted for improvements.

New Chicago Fund, Inc., is an expert at advising and leading organizations through all the steps necessary to establish an SSA with strong local support. Our experience acting as liaison among various neighborhood groups and individuals affected by an SSA helps us plan for and address the concerns of residents and property owners. In 2005, New Chicago Fund assisted the Uptown Community Development

Corporation with establishing an SSA in Uptown, Chicago. Uptown's commercial area was estimated to lose approximately $506 million annually in consumer expenditures to neighboring commercial districts and suburban shopping centers. Community leaders recognized that Uptown's sidewalks were uninviting with litter, hazardous with unshoveled snow, and unappealing in the lack of pedestrian-friendly amenities found in neighboring commercial districts. The Uptown SSA programs funded the transformation of the commercial area. The sidewalks are regularly cleaned and are litter-free. People no longer have to walk around uncleared snow mounds and risk slipping on the ice because maintenance programs provide full-service clearing. Additionally, SSA funds provided new pedestrian-friendly amenities such as benches, trash receptacles, flower planters, and street-pole banners. The Uptown area is now poised for commercial success.

1.   Double-underline the topic sentence.
2.   What subjects are being contrasted?
3.   What is the purpose of the paragraph?
4.   What are the points of contrast? How do these points relate to the purpose of the paragraph?

Student Comparison/Contrast Paragraph

Said Ibrahim

Eyeglasses vs. Laser Surgery: Benefits and Drawbacks

Although both eyeglasses and laser surgery can address vision problems successfully, each approach has particular benefits and drawbacks. Whereas one pair of eyeglasses is reasonably priced in comparison with laser surgery, eyeglass prescriptions often change over time, requiring regular lens replacements. As a result, over the wearer's lifetime, costs of eyeglasses can exceed $15,000. On the positive side, an accurate lens prescription results in clear vision with few or no side effects. Furthermore, glasses of just the right shape or color can be a great fashion accent. In contrast to eyeglasses, laser vision correction often has to be done only once. Consequently, although the costs average $2,500 per eye, the patient can save thousands of dollars over the following years. On the downside, some recipients of laser surgery report difficulties seeing at night, dry eyes, or infections. Fortunately, these problems are fairly rare. The final advantage of laser surgery applies to those who are happy to forgo the fashion benefits of eyeglasses. Most laser-surgery patients no longer have to wear any glasses other than sunglasses until later in life. At that point, they may need reading glasses. All in all, we are fortunate to live in a time when there are many good options for vision correction. Choosing the right one is a matter of carefully weighing the pros and cons of each approach.

1. Double-underline the topic sentence.
2. Is the purpose of the paragraph to help readers make a decision, to help them understand the subjects better, or both?
3. Underline and number each point of contrast in the sample paragraph. Then, give each parallel, or matched, point the same number.
4. Which organization (point by point or whole to whole) does Ibrahim use? Would another organization work as well? Explain.
5. Circle the transitions in the paragraph.

Professional Comparison/Contrast Essay

Mark Twain

Two Ways of Seeing a River

Born Samuel Langhorne Clemens, Mark Twain (1835–1910) is one of America's most admired writers, praised as much for his storytelling as for his humor and wit. He was also a sharp observer of society and politics, and he was known to criticize racial inequality, political corruption, and other injustices. Among the many books Twain wrote were *Tom Sawyer* (1876), *Huckleberry Finn* (1884), and *Life on the Mississippi* (1883), from which the following excerpt was taken.

1   Now when I had mastered the language of this water and had come to know every trifling feature that bordered the great river as familiarly as I knew the letters of the alphabet, I had made a valuable acquisition. But I had lost something, too. I had lost something which could never be restored to me while I lived. All the grace, the beauty, the poetry, had gone out of the majestic river! I still kept in mind a certain wonderful sunset which I witnessed when steamboating was new to me. A broad expanse of the river was turned to blood; in the middle distance the red hue

brightened into gold, through which a solitary log came floating, black and conspicuous; in one place a long, slanting mark lay sparkling upon the water; in another the surface was broken by boiling, tumbling rings that were as many-tinted as an opal; where the ruddy flush was faintest was a smooth spot that was covered with graceful circles and radiating lines, ever so delicately traced; the shore on our left was densely wooded, and the somber shadow that fell from this forest was broken in one place by a long, ruffled trail that shone like silver; and high above the forest wall a clean-stemmed dead tree waved a single leafy bough that glowed like a flame in the unobstructed splendor that was flowing from the sun. There were graceful curves, reflected images, woody heights, soft distances, and over the whole scene, far and near, the dissolving lights drifted steadily, enriching it every passing moment with new marvels of coloring.

2   I stood like one bewitched. I drank it in, in a speechless rapture. The world was new to me and I had never seen anything like this at home. But as I have said, a day came when I began to cease from noting the glories and the charms which the moon and the sun and the twilight **wrought** upon the river's face; another day came when I ceased altogether to note them. Then, if that sunset scene had been repeated, I should have looked upon it without rapture and should have commented upon it inwardly after this fashion: "This sun means that we are going to have wind to-morrow; that floating log means that the river is rising, small thanks to it; that slanting mark on the water refers to a **bluff reef** which is going to kill somebody's steamboat one of these nights, if it keeps on stretching out like that; those tumbling 'boils' show a dissolving bar and a changing channel there; the lines and circles in the slick water over yonder are a warning that that troublesome place is **shoaling up** dangerously; that silver streak in the shadow of the forest is the 'break' from a new snag and he has located himself in the very best place he could have found to fish for steamboats; that tall dead tree, with a single living branch, is not going to last long, and then how is a body ever going to get through this blind place at night without the friendly old landmark?"

3   No, the romance and beauty were all gone from the river. All the value any feature of it had for me now was the amount of usefulness it could furnish toward compassing the safe piloting of a steamboat. Since those days, I have pitied doctors from my heart. What does the lovely flush in a beauty's cheek mean to a doctor but a "break" that ripples above some deadly disease? Are not all her visible charms sown thick with what are to him the signs and symbols of hidden decay? Does he ever see her beauty at all, or doesn't he simply view her professionally and comment upon her unwholesome condition all to himself? And doesn't he sometimes wonder whether he has gained most or lost most by learning his trade?

> **wrought:** caused to appear

> **bluff reef:** a type of sandbar that is difficult to see and, therefore, dangerous to boats

> **shoaling up:** building up sediment, which causes the water to become shallower

1.   Double-underline the thesis statement. What is Twain's purpose in the essay?

2. What type of organization does this essay use (point by point or whole to whole)?

3. Why do you suppose Twain's perceptions of the river changed?

4. How is the writing in the "before" and "after" sections of the essay similar? How is it different?

Write Your Own Comparison and Contrast

Write a comparison/contrast paragraph or essay on one of the following topics or on one of your own choice. For help, refer to the How to Write Comparison and Contrast checklist on page 147.

College

- What surprised you most about starting courses at college? Describe similarities and differences between high school and college, and give examples.

- If you are still deciding on a major area of study, see if you can sit in on a class or two from programs that interest you. Then, compare and contrast the classes. If this process helped you decide on a program, explain the reasons for your choice.

Work

- Have you had experience working for both a bad supervisor and a good one? If so, compare and contrast their behaviors, and explain why you preferred one supervisor to another.

- Compare and contrast your work environment before and after a change in policies, management, or facilities. Use the comparison and contrast to show why the change was (or was not) beneficial.

Everyday Life

- Compare and contrast two businesses in your community. Write a review based on your comparison or contrast.

- Participate in a cleanup effort in your community, and then compare and contrast how the area looked before the cleanup with how it looked afterward.

CHECKLIST: How to Write Comparison and Contrast	
STEPS	**DETAILS**
☐ **Narrow and explore your topic.** See Chapter 2.	• Make the topic more specific. • Prewrite to get ideas about the narrowed topic.
☐ **Write a topic sentence (paragraph) or thesis statement (essay).** See Chapter 3.	• State the main point you want to make in your comparison/contrast.
☐ **Support your point.** See Chapter 3.	• Come up with points of comparison/ contrast and with details about each one.
☐ **Write a draft.** See Chapter 4.	• Make a plan that sets up a point-by-point or whole-to-whole comparison/contrast. • Include a topic sentence (paragraph) or thesis statement (essay) and all the support points.
☐ **Revise your draft.** See Chapter 4.	• Make sure it has *all* the Four Basics of Good Comparison and Contrast. • Make sure you include transitions to move readers smoothly from one subject or comparison/contrast point to the next.
☐ **Edit your revised draft.** See Chapters 15 through 18.	• Correct errors in grammar, spelling, word use, and punctuation.

12

Cause and Effect

Writing That Explains Reasons or Results

Understand What Cause and Effect Are

A **cause** is what made an event happen. An **effect** is what happens as a result of the event.

Four Basics of Good Cause and Effect

1 The main point reflects the writer's purpose: to explain causes, effects, or both.

2 If the purpose is to explain causes, the writing presents real causes; if the purpose is to explain effects, it presents real effects.

3 It gives readers detailed examples or explanations of the causes or effects.

4 It is organized logically — by space, time, or order of importance — according to its purpose.

In the following paragraph, the numbers and colors correspond to the Four Basics of Good Cause and Effect.

4 Causes arranged by order of importance.

Followers of college football recognize several outstanding programs, including Notre Dame, Michigan, Ohio State, and Florida State. However, in the past decade, one school in particular has dominated the college football rankings, with championships in 2009, 2011, 2012, and 2015: the University of Alabama, known as the Crimson Tide. **1** Several factors have led to Alabama's dominance. **2** First, there is a tradition of winning at Alabama, **3** which has had sixteen national titles in its history, with six under the legendary Paul "Bear" Bryant in the 1960s and 1970s, and four under current coach

Nick Saban. |2| That tradition of winning has led to outstanding recruiting: Alabama has brought some of the best talent in the country to the university. |3| The ability to recruit well means that Alabama's teams have depth: they can substitute outstanding players throughout the game, bringing fresh energy to the field. |2| Another reason for Alabama's success is the financial investment they have made in the team. |3| According to the NCAA, Alabama spent just under $1 million in 2012–2013 on recruiting, and in 2016, coach Nick Saban was the highest paid college football coach in the country, earning a staggering $7.09 million. Coach Saban does not coach alone: the university employs fourteen assistant coaches as well. |2| But perhaps more important than the tradition and the money spent, Alabama has a winning philosophy embraced by all the coaches: develop a solid defense, and treat every opponent with respect. |3| In a recent broadcast on ESPN, former Alabama quarterback Greg McElroy noted that Coach Saban and his staff expect the same preparation each week, both for the lowest-ranked opponent and for the championship game. |1| With tradition, financial support, strong coaching, and a solid team philosophy, Alabama should continue winning for years to come.

You read and write cause and effect in many situations.

COLLEGE	In a nutrition course, you are asked to identify the consequences (effects) of poor nutrition.
WORK	Sales are down in your group, and you explain the causes.
EVERYDAY LIFE	You explain to your child why a certain behavior is not acceptable by warning him or her about the negative effects of that behavior.

In college, writing assignments might include the words *discuss the causes (or effects) of*, but they might also use phrases such as *explain the results of*, *discuss the impact of*, and *how did* X *affect* Y? In all these cases, use the strategies discussed in this chapter.

First Basic: Main Point in Cause and Effect

The **main point** introduces causes, effects, or both. Here is an example of a topic sentence for a paragraph:

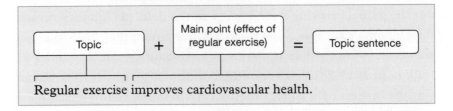

Remember that the main point for an essay can be a little broader than one for a paragraph (see pp. 152–153).

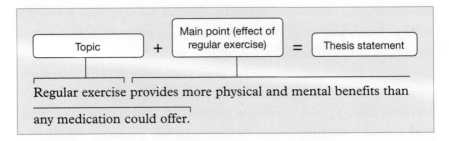

Whereas the topic sentence focuses on just one major benefit of regular exercise, the thesis statement considers multiple benefits.

Second and Third Basics: Support in Cause and Effect

The paragraph and essay models on pages 152–153 use the topic sentence (paragraph) and thesis statement (essay) from the Main Point section of this chapter. Both models include the primary and secondary support used in all cause-effect writing: statements that show real causes or effects backed up by detailed explanations or examples. In the essay plan, however, the major support points (statements of cause/effect) are topic sentences for individual paragraphs.

Avoid Logical Fallacies

When you are writing about causes and effects, make sure that you do not commit a logical fallacy, or a mistake in reasoning. There are two common mistakes made in writing about causes and effects: the post hoc fallacy and the slippery slope fallacy. The **post hoc fallacy** comes from a Latin phrase, *post hoc ergo propter hoc*, which literally means "after this, therefore because of this." We make this mistake when we look at two events and assume that the one that occurred first caused the second one. For example, if you have pizza on Monday and get the flu on Tuesday, eating the pizza is not the cause of the flu just because it happened before you got the flu.

The **slippery slope fallacy** occurs when someone suggests certain effects will occur following an action or event, but there is no logical basis for that belief. For example, the student who got the flu might have to miss a week of class. That student might say, "Now I am going to fail this course, and I won't graduate on time. Nobody will want to hire me." Having the flu can cause you to fall behind, but it probably won't affect your long-term job prospects. *Post hoc thinking* leads to illogical cause statements; *slippery slope thinking* leads to illogical effect statements.

Fourth Basic: Organization in Cause and Effect

Cause and effect can be organized in a variety of ways, depending on your purpose. (For more on the different orders of organization, see pp. 44–46.)

MAIN POINT	PURPOSE	ORGANIZATION
The "Occupy" protests of 2011 brought attention to the economic difficulties faced by low- and middle-income citizens.	to explain the effects of the protests	order of importance, saving the most important effect for last
A desire to remain at a protest site for an extended period led "Occupy" protesters to create miniature towns, with food service, libraries, and more.	to describe the places where protesters camped out	space order
The "Occupy" protests in New York City inspired other protests throughout the country.	to describe the spread of the protest movement over time	time order

PARAGRAPHS VS. ESSAYS IN CAUSE AND EFFECT

For more on the important features of cause and effect, see the Four Basics of Good Cause and Effect on page 148.

Paragraph Form

A   Regular exercise improves cardiovascular health. One
B   benefit of exercise is that it strengthens the heart. Like any
other muscle, the heart becomes stronger with use, and is able to pump blood through the body more efficiently. The result can be lower blood pressure, reducing the risk of heart
C   disease. Another benefit of exercise is that it lessens the toll that excessive weight can take on the heart. In seriously overweight individuals, the strain of carrying extra pounds can cause the heart to enlarge, interfering with its ability to pump blood. By losing weight through exercise and dietary changes, people can reduce the burden on their hearts and
D   also their cardiovascular risk. The most important cardiovascular benefit of exercise is that it lowers the risk of heart disease. As previously noted, exercise can reduce blood pressure and strain on the heart, both risk factors for heart attack, stroke, and heart failure. In addition, it can lower levels of "bad" cholesterol while raising levels of "good" cholesterol. Controlling bad cholesterol is important because when there is too much of this substance in the blood, it can build up on artery walls, causing reduced blood flow.

E   Regular and vigorous aerobic exercise is the best way to reap these cardiovascular benefits, but even a brisk walk a few times a week is better than no activity at all.

Main Point: Often narrower for a paragraph than for an essay: while the topic sentence (paragraph) focuses on just one major benefit of exercise, the thesis statement (essay) considers multiple benefits.

Support for the Main Point (Statements of Cause or Effect)

Detailed Explanations or Examples of Cause/Effect Statements: Usually, 1 to 3 sentences per statement for paragraphs and 3 to 8 sentences per statement for essays.

A   Topic sentence

B   Support 1 (cause 1 or effect 1)

C   Support 2 (cause 2 or effect 2)

D   Support 3 (cause 3 or effect 3)

E   Concluding sentence

Conclusion

Essay Format

1

Most people know how hard it is to start and stick with an exercise program. However, there is a good reason to build a significant amount of physical activity into every week: regular exercise provides more physical and mental benefits than any medication could offer. 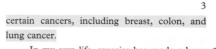 **A**

First, exercise helps people achieve and maintain a healthy weight. A nutritious diet that is not excessive in calories has a greater effect on weight loss than exercise does. However, regular exercise—ideally, interspersed throughout the day—can make an important contribution. For instance, people trying to lose weight might walk to work or to other destinations instead of driving. Or, they might take the stairs to their office instead of the elevator. If they go the gym at the end of the day, so much the better. Added up, all these efforts can make a difference. **B**

Second, exercise boosts mood and energy levels. For example, exercise causes the body to release endorphins, chemicals that give us a sense of well-being, even happiness. Accordingly, exercise can help reduce stress and combat **C**

2

depression. In addition, because exercise can make people look and feel more fit, it can improve their self-esteem. Finally, by improving strength and endurance, exercise gives individuals more energy to go about their lives.

The most important benefit of exercise is that it can help prevent disease. For example, exercise can improve the body's use of insulin and, as noted earlier, help people maintain a healthy weight. Therefore, it can help prevent or control diabetes. Additionally, exercise can lower the risk of heart attacks, strokes, and heart failure. For instance, exercise strengthens the heart muscle, helping it pump blood more efficiently and reducing high blood pressure, a heart disease risk factor. Also, exercise can lower levels of "bad" cholesterol while raising levels of "good" cholesterol. Controlling levels of bad cholesterol is important because when there is too much of this substance in the blood, it can build up in the walls of arteries, possibly blocking blood flow. Finally, some research suggests that regular exercise can reduce the risk of **D**

3

certain cancers, including breast, colon, and lung cancer.

In my own life, exercise has made a huge difference. Before starting a regular exercise program, I was close to needing prescription medications to lower my blood pressure and cholesterol. Thanks to regular physical activity, however, both my blood pressure and cholesterol levels are now in the normal range, and I have never felt better. Every bit of time spent at the gym or exchanging a ride in an elevator for a walk up the stairs has been well worth it. **E**

A Thesis statement

B Topic sentence 1 (cause 1 or effect 1)

C Topic sentence 2 (cause 2 or effect 2)

D Topic sentence 3 (cause 3 or effect)

E Concluding paragraph

NOTE: If you are explaining both causes and effects, you usually present the causes first and the effects later.

Use **transitions** to move readers smoothly from one cause to another, or from one effect to another, or from causes to effects. Because cause and effect can use any method of organization depending on your purpose, the following list shows just a few of the transitions you might use.

COMMON TRANSITIONS IN CAUSE AND EFFECT	
also	more important/serious cause or effect
as a result	most important/serious cause or effect
because	one cause/effect; another cause or effect
the final cause or effect	a primary cause; a secondary cause
the first, second, third cause or effect	a short-term effect; a long-term effect

Read and Analyze Cause and Effect

After you read each of the selections below, answer the questions that follow.

Cause and Effect in the Real World

Mary LaCue Booker, Singer/Actor

School Rules

Mary LaCue Booker studied both nursing and psychology in college before attending the competitive American Academy of Dramatic Arts in Los Angeles. Later, as the chair of the fine arts department in a Georgia middle school, Booker began writing rap songs to help motivate her students. Booker now has three CDs under her stage name La Q, and she has acted in the movie *We Must Go Forward*, about African American history. Booker writes songs, motivational speeches, and screenplays. Below are some lyrics from one of La Q's hit songs.

1   *Now get this, now get this, now get this.*
    If ya wanna be cool, obey the rules
    Cause if ya don't, it's your future you lose.
    I'm a school teacher from a rough school.
    I see students every day breakin' the rules.
    Here comes a new boy with a platinum grill
    Makin' trouble, ringin' the fire drill.

2   There goes anotha' fool wanna run the school,
    Breakin' all the damn school rules.
    Runnin' in the halls, writin' graffiti on the walls,
    Tellin' a lie without blinkin' an eye,
    Usin' profanity, pleadin' insanity,
    Callin' names, causin' pain,

3   Joinin' gangs like it's fame,
    Dissin' the teacha and each otha.
    Regardless of color, they're all sistas and brothas.

4   *Now get this, now get this, now get this, now get this.*
    Boys and girls are skippin' class,
    Cause they late with no hall pass.
    They wanna have their say, and that's okay,
    But they're outta their minds if they wanna have their way.

5   *Now get this, now get this, now get this.*
    If ya wanna be free, school's not the place ta be.
    But if ya wanna degree, you gotta feel me.
    So if you wanna be cool, obey the rules
    Cause if ya don't, it's your future you lose.

1.   What is La Q's purpose?
2.   What are the effects of breaking the rules?
3.   Underline the causes that lead to these effects.
4.   With a partner, or as a class, rewrite this rap into a formal English paragraph.

Student Cause/Effect Paragraph

Caitlin Prokop

A Difficult Decision with a Positive Outcome

Caitlin Prokop wrote the following paragraph as she was preparing to begin her studies at Brevard Community College in Florida. Later, she went on to pursue a degree in elementary education at the University of Hawaii. She was inspired to write this essay by her parents. Prokop understands the balance between inspiration and revision in writing and offers this advice: "Follow what the brain is telling the hand. Let it flow. If you cannot write about the topic that is given, put yourself in someone else's shoes and then write. Let your thoughts flow; then, revise and edit to get the finished copy."

When my mother made the decision to move back to New York, I made the choice to move in with my dad so that I could finish high school. This decision affected me in a positive way because I graduated with my friends, built a better relationship with my father, and had the chance to go to college without leaving home. Graduating with my friends was very important to me because I have known most of them since we were in kindergarten. It was a journey through childhood that we had shared, and I wanted to finish it with them. Accomplishing the goal of graduating from high school with my close friends, those who accompanied me through school, made me a stronger and more confident person. Another good outcome of my difficult decision was the relationship I built with my dad. We never saw eye to eye when I lived with both of my parents. For example, we stopped talking for five months because I always sided against him with my mom. Living together for the past five years has made us closer, and I cherish that closeness we have developed. Every Thursday is our day, a day when we talk to each other about what is going on in our lives, so that we will never again have a distant relationship. A third good outcome of my decision is that I can go to Brevard Community College, which is right down the street. In high school, I had thought that I would want to go away to college, but then I realized that I would miss my home. By staying here, I have the opportunity to attend a wonderful college that is preparing me for transferring to a four-year college and finding a good career. I have done some research and believe I would like to become a police officer, a nurse, or a teacher. Through the school, I can do volunteer work in each of these areas. Right now, I am leaning toward becoming a teacher, based on my volunteer work in a kindergarten class. There, I can explore what grades I want to teach. In every way, I believe that my difficult decision was the right one, giving me many opportunities that I would not have had if I had moved to a new and unfamiliar place.

1. Double-underline the topic sentence.
2. Does Prokop write about causes or effects? What is her purpose?
3. Circle the transitions Prokop uses to move readers from one point to the next.
4. Does the paragraph include the Four Basics of Good Cause and Effect (p.148)? Why or why not?
5. Have you made a difficult decision that turned out to be a good one? Why and how?

Professional Cause/Effect Essay

Kristen Ziman

Bad Attitudes and Glowworms

Paddock Publications

Kristen Ziman is a commander with the Aurora Police Department in Aurora, Illinois, and a columnist for the *Beacon News*. She holds a B.A. in criminal justice management from Aurora University and an M.A. in criminal justice/organizational leadership from Boston University. In addition to writing for the *Beacon News*, Ziman regularly posts to her blog, *Think Different*. In the following essay, Ziman discusses how keeping a positive attitude helps people maintain control over their lives.

1   In my third-grade classroom there was a poster on the wall that read:

I wish I were a glowworm,
A glowworm's never glum.
'Cuz how can you be grumpy
When the sun shines out your bum!

epiphany: a sudden flash of understanding or insight

contention: conflict; displeasure

2   I didn't understand what that poem meant until I was in my twenties, and I had an **epiphany** about attitude. I was partnered with a veteran officer, and two hours into our eight-hour shift, I began to realize that there was not a single thing he enjoyed about his job or his life. Being assigned to ride with me was also a source of **contention** for him, and he wasn't bashful about telling me so.

3   I found his disdain for life odd—especially given the fact that it was a beautiful summer day and the few calls we answered were relatively uneventful. As we patrolled the streets, I visualized a dark cloud exclusively over his head in contrast to the sunshine surrounding the rest of us, and I laughed out loud as the glowworm poem popped into my head. It was at that moment that I started to understand the effect our attitude has on our entire existence.

4   Throughout my life, I have been bombarded with lessons about attitude. It's not what happens to us in life, but the way we respond that makes a difference. If you can't change a situation, you must change the way you see the situation. I understand these lessons on an intellectual level, but conceptually, there are times I find it difficult to find the light when darkness seems to be so overwhelming.

metamorphosis: transformation

5   As I gained more experience as a police officer, I began to understand how the **metamorphosis** from an optimist to a pessimist occurs. I became distrusting of other human beings, though not without reason. I had been lied to, spit on, and physically attacked while doing my job. I saw the evil human beings did to one another and started to become suspicious of the motives all around me. There was a moment when I quietly challenged my decision to make this my career, and I felt my own dark cloud begin to hover.

validated: confirmed; supported

proverbial: related to a proverb or common saying. ("Look at yourself in the mirror" is a common saying.)

6   Because I've always been very analytical and self-aware [by my own estimation], I started to pay attention to the negativity of my coworkers, and it suddenly became clear that the miserable ones seemed to feed off each other like vultures. They gravitated towards one another because they **validated** each other's thoughts and beliefs. They were always victims, and they effortlessly found someone else to blame for all that was wrong. Never did they stop to look in the **proverbial** mirror and ask themselves if they might be part of the problem.

7   My favorite book is *Man's Search for Meaning* by Viktor Frankl. In his book, Frankl writes about his experiences in the concentration camps of Nazi Germany. He took particular interest in how some of his fellow prisoners seemed to endure and even thrive, while others gave up and laid down to die. From this, he concluded that "everything can be taken from a man but one thing: the last of human freedom is to choose one's attitude in any given set of circumstances—to choose one's own way."

8   We all struggle in some way with things that are completely out of our control. But the way we gain control over these things—even if only attitudinally—is where our freedom lies. We don't have to experience torture in a concentration camp to apply Frankl's teachings to our own

lives. We each have the freedom to make choices that liberate us from our self-imposed prisons.

9   If Frankl's story doesn't motivate you to choose the way you look at things, maybe you need to surround yourselves with more glowworms.

1.   Double-underline the thesis statement. What is Ziman's purpose?

2.   Does this essay present causes, effects, or both? Explain how you came to your conclusion.

3.   Does this essay follow the Four Basics of Good Cause and Effect (p. 148)? Why or why not?

Write Your Own Cause and Effect

Write a cause/effect paragraph or essay on one of the following topics or on one of your own choice. For help, refer to the How to Write Cause and Effect checklist on page 160.

College

■   Explore the causes or effects of cheating on your campus. What motivates a student to cheat, and how do professors respond to cheating? Interview professors and students as you prepare your essay.

■   If you have chosen a major or program of study, explain the factors that led to your decision. Or, explain how you think this choice will shape your future.

Work

■   Write about the causes, effects, or both of stress at work. Think about a practical purpose for your analysis: could your employer change the situation?

■   Identify a friend or acquaintance who has been successful at work. Write about the factors behind this person's success.

Everyday Life

■   Try to fill in this blank: "_____ changed my life." Your response can be an event, an interaction with a particular person, or anything significant to you. It can be something positive or negative. After you fill in the blank, explain how and why this event, interaction, or time had so much significance.

■ Arrange to spend a few hours at a local soup kitchen or food pantry, or on another volunteer opportunity that interests you. (You can search online for volunteer opportunities in your area.) Write about how the experience affected you.

CHECKLIST: How to Write Cause and Effect	
STEPS	**DETAILS**
☐ **Narrow and explore your topic.** See Chapter 2.	• Make the topic more specific. • Prewrite to get ideas about the narrowed topic.
☐ **Write a topic sentence (paragraph) or thesis statement (essay).** See Chapter 3.	• State your subject and the causes, effects, or both that your paper will explore.
☐ **Support your point.** See Chapter 3.	• Come up with explanations/examples of the causes, effects, or both.
☐ **Write a draft.** See Chapter 4.	• Make a plan that puts the support points in a logical order. • Include a topic sentence (paragraph) or thesis statement (essay) and all the supporting explanations/examples.
☐ **Revise your draft.** See Chapter 4.	• Make sure it has *all* the Four Basics of Good Cause and Effect. • Make sure you include transitions to move readers smoothly from one cause/effect to the next.
☐ **Edit your revised draft.** See Chapters 15 through 18.	• Correct errors in grammar, spelling, word use, and punctuation.

13

Argument

Writing That Persuades

Understand What Argument Is

Argument is writing that takes a position on an issue and gives supporting evidence to persuade someone else to accept, or at least consider, the position. Argument is also used to convince someone to take (or not take) an action.

Four Basics of Good Argument

1 It takes a strong and definite position.

2 It gives good reasons to defend the position.

3 It provides valid supporting evidence and considers opposing views thoughtfully.

4 It organizes support logically according to the writer's purpose.

In the following paragraph, the numbers and colors correspond to the Four Basics of Good Argument.

1 Even though I write this blog post on an 88-degree day, I am truly glad that I stopped using my air conditioner, and I urge you to follow my lead. **2** For one thing, going without air conditioning can save a significant amount of money. **3** Last summer, this strategy cut my electricity costs by nearly $2,000, and I am on my way to achieving even higher savings this summer. **2** For another thing, living without air conditioning reduces humans' effect on the environment. **3** Agricultural researcher Stan Cox estimates that air conditioning creates 300 million tons of carbon dioxide (CO_2)

4 Support is organized logically according to the writer's purpose.

emissions each year. This amount, he says, is the equivalent of every U.S. household buying an additional car and driving it 7,000 miles annually. Because CO_2 is one of the greenhouse gases responsible for trapping heat in our atmosphere, reducing CO_2 emissions is essential to curbing climate change. **2** The final reason for going without air conditioning is that it is actually pretty comfortable. **3** The key to staying cool is keeping the blinds down on south-facing windows during the day. It is also a good idea to open windows throughout the home for cross ventilation while turning on ceiling fans to improve air circulation. **3** Although some people argue that using fans is just as bad as switching on the air conditioner, fans use far less electricity. In closing, let me make you a promise: the sooner you give up air conditioning, the sooner you will get comfortable with the change—and the sooner you and the planet will reap the rewards.

Knowing how to understand and construct a good argument is one of the most useful skills you can develop.

COLLEGE	You argue for or against makeup exams for students who do not do well the first time.
WORK	You need to leave work an hour early 1 day a week for 12 weeks to take a course. You persuade your boss to allow you to do so.
EVERYDAY LIFE	You try to negotiate a better price on an item you want to buy.

In college, writing assignments might include questions or statements such as the following: *Do you agree or disagree with* _____? *Defend or refute* _____. *Is* _____ *fair and just?* In all these cases, use the strategies discussed in this chapter.

First Basic: Main Point in Argument

Your **main point** in argument is the position you take on the issue (or topic) about which you are writing. The main point in argument is often called a **claim**. When you are free to choose an issue, choose something that matters to you. When you are assigned an issue, try to find some part of it that matters to you.

In argument, the topic sentence (in a paragraph) or thesis statement (in an essay) usually includes the issue / topic and your position about it. Here is an example of a topic sentence for a paragraph:

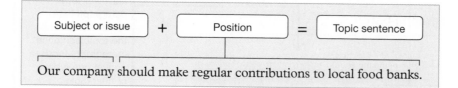

Remember that the main point for an essay can be a little broader than one for a paragraph (see pp. 164–165).

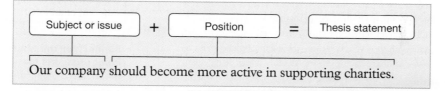

Whereas the topic sentence focuses on just one type of charitable organization, the thesis statement sets up a discussion of different ways to help different charities.

Second and Third Basics: Support in Argument

The paragraph and essay models on pages 164–165 use the topic sentence (paragraph) and thesis statement (essay) from the Main Point section of this chapter. Both models include the primary and secondary support used in all argument writing: the **reasons** for the writer's position backed up by **evidence**. In the essay model, however, the major support points (reasons) are topic sentences for individual paragraphs.

Support in argument also includes consideration of opposing points of view. An opposing position is called a **counterclaim**, and the opposing reasons are called **counterarguments**. You can support your argument by presenting opposing points of view fairly and responding to them thoughtfully.

Types of Evidence

- **Facts:** Statements or observations that can be proved. Statistics — real numbers from actual studies — can be persuasive factual evidence. (List of types of evidence continues on p. 166.)

PARAGRAPHS VS. ESSAYS IN ARGUMENT

For more on the important features of argument, see the Four Basics of Good Argument on page 161.

Paragraph Form

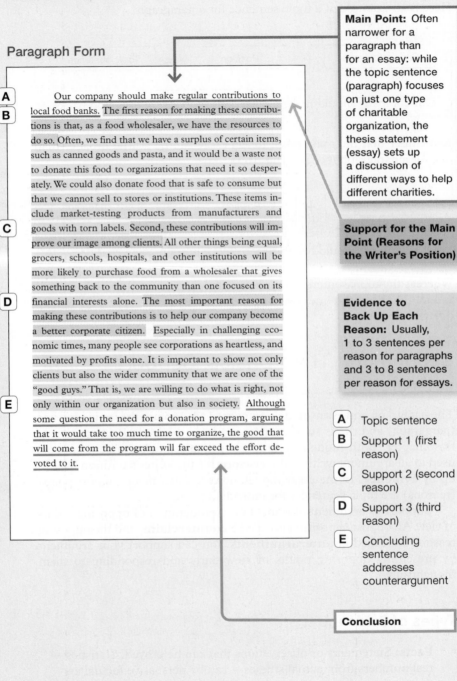

A Our company should make regular contributions to local food banks. **B** The first reason for making these contributions is that, as a food wholesaler, we have the resources to do so. Often, we find that we have a surplus of certain items, such as canned goods and pasta, and it would be a waste not to donate this food to organizations that need it so desperately. We could also donate food that is safe to consume but that we cannot sell to stores or institutions. These items include market-testing products from manufacturers and goods with torn labels. **C** Second, these contributions will improve our image among clients. All other things being equal, grocers, schools, hospitals, and other institutions will be more likely to purchase food from a wholesaler that gives something back to the community than one focused on its financial interests alone. **D** The most important reason for making these contributions is to help our company become a better corporate citizen. Especially in challenging economic times, many people see corporations as heartless, and motivated by profits alone. It is important to show not only clients but also the wider community that we are one of the "good guys." That is, we are willing to do what is right, not only within our organization but also in society. **E** Although some question the need for a donation program, arguing that it would take too much time to organize, the good that will come from the program will far exceed the effort devoted to it.

Main Point: Often narrower for a paragraph than for an essay: while the topic sentence (paragraph) focuses on just one type of charitable organization, the thesis statement (essay) sets up a discussion of different ways to help different charities.

Support for the Main Point (Reasons for the Writer's Position)

Evidence to Back Up Each Reason: Usually, 1 to 3 sentences per reason for paragraphs and 3 to 8 sentences per reason for essays.

A Topic sentence

B Support 1 (first reason)

C Support 2 (second reason)

D Support 3 (third reason)

E Concluding sentence addresses counterargument

Conclusion

Essay Form

1

At the last executive meeting, we discussed several possible ways to improve our company's marketing and advertising and to increase employee morale. Since attending the meeting, I have become convinced that one effort would help in those areas and more: our company should become more active in supporting charities. **A**

First, giving time and money to community organizations is a good way to promote our organization. This approach has worked well for several of our competitors. For example, Lanse Industries is well known for sponsoring Little League teams throughout the city. Its name is on the back of each uniform, and banners promoting Lanse's new products appear on the ball fields. Lanse gets free promotion of these efforts through articles in the local papers, and according to one company source quoted in the Hillsburg Gazette, Lanse's good works in the community have boosted its sales by 5 to 10 percent. Another competitor, Great Deals, has employees serve meals at soup kitchens over the holidays and at **B**

2

least once during the spring or summer. It, too, has gotten great publicity from these efforts, including a spot on a local TV news show. It is time for our company to start reaping these kinds of benefits.

Second, activities like group volunteering will help employees feel more connected to one another and to their community. Kay Rodriguez, a manager at Great Deals and a good friend of mine, organized the company's group volunteering efforts at the soup kitchens, and she cannot say enough good things about the results. Aside from providing meals to the needy, the volunteering has boosted the morale of Great Deals employees because they understand that they are supporting an important cause in their community. Kay has also noticed that as employees work together at the soup kitchens, they form closer bonds. She says, "Some of these people work on different floors and rarely get to see each other during the work week. Or they just do not have time to talk. But while they work together on the volunteering, I see real **C**

3

connections forming." I know that some members of our executive committee might think it would be too time-consuming to organize companywide volunteering efforts. Kay assures me, however, that this is not the case and that the rewards of such efforts far exceed the costs in time. **D**

The most important reason for supporting charities is that it is the right thing to do. As a successful business that depends on the local community for a large share of revenue and employees, I believe we owe that community something in return. If our home city does not thrive, how can we? By giving time and money to local organizations, we provide a real service to people, and we present our company as a good and caring neighbor instead of a faceless corporation that could not care less if local citizens went hungry, had trash and graffiti in their parks, or couldn't afford sports teams for their kids. We could make our community proud to have us around. **E**

4

I realize that our main goal is to run a profitable and growing business. I do not believe, however, that this aim must exclude doing good in the community. In fact, I see these two goals moving side-by-side, and hand-in-hand. When companies give back to local citizens, their businesses benefit, the community benefits, and everyone is pleased by the results. **F**

A	Thesis statement
B	Topic sentence 1 (reason 1)
C	Topic sentence 2 (reason 2)
D	Addresses counterargument
E	Topic sentence 3 (reason 3)
F	Concluding paragraph

- **Examples:** Specific information or experiences that support your position.

- **Expert opinions:** The opinions of people considered knowledgeable about your topic because of their educational or work background, their research into the topic, or other qualifications. It is important to choose these sources carefully. For example, an economics professor might be very knowledgeable about the possible benefits and drawbacks of beverage taxes. He or she probably wouldn't be the best source of information on the health effects of soda, however.

- **Predictions:** Forecasts of the possible outcomes of events or actions. These forecasts are the informed views of experts, not the best guesses of non-experts.

Once you have assembled your evidence, test it to see if it is the right evidence for the writing situation and audience.

Testing Evidence

- Consider your audience's view of the issue. Are audience members likely to agree with you, to be uncommitted, or to be hostile? Then, make sure your evidence would be convincing to a typical member of your audience.

- Reread your evidence from an opponent's perspective, looking for possible counterarguments. Anticipate your opponent's objections, and include evidence to answer them.

- Do not overgeneralize. Statements about what everyone else does or what always happens are easy to disprove. It is better to use facts (including statistics), specific examples, expert opinions, and informed predictions.

- Make sure you have considered every important angle of the issue.

- Reread the evidence to make sure it provides good support for your position. Also, the evidence must be relevant to your argument.

Fourth Basic: Organization in Argument

Most arguments are organized by **order of importance**, starting with the least important evidence and saving the most convincing reason and evidence for last. (For more on order of importance, see p. 46.)

Use **transitions** to move your readers smoothly from one supporting reason to another. Here are some of the transitions you might use in your argument.

COMMON TRANSITIONS IN ARGUMENT	
above all	more important
also	most important
best of all	one fact / another fact
especially	one reason / another reason
for example	one thing / another thing
in addition	remember
in fact	the first (second, third) point
in particular	worst of all
in the first (second, third) place	

Read and Analyze Argument

After you read each of the selections below, answer the questions that follow.

Argument in the Real World

Diane Melancon, Oncologist

The Importance of Advance Directives

In part because her family never expected her to pursue a career, Diane Melancon took what she describes as a "curvy path" to her medical degree and her current practice in oncology (the treatment of cancer). After high school, she worked her way through a number of educational programs, earning a certificate in medical assistance from Diman Regional Vocational Technical High School, an A.S. in X-ray technology from Northeastern University, a B.A. from Wellesley College, and an M.D. from Dartmouth Medical School. In her medical practice today, she writes patient assessments and treatment plans. In the following piece, she argues for the importance of advance directives, in which patients spell out how they wish their medical treatment to be handled in life-threatening situations.

1   Consider these difficult situations: (1) A car accident seriously damages a young man's brain, leaving his family to decide whether or not he should be kept on life support. (2) A patient's cancer is not responding well to chemotherapy. She must decide whether to continue with the therapy, despite its physical and emotional strains, or to receive only care that reduces pain and provides comfort. Nothing will make such decisions any easier for these patients or their families. However, people who are able to provide guidance for their treatment in advance of a medical crisis can help ensure that their wishes are followed, even under the most difficult circumstances. Therefore, everyone should seriously consider preparing advance directives for medical care.

2   One major reason for preparing advance directives is that they make it clear to care providers, family, and other loved ones which medical measures patients do or do not want to be taken during a health crisis. Directives specify these wishes even after patients are no longer able to do so themselves—because, for example, they have lost consciousness. Advance directives include living wills, legal documents that indicate which life-sustaining measures are acceptable to patients and under what circumstances. These measures include the use of breathing aids, such as ventilators, and of feeding aids, such as tube-delivered nutrition. Living wills may also indicate a point at which a patient wishes to receive only comfort care, as opposed to aggressive treatment. Furthermore, living wills may specify whether patients wish to receive cardiopulmonary resuscitation if their heart and breathing stop. Finally, through a legal document known as a medical power of attorney, patients may select another person to make medical decisions on their behalf if they become incapable of doing so themselves. All of these parts of advance directives help reduce the risk that patients' wishes will be overlooked or contradicted during any point of the treatment process.

3   Another important reason for preparing advanced directives is that they can reduce stress and confusion in the delivery of care. Ideally, patients should complete these directives while they are still relatively healthy in mind and body and capable of giving thoughtful and informed instructions for their own medical care. In contrast, waiting until a health problem is far advanced can increase the difficulty and stress of making medical decisions; at this point, patients and their loved ones may be feeling too overwhelmed to think carefully through the various options. In the worst-case scenario, patients may have moved beyond the ability to contribute to medical decisions at all. In such cases, family members and others close to patients may be forced to make their own judgments about which treatments should or should not be given, possibly resulting in disagreements and confusion. However, when patients have made their preferences clear in advance, care delivery moves more smoothly for them and everyone else.

4   Some people may believe that advance directives are too depressing to think about or that they are even unnecessary. They may take the attitude "Let's cross that bridge when we come to it." However, as has been noted, by the time the bridge is in sight it might already be too late. Although making advance plans for life-threatening medical situations can be difficult and emotional, avoiding such planning can create more stress for patients and their loved ones. Worse, it may mean that the patients' true wishes are never known or acted upon.

1.   Double-underline the thesis statement. Can you paraphrase her claim?

2.   Circle the transitions that introduce the different reasons supporting the argument.

3.   Underline the part of the essay that presents an opposing view.

4.   Does this essay follow the Four Basics of Good Argument (p. 161)? Why or why not?

5.   Who is Melancon's audience? How does her argument pay attention to the needs of her readers?

The next two student essays argue about the wisdom of using social media, like Facebook and Twitter, as educational aids in college. Read both essays, and answer the questions after the second one.

Student Argument Essay 1: "Yes" to Social Media in Education

Jason Yilmaz

A Learning Tool Whose Time Has Come

1   Efforts to incorporate social media into courses at our college have drawn several complaints. A major objection is that Facebook and Twitter are distractions that have no place in the classroom. Based on my own experiences, I must completely disagree. Social media, when used intelligently, will get students more involved with their courses and help them be more successful in college.

2   In the first place, social media can help students engage deeply with academic subjects. For example, in a sociology class that I took in high school, the instructor encouraged students to use Twitter in a research assignment. This assignment called for us to record, over one week, the number of times we observed students of different races and ethnic groups interacting outside of the classroom. Each of us made observations in the lunch room, in the courtyard where students liked to hang

out between classes, and in other public areas. We tweeted our findings as we did our research, and in the end, we brought them together to write a group report. The Twitter exchanges gave each of us new ideas and insights. Also, the whole process helped us understand what a research team does in the real world.

3   In the second place, social media are a good way for students to get help and support outside of class. As a commuter student with a job, it is hard for me to get to my instructors' office hours, let alone meet with other students. Therefore, I would value Facebook groups that would let me post questions about assignments and other homework and get responses from instructors and other students. Also, I would be able to form online study groups with classmates.

4   Finally, social networking can make students feel more confident and connected. In the sociology course where I used Twitter, I found that other students valued and respected the information that I shared, just as I valued their contributions. Also, all of us felt like we were "in this together"—an uncommon experience in most classrooms. I have heard that feeling connected to other students and to the larger college community can make people less likely to drop out, and I believe it.

5   New things often scare people, and the use of social media in education is no exception. However, I would hate to see fears about social media get in the way of efforts to make students more engaged with and successful in college. We owe it to students to overcome such fears.

Student Argument Essay 2: "No" to Social Media in Education

Shari Beck

A Classroom Distraction — and Worse

1   Last week, I saw the campus newspaper's story about new efforts to incorporate Twitter, Facebook, and other social media into courses. What did I think about these efforts? To get my answer, I only had to lower the newspaper. Across the table from me was my fourteen-year-old son, whom I'd just told, for the third time, to go upstairs and do his homework. Instead, he was still under the spell of his phone, thumbs flying as he continued to text a friend about who knows what.

2   As you might have guessed already, my answer to my own question is this: Making social media part of a college education is a terrible idea, for a whole lot of reasons.

3   One reason is the distraction factor, illustrated by my phone-addicted son. I am confident that he is not the only person incapable of turning

his full attention to any subject when the competition is an incoming or outgoing text message, or anything happening on a computer screen. Supporters of the college's social-media initiative say that students will benefit from discussing course material on Facebook or Twitter. I am concerned, however, that such discussions—when and if they ever take place—would quickly go off-topic, turning into social exchanges. Also, participants' attention could easily wander to other links and news flashes.

4   Another reason I am opposed to social media in education is that students' postings on Facebook or Twitter might compromise their privacy. I am not confident that all teachers will educate students about the importance of limiting the personal information that they make available in public forums. Tech-savvy students probably know how to maximize their privacy settings, but I doubt that all students do.

5   My biggest concern is that students will use social media to cheat. According to proponents of the social-media initiative, one of the biggest educational advantages of Facebook and Twitter is that students can exchange information and form study groups. But it is also possible that they will share answers to homework or test questions or take credit for information posted or tweeted by others. They may not realize that such information theft is plagiarism—something that could cause them to fail a course, or worse. In responding to a 2011 survey by the Pew Research Center, 55 percent of college presidents said that student plagiarism had increased over the previous ten years. Of those who reported this increase, 89 percent said computers and the internet played "a major role." It would be a shame to make this growing problem even worse through programs like the college's social-media initiative.

6   From where I sit—once again, across the table from my phone-distracted son—the disadvantages of this initiative far outweigh the benefits. I plan to send an email opposing it to the Student Affairs Office. First, though, I'm taking my son's phone away for the night.

1.   Double-underline the thesis statement in both essays.

2.   Underline the reasons for the position taken in each essay.

3.   Does each essay follow the Four Basics of Good Argument (p. 161)? Give examples to support your answer.

4.   Write down at least one additional support point / reason that one of the authors might have included. Then, describe the types of evidence that could be used to back up this support point.

5.   Who is the audience for these essays? How do you know?

6.   Write a brief summary of both essays.

Write Your Own Argument

Write an argument paragraph or essay on one of the following topics or on one of your own choice. For help, refer to the How to Write Argument checklist on page 173.

College

- Take a position on a controversial issue on your campus. If you need help coming up with topics, you might consult the campus newspaper.

- Argue for or against the use of standardized tests or placement tests. Make sure to research different positions on the tests to support your argument and address opposing views. One website you might consult is standardizedtests.procon.org. If you use research to develop your argument, be sure to take careful notes. For more on research, see Chapter 14.

Work

- Argue for something that you would like to get at work, such as a promotion, a raise, or a flexible schedule. Explain why you deserve what you are asking for, and give specific examples.

- Argue for an improvement in your workplace, such as the addition of a bike rack, new chairs in the break room, or a place to swap books or magazines. Make sure your request is reasonable in cost and will be beneficial to a significant number of employees.

Everyday Life

- Read and respond to an argument in your local print or online newspaper.

- Choose a community organization that you belong to, and write about why it is important. Try to persuade your readers to join.

CHECKLIST: How to Write Argument

STEPS	DETAILS
☐ **Narrow and explore your topic.** See Chapter 2.	• Make the topic more specific. • Prewrite to get ideas about the narrowed topic.
☐ **Write a topic sentence (paragraph) or thesis statement (essay).** See Chapter 3.	• State your position on your topic.
☐ **Support your point.** See Chapter 3.	• Come up with reasons and evidence to back up your position. Consider and address counterarguments.
☐ **Write a draft.** See Chapter 4.	• Make a plan that puts the reasons in a logical order. • Include a topic sentence (paragraph) or thesis statement (essay) and all the reasons and supporting evidence.
☐ **Revise your draft.** See Chapter 4.	• Make sure it has *all* the Four Basics of Good Argument (p. 161). • Make sure you include transitions to move readers smoothly from one reason to the next.
☐ **Edit your revised draft.** See Chapters 15 through 18.	• Correct errors in grammar, spelling, word use, and punctuation.

14

Research

Writing That Explores a Question and Synthesizes Information

Understand What Research Is

In all areas of your life, and especially in college, you will do **research**—looking for information so that you can understand an issue or make an informed decision about it.

Four Basics of Good Research

1 It is a process that begins with a research question.

2 It involves searching libraries and the internet to find relevant, timely, and credible sources.

3 It requires evaluating sources to ensure they are reliable and synthesizing them to create a thesis that answers your research question.

4 It requires you to use sources fairly and honestly so that you avoid plagiarism.

Knowing how to choose a topic; find, evaluate, and synthesize relevant sources; and correctly cite and document sources for a research project is crucial to success in all parts of your life.

COLLEGE	You search online for information to help you determine whether or not the death penalty deters crime, or you might conduct an online poll to determine the political views of students on your campus.
WORK	You investigate how other companies have reviewed a major office product before you invest in it.
EVERYDAY LIFE	You research potential side-effects for your medication online, or you might interview potential babysitters before hiring someone to stay with your daughter.

Writing a research paper involves completing a number of steps. To make sure you allow enough time to complete a research paper, make a schedule in advance and stick to it. Before you begin, review your assignment, making a note of the requirements and the due date.

First Basic: Begin with a Question

Whether you choose a topic or are assigned a specific one, you can do some prewriting activities (see Chapter 2) to help you narrow and refine your topic before you begin to do research. As you prewrite, you should develop a **guiding research question**, which is often a variation of "What do I want to find out about my topic?" This question will help direct and focus your research.

Second Basic: Find Appropriate Sources

Research requires you to find and use appropriate sources to answer your guiding question. With both the internet and libraries available to you, finding information is not a problem. However, knowing how to find *appropriate* sources — those that are relevant, timely, and reliable — can be a challenge. The following strategies will help you.

- **Consult a reference librarian**. Learn from him or her how to use your library's catalog, databases, and reference tools.

- **Use the online catalog**. Search by keyword, title, author, subject, publication data, or call number. A *call number* is an identification number that helps you locate a book in the library. If you are just beginning your research, use the keyword search.

- **Use library resources**. Look at your library's website for links to free electronic research sources that the library subscribes to, including periodical databases. A *periodical database* is a searchable collection of magazines, journals, and newspapers (also called *periodicals*). These databases are usually reliable and legitimate sources of information. The library home page may also list the library's hours, provide search tools, and offer research tips and other valuable information.

- **Use search engines**. Use search engines (such as Google, www.google.com) to explore information on the internet. To use a search engine, type in keywords related to your subject. Adding more specific keywords or phrases and using an advanced-search option may narrow the number of entries (called *hits*) you have to sift through to find relevant information. (With many search engines, you get the best results by enclosing phrases in quotation marks.) When you discover a website to which you might want to return, save the web address so that you do not have to remember it each time you want to go to the site.

■ **Interview experts or people directly affected by your research topic**. Schedule your interview and plan five to ten *open-ended questions*, such as "What do you think of the proposal to build a new library?" Avoid *closed questions*, which only require yes or no as an answer. Using a small recorder during the interview can be helpful. If you want to do so, make sure that you first ask the person for permission.

Third Basic: Evaluate and Synthesize Sources

Whether you are doing research for a college course, a work assignment, or personal reasons, make sure the sources you use are reliable. Reliable sources present accurate, up-to-date information written by authors with appropriate credentials for the subject matter.

Here are some questions you can ask to evaluate a source. If you answer "no" to any of these questions, do not use the source.

QUESTIONS FOR EVALUATING A PRINT OR ELECTRONIC SOURCE

■ **Is the source reliable?** It should be from a well-known magazine or publisher or from a reputable website. (For websites, also consider the internet address extension; see the box that follows for guidance.)

■ **Is the author qualified to write reliably about the subject?** If there is no biographical information, do an online search using the author's name to learn more about the author's qualifications.

■ **Do you know who sponsored the publication or website?** Be aware of the sponsor's motives (for example, to market a product).

■ **Does the author provide adequate support for key points?** Does he or she cite the sources of this support?

Guide to Internet Address Extensions

EXTENSION	SPONSOR OF SITE	HOW RELIABLE?
.com	A commercial or business organization	Varies. Consider whether you have heard of the organization, and be sure to read its home page or "About us" link carefully.
.edu	An educational institution	Reliable, but may include materials of varying quality.
.gov	A government agency	Reliable.
.net	A commercial organization	Varies. See the advice for ".com" extensions.
.org	A nonprofit organization	Generally reliable, although each volunteer or professional group promotes its own interests.

Synthesize Information to Support a Thesis Statement

Once you have gathered enough information, you can begin to synthesize your sources to form an answer to your research question. To **synthesize** means to combine or put together, drawing information from different places to create a unified idea. To synthesize effectively, think about how the information in your sources connects: do the ideas confirm, contradict, expand, or complicate each other?

Fourth Basic: Cite and Document Sources to Avoid Plagiarism

Plagiarism is presenting someone else's ideas and information as your own. Turning in a paper written by someone else, whether it is from the internet or from a friend or family member who gives you permission, is deliberate plagiarism. Sometimes, however, students plagiarize by mistake because the notes they have taken do not indicate which ideas are theirs and which were taken from outside sources. The following strategies will help you avoid accidental plagiarism.

- Take accurate notes: annotate carefully, paraphrase key ideas in your own words, and summarize what you read (see Chapter 1).
- Put quotation marks around phrases and sentences that you copy word for word in your notes.
- Keep a **running bibliography**, or list of sources, that you consult or use as you research a topic. Record complete publication information for each source at the time you consult it.
- Organize research notes in a notebook or electronic file.

Here is a list of information to record for each source while you are taking notes.

BOOKS	ARTICLES	WEBSITES
Author name(s) and names of any other contributors (editors, translators, etc.)	Author name(s)	Author name(s) (if any)
Title and subtitle	Title of article	Title of page or site
Publisher	Title of magazine, journal, or newspaper	Publisher (if different from site title)
Year of publication	Day, month, year of publication (4 Jan. 2016)	Date of online publication or latest update (day / month / year, e.g., 4 Jan. 2016)
Volume number (if relevant) and page number(s)	Volume, issue, and page number(s)	Digital Object Identifier (DOI) number: a permanent number for some online documents (preferred) OR Web address (URL): omit *http://* or *https://*.
All relevant information for a source that contains the short story, book, article, TV episode, etc., that you are referencing, e.g., if you access an article through JSTOR, note the title of the site and any other relevant information, including other contributors, version, number, publisher, publication date, and location.		

One of the most common mistakes students make is to find sources, use sources, and write the paper at the same time. Taking notes, summarizing, and responding to each individual source before writing the paper are essential steps in the research process.

Use MLA Format to Cite and Document Sources

There are several different systems of documentation. Most English instructors prefer the Modern Language Association (MLA) system. When you are writing a research paper in another course, you may be required to use another system. When you use MLA style, you provide in-text citations of sources as you use them in an essay and a complete, alphabetized list of sources at the end in a Works Cited page.

Use In-Text Citations within Your Essay

In-text citations show the reader information that comes from a source. In MLA style, in-text citations usually include a signal (introductory) phrase and a page number in parentheses. For websites and other electronic sources, you typically will not be able to include page numbers, although you can note any paragraph, chapter, or part numbers that appear in the source.

Direct Quotation: In an article by Alan Bavley, veteran and PTSD sufferer Chris Kornkven was quoted as saying the following about service dogs he had observed: "They seemed like they would be really helpful, particularly for individuals living alone" (5).

Paraphrase: In an article by Alan Bavley, veteran and PTSD sufferer Chris Kornkven expressed the belief that service dogs would be especially beneficial to vets who live by themselves (5).

When you do not refer to the author(s) in an introductory phrase, write the author's name followed by the page number(s), if available, at the end of the quotation. If an author is not named, use the title of the source.

Direct Quotation: "Today's all-volunteer military is far smaller than past draftee-fed forces, requiring troops to be repeatedly recycled through combat zones" (*Issues in Peace and Conflict Studies* 395).

Paraphrase: Because the current wars are not supported by a draft, military forces are smaller than in past wars, and troops are being deployed multiple times (*Issues in Peace and Conflict Studies* 395).

For more detailed information on how to format in-text citations for different types of sources, consult *Writing Essentials Online: A Macmillan LaunchPad*.

Use a Works Cited List at the End of Your Essay

The list of works cited includes all the sources used in your paper, alphabetized by the author's last name (or by the first word in the entry, if there is no author). The Works Cited page starts on a new page at the end of your essay. Entries in the Works Cited list should follow the MLA guidelines, using a hanging indent, as in the example below:

> Dickinson, Emily. "Two Voyagers." *Selected Poems*, edited by Stanley Appelbaum, Dover Publications Inc., 1990, p. 24.
>
> Coles, Kimberly Anne. "The Matter of Belief in John Donne's Holy Sonnets." *Renaissance Quarterly*, vol. 68, no. 3, Fall 2015, pp. 899–931.
>
> Levy, Shawn, producer. *Stranger Things*, written and directed by Matt and Ross Duffer, season 1, episode 3, Holly Jolly, 2016.

The two most basic elements of any citation are the author's name and the title of the work, both of which are followed by a period. For additional information on what to include in a works cited entry, consult *Writing Essentials Online: A Macmillan LaunchPad*.

Write Your Own Research

If your instructor has not assigned a topic, then choose one from the list below and write a researched essay. For help, refer to the Checklist: How to Write Research on page 187.

• Challenges and benefits of your chosen career	• How to get involved in local government
• Paying for higher education	• Bias in media
• Online dating services	• Bilingualism
• Mental health disorders and treatments	• Food labels and regulations
	• Gluten-free or vegan diets

Read and Analyze Research:
Student Research Essay

Dara Riesler
Professor Gomes
English 99
4 October 2017

Service Dogs Help Heal the Mental Wounds of War

Whenever Ken Costich, a former army colonel, is on the edge of a panic attack, his dog, Bandit, senses it immediately, nuzzling Costich until he feels calm again (Caprioli). Across the country, another dog, Maya, is also looking out for her owner, veteran Jacob Hyde. When Hyde, feeling nervous in a crowd, gives the command "block," Maya stands between him and other people, easing Hyde's fears (Lorber). Elsewhere, Mush, a Siberian husky, is helping her owner, Margaux Vair, get out and meet people—something Vair had avoided since returning from her service in Iraq (Albrecht). "Because [Mush] is a Husky and very pretty, everybody wants to pet her," Vair says. "What's happening is that people are coming up and talking to me, and it's helping with my confidence" (qtd. in Albrecht).

Bandit, Maya, and Mush—specially trained service dogs—are making a significant difference in the lives of their owners, all of whom suffer from post-traumatic stress disorder (PTSD) as a result of military service. As the benefits of service dogs become clearer and as more PTSD sufferers return from the wars in Iraq and Afghanistan, demand for these helpful and caring pets is growing; in fact, at the present time, demand far exceeds supply.

PTSD, as defined by the United States Department of Veterans Affairs (VA), is an anxiety disorder that can result from a traumatic experience, such as personal injury in combat or witnessing the deaths or injuries of others ("What is PTSD?"). According to the VA, symptoms of the condition include flashbacks of the trauma or nightmares about it. PTSD sufferers may also have difficulty forming or maintaining relationships with others.

½" margin between top of page and header

Student's last name and page number on top of each page

Identification of student, professor, course, and date

Title centered; not set in bold or italics or underlined

Introduction

Indirect and direct quotations with in-text citations

Thesis statement

Topic sentence

Titles used for in-text citations of sources without authors

Additionally, some of them are constantly "keyed up" and "on the lookout for danger," as if they are still in a war zone ("Symptoms of PTSD?"). According to the RAND Corporation, a nonprofit research group, an estimated 300,000 veterans from the wars in Afghanistan and Iraq suffer from PTSD or major depression ("Invisible Wounds"). In attempts to escape or to numb the effects of PTSD, sufferers may turn to alcohol or drugs, possibly leading to addiction ("PTSD and Problems with Alcohol Use"). Worse, they may decide to end their lives, as an estimated 6,500 veterans do each year (Williams).

A variety of treatments are available to veterans with PTSD. They include one-on-one discussions with a therapist, group therapy, and medicines—usually antidepressants—that address the symptoms of the condition ("Treatment of PTSD"). The use of service dogs as an additional therapy for PTSD is a relatively new practice. According to researchers Joan Esnayra and Craig Love, a key benefit of these dogs is that they are constant companions to PTSD sufferers, helping them go about their daily lives and directly addressing their symptoms. For example, service dogs may be trained to alert easily startled veterans that someone is approaching, to scan surroundings for possible threats, or to turn on the lights and wake up veterans suffering from nightmares (Esnayra and Love). These pets can also soothe veterans experiencing panic attacks and remind their owners when it is time to take medications (Caprioli).

Some veterans, however, find that their dog companions outshine medication as a PTSD treatment. "This dog [did] more for me in three weeks than any medication," says Ken Costich (qtd. in Caprioli; see fig. 1). Alicia Miller, an Army veteran who cofounded an organization that donates and trains service dogs for vets, agrees. "Medication works 50 percent of the time," says Miller, who also experiences symptoms of PTSD. "Talk therapy, alone, works 30 percent of the time, and dogs work 84.5 percent of the time" (qtd. in Caprioli).

In a recent study, Esnayra and Love found that among 39 PTSD sufferers paired with service dogs, 82 percent reported fewer PTSD symptoms (Bavley 5). In addition, 40 percent reported that they were able to reduce their use of medications. Recognizing that more research into the effectiveness of service-dog therapy is needed, the United States Department of Defense is funding a $300,000 study on this topic (Bavley 5). Esnayra and Love are conducting the research.

Although service-dog therapy has many benefits, organizations that train these dogs have trouble keeping up with the demand created by the thousands of veterans who have returned from Iraq or Afghanistan with PTSD (Dreazen). Training is time-consuming and demanding; the dogs are taught to respond to as many as 150 commands and to notice subtle changes in vets — such as a quickening pulse — that signal emotional distress (Montalván and Witter 4). During a two-year period that ended in the spring of 2010, Puppies Behind Bars, a program in which prisoners train service dogs, placed 23 dogs with veterans suffering from PTSD (Lorber). Other nonprofit training organizations report similar, or lower, numbers of vet-ready dogs (Caprioli). Given the labor-intensive training, these numbers are understandable; however, the need remains.

Topic sentence

Another challenge is the expense of the training, which in the case of many nonprofit organizations, like Puppies Behind Bars, is paid for by donations, not by the veterans (Caprioli; Dreazen). At Puppies Behind Bars, $26,000 is needed to train each dog. Other training organizations report similar expenses.

Topic sentence

Some lawmakers are taking steps to meet vets' growing need for helper dogs. In 2009, President Obama signed into law the Service Dogs for Veterans Act, which was sponsored by Senator Al Franken and Senator Johnny Isakson. According to Franken's office, this legislation matches at least 200 veterans with

Topic sentence

VA-funded service dogs, and it requires that at least 50 percent of these vets suffer mainly from mental-health problems, as opposed to physical disabilities. It also calls for a study of the participating veterans to learn more about the therapeutic and economic benefits of service dogs ("Franken-Isakson Service Dogs"). Additionally, in January 2011, the Veterans Dog Training Therapy Act was introduced in the U.S. House of Representatives. Under this legislation, vets with PTSD would be taught how to train service dogs that, in turn, would be used by other vets (Peters).

Conclusion

With luck, and with the continuing efforts of legislators and concerned citizens, more helper dogs will find homes with veterans, providing not only valued service but also lasting friendship. As Army veteran Luis Carlos Montalván says of his service dog, Tuesday: "We are bonded, dog and man, in a way able-bodied people can never understand, because they will never experience anything like it. As long as Tuesday is alive, he will be with me. Neither of us will ever be alone. We will never be without companionship" (Montalván and Witter 6).

Works Cited

Albrecht, Brian. "Psychiatric Service Dogs Aid Northeast
Ohio Veterans." *Cleveland.com*, 13 July 2011, blog.
cleveland.com/metro/2011/07/psychiatric_service_dogs_
aid_l.html.

Bavley, Alan. "PTSD Treatment Goes to the Dogs: DOD
Research Pairs Soldiers with K-9s." *Stars and Stripes*,
10 Sept. 2009, p. 5.

Caprioli, Jennifer M. "Dogs Go the Distance: Program Provides
Service to Veterans with PTSD." United States Army,
4 Mar. 2010, www.army.mil/article/35297/dogs-go-the-
distance-program-provides-service-to-veterans-with-ptsd.

Dreazen, Yochi J. "'Sit! Stay! Snuggle!': An Iraq Vet Finds His
Dog Tuesday." *The Wall Street Journal*, 11 July 2009,
www.wsj.com/articles/SB124727385749826169.

Esnayra, Joan, and Craig Love. "A Survey of Mental Health
Patients Utilizing Psychiatric Service Dogs." *PSD Lifestyle*,
Psychiatric Service Dog Society, 2008, VeteranVoice.info,
www.veteranvoice.info/ARCHIVE/info_12apr_A Survey of
Mental Health Patients Utilizing Psychiatric Service Dogs.
pdf.

"Franken-Isakson Service Dogs for Veterans Act Passes Senate."
Al Franken: U.S. Senator for Minnesota, 24 July 2009,
www.franken.senate.gov/?p=hot_topic&id= 592.

"Invisible Wounds: Mental Health and Cognitive Care Needs
of America's Returning Veterans." *RAND Corporation*,
2008, www.rand.org/content/dam/rand/ pubs/research_
briefs/2008/RAND_RB9336.pdf.

Article from online news site

Article from print newspaper

Part of larger website

Article from online newspaper

Parts of larger websites

Article from online newspaper

Lorber, Janie. "For the Battle-Scarred, Comfort at Leash's End." *The New York Times*, 3 Apr. 2010. Web, www.nytimes.com/2010/04/04/us/04dogs.html?_r=0.

Book with two authors

Montalván, Luis Carlos, and Bret Witter. *Until Tuesday: A Wounded Warrior and the Golden Retriever Who Saved Him.* Hyperion, 2011.

Article from online newspaper

Peters, Sharon L. "Man's Best Friend Could Soon Be Veteran's Best Medicine." *USA Today*, 19 Jan. 2011, usatoday30.usatoday.com/yourlife/health/healthcare/2011-01-20-verantherapy20_ST_N.htm.

Online government publications. Note: Three hyphens used in place of government and department names in each entry after the first

United States Department of Veterans Affairs, National Center for PTSD. "PTSD and Problems with Alcohol Use." *National Center for PTSD*, Department of Veterans Affairs, 1 Jan. 2007, www.ptsd.va.gov/public/problems/ptsd-alcohol-use.asp.

—. "Symptoms of PTSD." *National Center for PTSD*, Department of Veterans Affairs, 1 Jan. 2007, www.ptsd.va.gov/public/PTSD-overview/basics/symptoms_of_ptsd.asp.

—. "Treatment of PTSD?" *National Center for PTSD*, Department of Veterans Affairs, 1 Jan. 2007, www.ptsd.va.gov/public/treatment/therapy-med/treatment-ptsd.asp.

—. "What Is PTSD?" *National Center for PTSD*, Department of Veterans Affairs, 1 Jan. 2007, www.ptsd.va.gov/public/PTSD-overview/basics/what-is-ptsd.asp.

Article from online newspaper

Williams, Carol J. "Court Orders Major Overhaul of VA's Mental Health System." *Los Angeles Times*, 11 May 2011, articles.latimes.com/2011/may/11/local/la-me-0511-veterans-ptsd-20110511.

1. Double underline the thesis of the essay.

2. Can you match each source in the Works Cited list to an in-text citation?

3. Does Riesler's essay follow the Four Basics of Good Research? Explain.

CHECKLIST: How to Write Research	
STEPS	**DETAILS**
☐ **Make a schedule.**	• Include the due date, research dates, and dates for completion and revision of a draft.
☐ **Narrow and explore your topic.** See Chapter 2.	• Make the topic more specific. • Prewrite to get ideas about the narrowed topic.
☐ **Write a research question** (see p. 175).	• Ask a question for your research to answer.
☐ **Find and evaluate sources** (see p. 175).	• Use the library and the internet to find sources. • Consider an interview or a survey.
☐ **Read and annotate sources.** See Chapter 1.	• Use a note-taking strategy. • Record bibliographic information for all sources. • Summarize, paraphrase, and quote carefully, making sure you use quotation marks and page numbers where needed.
☐ **Write a thesis statement.** See Chapter 3.	• Use the answer to your guiding research question to draft your thesis statement.
☐ **Support your point.** See Chapter 3.	• Make a chart that shows which sources support your point. • Select the best support for use in your paper. • If you do not have enough support, continue with research and reading (prewriting).

☐ **Write a draft.** See Chapters 4 and 14.	• Make a plan that organizes your support logically. • Write an introduction, and make sure your thesis is clear. • Draft topic sentences for each supporting paragraph. • Add a concluding paragraph. • Use in-text citations. • Draft a Works Cited list. Make sure each source used in your paper appears in the alphabetized Works Cited list.
☐ **Revise your draft.** See Chapter 4.	• Make sure you have covered the Four Basics of Good Research. • Make sure your readers have all the information they need to understand the support. • Make sure you have included transitions. • Make sure readers can identify where source material is used in the paper.
☐ **Edit your revised draft.** See Chapters 15 through 18.	• Correct errors in grammar, spelling, word use, and punctuation.

Basic Grammar

An Overview

This chapter reviews the basic sentence elements that you will need to understand to find and fix most grammatical errors.

NOTE: In the examples in this chapter, subjects are underlined once, and verbs are underlined twice.

The Parts of Speech

There are seven basic parts of speech:

1. **Noun:** names a person, place, thing, or idea.

   Jaime dances.

2. **Pronoun:** replaces a noun in a sentence. *He, she, it, we,* and *they* are pronouns.

   She dances.

3. **Verb:** tells what action the subject does or links a subject to another word that describes it.

   Jaime **dances**. [The verb *dances* is what the subject, Jaime, does.]

   She **is** a dancer. [The verb *is* links the subject, Jaime, to a word that describes her, *dancer*.]

4. **Adjective:** describes a noun or a pronoun.

   Jaime is **thin**. [The adjective *thin* describes the noun *Jaime*.]

   She is **graceful**. [The adjective *graceful* describes the pronoun *She*.]

5. **Adverb:** describes an adjective, a verb, or another adverb. Adverbs often end in *-ly*.

    Jaime is **extremely** graceful.   [The adverb *extremely* describes the adjective *graceful*.]

    She practices **often**.   [The adverb *often* describes the verb *practices*.]

    Jaime dances **quite** beautifully.   [The adverb *quite* describes another adverb, *beautifully*.]

6. **Preposition:** connects a noun, pronoun, or verb with information about it. *Across, around, at, in, of, on,* and *out* are prepositions (there are many others).

    Jaime practices **at** the studio.   [The preposition *at* connects the verb *practices* with the noun *studio*.]

7. **Conjunction:** connects words to each other. An easy way to remember seven common conjunctions is to connect them in your mind to **FANBOYS:** *for, and, nor, but, or, yet, so.*

    The studio is expensive **but** good.

The Basic Sentence

A **sentence** is the basic unit of written communication. A complete sentence in written standard English must have these three elements:

- A verb
- A subject
- A complete thought

Verbs

Every sentence has a **main verb,** the word or words that tell what the subject does or that link the subject to another word that describes it. The main verb in a sentence will show the tense (or time) the action occurs: past, present, or future. In analyzing a sentence, find the main verb first; then you will be able to identify the subject more easily.

There are three kinds of verbs: *action verbs*, *linking verbs*, and *helping verbs*.

Action Verbs

An **action verb** tells what action the subject performs.

To find the main action verb in a sentence, ask yourself this question: *What action occurs in this sentence?*

> **ACTION VERBS**　　The <u>band</u> <u>played</u> all night.　[*The action = playing*]
>
> 　　　　　　　　　　The <u>alarm</u> <u>rings</u> loudly.　[*The action = ringing*]

Linking Verbs

A **linking verb** connects (links) the subject to another word or group of words that describes the subject. Linking verbs show no action. The most common linking verb is *be* (*am, is, are,* and so on). Other linking verbs, such as *seem* and *become,* can usually be replaced by a form of the verb *be,* and the sentence will still make sense.

To find linking verbs, ask yourself this question: *What word joins the subject and the words that describe the subject?* You may also ask this: *Which word shows the past, present, or future in this sentence?*

> **LINKING VERBS**　　The <u>bus</u> <u>is</u> late. [is *connects* bus *and* late *in the present*]
>
> 　　　　　　　　　　My new <u>shoes</u> <u>look</u> shiny. (My new <u>shoes</u> <u>are</u> shiny.)
>
> 　　　　　　　　　　The <u>milk</u> <u>tastes</u> sour. (The <u>milk</u> <u>is</u> sour.)

Some words can be used as either action verbs or linking verbs, depending on how the verb is used in a particular sentence.

> **ACTION VERB**　　<u>Justine</u> <u>smelled</u> the flowers.
>
> **LINKING VERB**　　The <u>flowers</u> <u>smelled</u> wonderful.

Common Linking Verbs

FORMS OF *BE*	FORMS OF *SEEM* AND *BECOME*	FORMS OF SENSE VERBS
am are is was were	seem, seems, seemed become, becomes, became	look, looks, looked appear, appears, appeared smell, smells, smelled taste, tastes, tasted feel, feels, felt

Helping Verbs

A **helping verb** joins the main verb in a sentence to form the **complete verb** (also known as a verb phrase—the main verb and all of its helping verbs). The helping verb is often a form of the verb *be, have,* or *do*. A sentence may have more than one helping verb along with the main verb.

> Helping verb **+** Main verb **=** Complete verb

Sharon was listening to the radio as she was studying for the test.
[The helping verb is *was*; the complete verbs are *was listening* and *was studying*.]

I am saving my money for a car.

Colleen might have borrowed my sweater.

You must pass this course before taking the next one.

You should stop smoking.

Common Helping Verbs

FORMS OF *BE*	FORMS OF *HAVE*	FORMS OF *DO*	OTHER
am are been being is was were	have has had	do does did	can could may might must should will would

Subjects

The **subject** of a sentence is the person, place, thing, or idea described in the sentence or performing the action of the sentence. The subject of a sentence is usually a noun or a pronoun. For a list of common pronouns, see page 224.

To find the subject, identify the verb. If it is an action verb, ask yourself, *Who or what is doing the action?* If it is a linking verb, ask yourself, *Who or what is being described?*

> **PERSON AS SUBJECT**   Isaac arrived last night.
>
> [**Who** arrived? *Isaac*]
>
> **THING AS SUBJECT**   The restaurant has closed.
>
> [**What** has closed? The *restaurant*]

A **compound subject** consists of two or more subjects joined by *and, or,* or *nor.*

> **TWO SUBJECTS**   Kelli and Kate love animals of all kinds.
>
> **SEVERAL SUBJECTS**   The baby, the cats, and the dog play well together.

The subject of a sentence is *never* in a **prepositional phrase**, a word group that begins with a preposition and ends with a noun or pronoun, called the **object of a preposition**.

> Subject   Preposition   Object of preposition
>
> The stars of that television series will attend the comic-con.
>
> Prepositional phrase

PREPOSITION	OBJECT	PREPOSITIONAL PHRASE
from	the bakery	from the bakery
to	the next corner	to the next corner
under	the table	under the table

COMMON PREPOSITIONS				
about	after	among	because of	below
above	against	around	before	beneath
across	along	at	behind	beside
between	in	of	past	until
by	inside	off	since	up
down	into	on	through	upon
during	like	out	to	with
except	near	outside	toward	within
for	next to	over	under	without
from				

See if you can identify the subject of the following sentence.

> One of my best friends races cars.

Although you might think that the word *friends* is the subject, it isn't. *One* is the subject. Only one friend races cars, not all of them. The word *friends* cannot be the subject because it is in the prepositional phrase *of my best friends*. When you are looking for the subject of a sentence, cross out the prepositional phrase.

PREPOSITIONAL PHRASE CROSSED OUT

> One ~~of the students~~ won the science prize.
> The rules ~~about the dress code~~ are very specific.

Complete Thoughts

A **complete thought** is an idea, expressed in a sentence, that makes sense by itself, without additional words. An incomplete thought leaves readers wondering what's going on.

INCOMPLETE THOUGHT	because my alarm did not go off
COMPLETE THOUGHT	I was late because my alarm did not go off.
INCOMPLETE THOUGHT	the people who won the lottery
COMPLETE THOUGHT	The people who won the lottery were old.

To determine whether a thought is complete, ask yourself this question: *Do I have to ask a question to understand it?*

> **INCOMPLETE THOUGHT**   in my wallet
>
> [You would have to ask a question to understand, so it is not a complete thought.]
>
> **COMPLETE THOUGHT**   My <u>ticket</u> <u>is</u> in my wallet.

Six Basic English Sentence Patterns

In English, there are six basic sentence patterns, some of which you have just worked through in this chapter. Although there are other patterns, they build on these six.

1. **Subject-Verb (S-V).** This pattern is the most basic one, as you have already seen.

   > S   V
   > <u>Babies</u> <u>cry</u>.

2. **Subject-Linking Verb-Noun (S-LV-N)**

   > S   LV   N
   > <u>They</u> <u>are</u> children.

3. **Subject-Linking Verb-Adjective (S-LV-ADJ)**

   > S   LV ADJ
   > <u>Parents</u> <u>are</u> tired.

4. **Subject-Verb-Adverb (S-V-ADV)**

   > S   V   ADV
   > <u>They</u> <u>sleep</u> poorly.

5. **Subject-Verb-Direct Object (S-V-DO).** A *direct object* directly receives the action of the verb.

   > S   V   DO
   > <u>Teachers</u> <u>give</u> tests.   [The *tests* are given.]

6. **Subject-Verb-Direct Object-Indirect Object.** An *indirect object* does not directly receive the action of the verb.

>   **S**   **V** **DO**   **IO**
>
> <u>Teachers</u> <u>give</u> tests to students.   [The *tests* are given; the
>   *students* are not.]

This pattern can also have the indirect object before the direct object.

>   **S**   **V**   **IO**   **DO**
>
> <u>Teachers</u> <u>give</u> students tests.

16

The Four Most Serious Errors

Fragments, Run-Ons, Subject-Verb Agreement
Problems, and Verb-Tense Problems

This chapter of the book focuses first on four grammar errors that people most often notice.

THE FOUR MOST SERIOUS ERRORS

1. Fragments

2. Run-ons and comma splices

3. Problems with subject-verb agreement

4. Problems with verb form and tense

If you can edit your writing to correct these four errors, your grades will improve.

NOTE: In the examples in this chapter, subjects are underlined once, and verbs are underlined twice.

Fragments

A **fragment** is a group of words that is missing one or more parts of a complete sentence: a subject, a verb, or a complete thought.

SENTENCE	I was hungry, so I ate some cold pizza and drank a soda.
FRAGMENT	I was hungry, so I ate some cold pizza. *And drank a soda.*
	[*And drank a soda* contains a verb (*drank*) but no subject.]

To find fragments in your own writing, look for the five trouble spots in this chapter. When you find a fragment in your own writing, you can usually correct it in one of two ways.

BASIC WAYS TO CORRECT A FRAGMENT

■ Add what is missing (a subject, a verb, or both).

■ Attach the fragment to the sentence before or after it.

1. Fragments That Start with Prepositions

Whenever a preposition starts what you think is a sentence, check for a subject, a verb, and a complete thought. If the group of words is missing any of these three elements, it is a fragment. You can correct the fragment by connecting it to the sentence either before or after it.

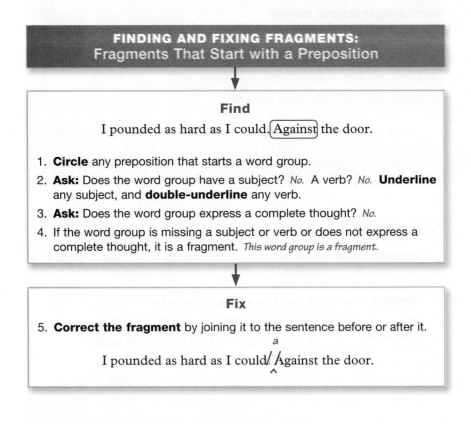

FINDING AND FIXING FRAGMENTS:
Fragments That Start with a Preposition

Find

I pounded as hard as I could. Against the door.

1. **Circle** any preposition that starts a word group.
2. **Ask:** Does the word group have a subject? *No.* A verb? *No.* **Underline** any subject, and **double-underline** any verb.
3. **Ask:** Does the word group express a complete thought? *No.*
4. If the word group is missing a subject or verb or does not express a complete thought, it is a fragment. *This word group is a fragment.*

Fix

5. **Correct the fragment** by joining it to the sentence before or after it.

I pounded as hard as I could. a Against the door.

For a list of common prepositions, see page 194.

2. Fragments That Start with Dependent Words

A **dependent word** (also called a **subordinating conjunction**) is the first word in a dependent clause. A dependent clause cannot be a sentence because it does not express a complete thought, even though it has a subject and a verb. Whenever a dependent word starts what you think is a sentence, stop to check for a subject, a verb, and a complete thought.

Common Dependent Words

after	if / if only	until
although	now that	what (whatever)
as / as if / as though	once	when (whenever)
as long as / as soon as	since	where (wherever)
because	so that	whether
before	that	which
even if / even though	though	while
how	unless	who / whose

You can correct a fragment by connecting it to the sentence before or after it. If the dependent clause is joined to the sentence after it, put a comma after the dependent clause.

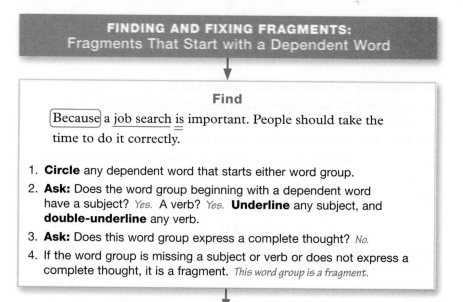

FINDING AND FIXING FRAGMENTS:
Fragments That Start with a Dependent Word

Find

Because a job search is important. People should take the time to do it correctly.

1. **Circle** any dependent word that starts either word group.
2. **Ask:** Does the word group beginning with a dependent word have a subject? *Yes.* A verb? *Yes.* **Underline** any subject, and **double-underline** any verb.
3. **Ask:** Does this word group express a complete thought? *No.*
4. If the word group is missing a subject or verb or does not express a complete thought, it is a fragment. *This word group is a fragment.*

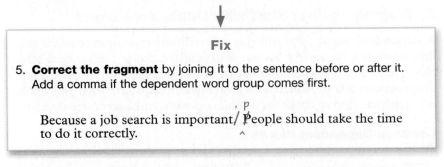

Fix

5. **Correct the fragment** by joining it to the sentence before or after it. Add a comma if the dependent word group comes first.

> Because a job search is important,/ People should take the time to do it correctly.

3. Fragments That Start with *-ing* Verb Forms

An *-ing* **verb form** ends in *-ing: walking, writing, running*. Sometimes, an *-ing* verb form introduces a fragment. When an *-ing* verb form starts what you think is a sentence, stop and check for a subject, a verb, and a complete thought.

You can correct this type of fragment either by adding whatever sentence elements are missing (usually a subject and a helping verb) or by connecting the fragment to the sentence before or after it. Usually, you will need to put a comma before or after the fragment to join it to the complete sentence.

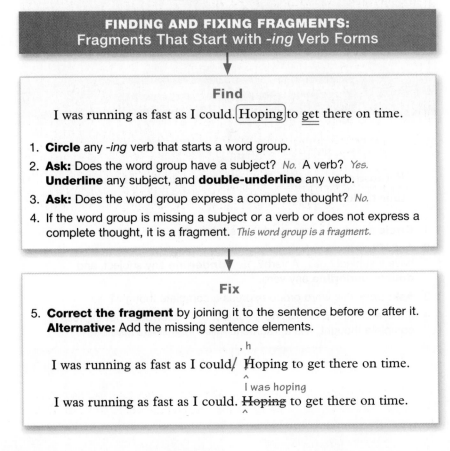

FINDING AND FIXING FRAGMENTS:
Fragments That Start with *-ing* Verb Forms

Find

I was running as fast as I could. Hoping to get there on time.

1. **Circle** any *-ing* verb that starts a word group.
2. **Ask:** Does the word group have a subject? *No.* A verb? *Yes.* **Underline** any subject, and **double-underline** any verb.
3. **Ask:** Does the word group express a complete thought? *No.*
4. If the word group is missing a subject or a verb or does not express a complete thought, it is a fragment. *This word group is a fragment.*

Fix

5. **Correct the fragment** by joining it to the sentence before or after it. **Alternative:** Add the missing sentence elements.

> I was running as fast as I could,/ Hoping to get there on time.
>
> I was hoping
> I was running as fast as I could. ~~Hoping~~ to get there on time.

4. Fragments That Start with *to* and a Verb

If a word group begins with *to* and a verb, it must have another verb (which shows tense); if not, it is not a complete sentence. When you see a word group that begins with *to* and a verb, first check to see if there is another verb. If there is no other verb, the word group is a fragment.

To correct a fragment that starts with *to* and a verb, join it to the sentence before or after it, or add the missing sentence elements.

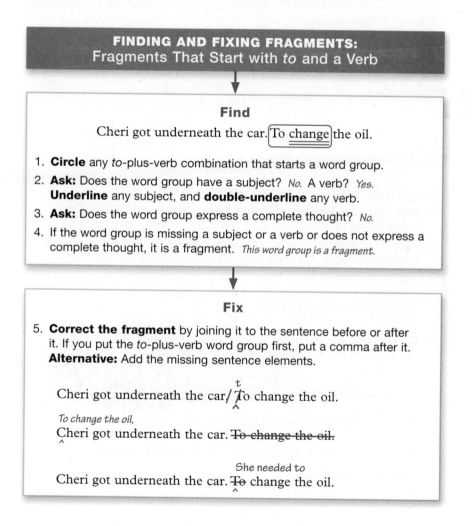

FINDING AND FIXING FRAGMENTS:
Fragments That Start with *to* and a Verb

Find

Cheri got underneath the car. To change the oil.

1. **Circle** any *to*-plus-verb combination that starts a word group.
2. **Ask:** Does the word group have a subject? *No.* A verb? *Yes.* **Underline** any subject, and **double-underline** any verb.
3. **Ask:** Does the word group express a complete thought? *No.*
4. If the word group is missing a subject or a verb or does not express a complete thought, it is a fragment. *This word group is a fragment.*

Fix

5. **Correct the fragment** by joining it to the sentence before or after it. If you put the *to*-plus-verb word group first, put a comma after it. **Alternative:** Add the missing sentence elements.

Cheri got underneath the car/ To change the oil.

To change the oil,
Cheri got underneath the car. To change the oil.

She needed to
Cheri got underneath the car. To change the oil.

5. Fragments That Are Examples or Explanations

When a group of words gives an example or explanation connected to the previous sentence, stop to check it for a subject, a verb, and a complete thought.

The following words may signal a fragment that is an example or explanation.

TIP *Such as* and *like* do not often begin complete sentences.

especially	for example	like	such as

Correct a fragment that starts with an example or explanation by connecting it to the sentence before or after it. Sometimes, you can add whatever sentence elements are missing (a subject, a verb, or both) instead. When you connect the fragment to a sentence, you may need to change some punctuation. For example, fragments that are examples are often set off by a comma.

FINDING AND FIXING FRAGMENTS:
Fragments That Are Examples or Explanations

Find

Freecycle.org recycles usable items. Such as clothing.

1. **Circle** the word group that is an example or explanation.
2. **Ask:** Does the word group have a subject, a verb, and a complete thought? *No.*
3. If the word group is missing a subject or a verb or does not express a complete thought, it is a fragment. *This word group is a fragment.*

Fix

4. **Correct the fragment** by joining it to the sentence before or after it or by adding the missing sentence elements.

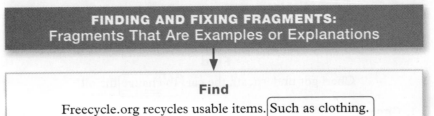

Freecycle.org recycles usable items. Such as clothing.

You may need to add some words to correct fragments:

I should list some things on freecycle.org. The sweaters
I never wear. *could keep others warm*

Run-Ons

A **run-on** is two complete sentences **(independent clauses)** joined incorrectly as one sentence. (For help identifying a complete sentence, see Chapter 15.) There are two kinds of run-ons: **fused sentences** and **comma splices**. A **fused sentence** is two complete sentences joined without any punctuation.

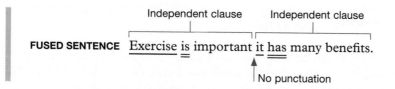

A **comma splice** is two complete sentences joined by only a comma.

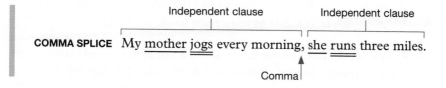

When you join two sentences, use the proper punctuation.

CORRECTIONS   Exercise is important; it has many benefits.

My mother jogs every morning; she runs three miles.

To find run-ons, focus on each sentence in your writing, one at a time. Once you have found a run-on, there are three ways to correct it.

WAYS TO CORRECT RUN-ONS

1. Add a period or a semicolon.
2. Add a comma and a coordinating conjunction.
3. Add a dependent word.

1. Correct Run-Ons by Adding a Period or a Semicolon

You can correct run-ons by adding a period to make two separate sentences. After adding the period, capitalize the letter that begins the new sentence. Reread your two sentences to make sure they each contain a subject, a verb, and a complete thought.

> **RUN-ON (CORRECTED)**   I interviewed a candidate for a job ᵗ⁵he gave me the "dead fish" handshake.

A semicolon (;) can be used instead of a period to join two closely related sentences. Do not capitalize the word that follows a semicolon unless it is the name of a specific person, place, or thing that is usually capitalized—for example, Mary, New York, or the Eiffel Tower.

> **RUN-ON (CORRECTED)**   It is important in an interview to hold your head up;/ it is just as important to sit up straight.

NOTE: The semicolon may be followed by a **conjunctive adverb**—such as *however, indeed, instead, moreover, nevertheless,* and *similarly*—and a comma.

> Semicolon   Conjunctive adverb   Comma
>
> I stopped by the market; however, it was closed.

FINDING AND FIXING RUN-ONS: Adding a Period or a Semicolon

↓

Find

Few people know the history of many popular holidays Valentine's Day is one of these holidays.

1. To see if there are two independent clauses in a sentence, **underline** the subjects, and **double-underline** the verbs.
2. **Ask:** If the sentence has two independent clauses, are they separated by either a period or a semicolon? *No. It is a run-on.*

↓

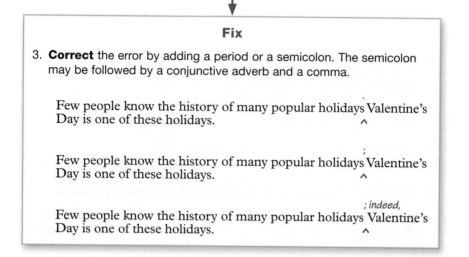

Fix

3. **Correct** the error by adding a period or a semicolon. The semicolon may be followed by a conjunctive adverb and a comma.

Few people know the history of many popular holidays Valentine's Day is one of these holidays.

Few people know the history of many popular holidays Valentine's Day is one of these holidays.

Few people know the history of many popular holidays Valentine's Day is one of these holidays.

2. Correct Run-Ons by Adding a Comma and a Coordinating Conjunction

Another way to correct run-ons is to add a comma and a **coordinating conjunction**: a link that joins independent clauses to form one sentence. The seven coordinating conjunctions are *for, and, nor, but, or, yet, so,* which some people remember by thinking of the acronym **FANBOYS**.

RUN-ON (CORRECTED)
Nakeisha was qualified for the job she hurt her chances by mumbling.

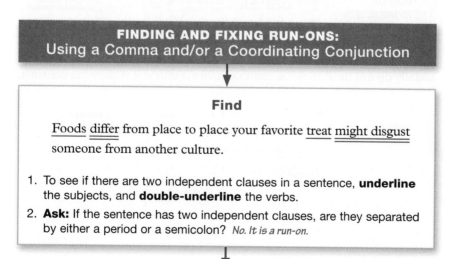

FINDING AND FIXING RUN-ONS:
Using a Comma and/or a Coordinating Conjunction

Find

Foods differ from place to place your favorite treat might disgust someone from another culture.

1. To see if there are two independent clauses in a sentence, **underline** the subjects, and **double-underline** the verbs.
2. **Ask:** If the sentence has two independent clauses, are they separated by either a period or a semicolon? *No. It is a run-on.*

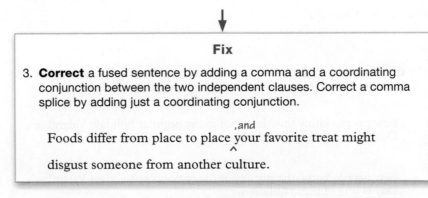

Fix

3. **Correct** a fused sentence by adding a comma and a coordinating conjunction between the two independent clauses. Correct a comma splice by adding just a coordinating conjunction.

....,and
Foods differ from place to place your favorite treat might
....^

disgust someone from another culture.

3. Correct Run-Ons by Adding a Dependent Word

A third way to correct run-ons is to make one of the complete sentences a dependent clause by adding a dependent word (a **subordinating conjunction** or a **relative pronoun**), such as *after, because, before, even though, if, that, though, unless, when, who,* and *which.* (For a more complete list of these words, see the chart on p. 199.)

> **RUN-ON**   It is important to end an interview on a positive note/
> **(CORRECTED)**   *because*
>   that final <u>impression</u> <u>is</u> what the interviewer will
>   ^
>   remember.

You can also put the dependent clause first. When the dependent clause comes first, be sure to put a comma after it.

>   When the   ,
> **RUN-ON**   ~~The~~ <u>interviewer</u> <u>stands</u> the <u>candidate</u> <u>should shake</u>
> **(CORRECTED)**   ^   ^
>   his or her hand firmly.

When the dependent clause is the second clause in a sentence, you usually do not need to put a comma before it unless it is showing contrast.

>   , though
> **RUN-ON**   Many <u>holidays</u> <u>have</u> religious origins some
> **(CORRECTED)**   ^
>   <u>celebrations</u> <u>have</u> moved away from their
>   religious roots.

Dependent words

after	now that	what(ever)
although	once	when(ever)
as	since	where
because	so that	whether
before	that	which(ever)
even if / though	though	while
how	unless	who
if / if only	until	

FINDING AND FIXING RUN-ONS:
Making a Dependent Clause

Find

Alzheimer's disease is a heartbreaking illness, it causes a

steady decrease in brain capacity.

1. To see if there are two independent clauses in a sentence, **underline** the subjects, and **double-underline** the verbs.
2. **Ask:** If the sentence has two independent clauses, are they separated by a period, a semicolon, or a comma and a coordinating conjunction? *No. It is a run-on.*

Fix

3. If one part of the sentence is less important than the other, or if you want to make it so, add a dependent word to the less important part.

    because
    Alzheimer's disease is a heartbreaking illness/it causes a
    steady decrease in brain capacity.
    ^

NOTE: You can use the word *then* to join two sentences, but if you add it without the correct punctuation or added words, your sentence will be a run-on.

> **COMMA SPLICE**   I picked up my laundry, then I went home.

Correct errors caused by *then* just as you would correct any other run-on.

. T
I picked up my laundry, then I went home.
                    ^

;
I picked up my laundry, then I went home.
                    ^

                    and
I picked up my laundry, then I went home.
                 ^

                    before
I picked up my laundry, ~~then~~ I went home.
                    ^

Problems with Subject-Verb Agreement

In any sentence, the subject and the verb must **match—or agree**—in number. If the subject is singular (one person, place, or thing), the verb must also be singular. If the subject is plural (more than one), the verb must also be plural.

> **SINGULAR**   The skydiver jumps out of the airplane.

> **PLURAL**   The skydivers jump out of the airplane.

Regular Verbs, Present Tense

	Singular		Plural
FIRST PERSON	I walk.	} no -*s*	We walk.
SECOND PERSON	You walk.		You walk.
THIRD PERSON	He (she, it) walks.	} all end in -*s*	They walk.
	Joe walks.		Joe and Alice walk.
	The student walks.		The students walk.

Regular verbs (with forms that follow Standard English patterns) have two forms in the present tense: one that ends in -*s* and one that has no ending. The third-person subjects—*he, she, it*—and singular nouns always use the form that ends in *-s*. First-person subjects (*I*), second-person subjects (*you*), and plural subjects use the form with no ending.

To find problems with subject-verb agreement in your own writing, look for five trouble spots that often signal these problems.

1. The Verb Is a Form of *Be, Have,* or *Do*

The verbs *be, have,* and *do* do not follow the rules for forming singular and plural forms; they are **irregular verbs**.

Forms of the Verb *Be*

Present Tense	Singular	Plural
FIRST PERSON	I am	we are
SECOND PERSON	you are	you are
THIRD PERSON	she, he, it is	they are
	the student is	the students are
Past Tense		
FIRST PERSON	I was	we were
SECOND PERSON	you were	you were
THIRD PERSON	she, he, it was	they were
	the student was	the students were

Forms of the Verb *Have,* Present Tense

	Singular	Plural
FIRST PERSON	I have	we have
SECOND PERSON	you have	you have
THIRD PERSON	she, he, it has	they have
	the student has	the students have

Forms of the Verb *Do*, Present Tense

	Singular	Plural
FIRST PERSON	I do	we do
SECOND PERSON	you do	you do
THIRD PERSON	she, he, it does	they do
	the student does	the students do

These verbs cause problems for writers who are used to using the same form in all cases in conversation: *he do the cleaning; they do the cleaning*. People also sometimes use the word *be* instead of the correct form of *be*: *She be on vacation*.

In college and at work, use the correct forms of the verbs *be, have,* and *do* as shown in the charts above.

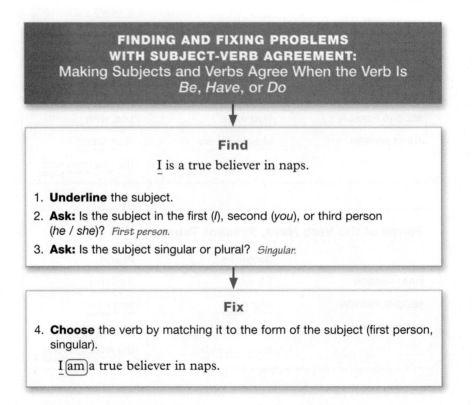

FINDING AND FIXING PROBLEMS WITH SUBJECT-VERB AGREEMENT:
Making Subjects and Verbs Agree When the Verb Is *Be, Have,* or *Do*

Find

I is a true believer in naps.

1. **Underline** the subject.
2. **Ask:** Is the subject in the first (*I*), second (*you*), or third person (*he / she*)? *First person.*
3. **Ask:** Is the subject singular or plural? *Singular.*

Fix

4. **Choose** the verb by matching it to the form of the subject (first person, singular).

   I am a true believer in naps.

2. Words Come between the Subject and the Verb

When the subject and verb are not directly next to each other, it is more difficult to find them to make sure they agree. Most often, either a prepositional phrase or a dependent clause comes between the subject and the verb.

Prepositional Phrase between the Subject and the Verb

A **prepositional phrase** starts with a preposition and ends with a noun or pronoun: I took my bag *of books* and threw it *across the room*. (For a list of common prepositions, see p. 194.)

The subject of a sentence is never in a prepositional phrase. When you are looking for the subject of a sentence, you can cross out any prepositional phrases.

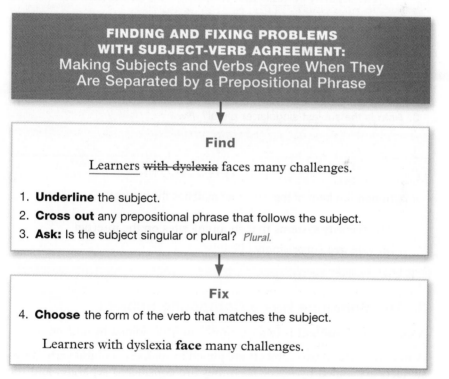

FINDING AND FIXING PROBLEMS WITH SUBJECT-VERB AGREEMENT:
Making Subjects and Verbs Agree When They Are Separated by a Prepositional Phrase

Find

Learners ~~with dyslexia~~ faces many challenges.

1. **Underline** the subject.
2. **Cross out** any prepositional phrase that follows the subject.
3. **Ask:** Is the subject singular or plural? *Plural.*

Fix

4. **Choose** the form of the verb that matches the subject.

Learners with dyslexia **face** many challenges.

Dependent Clause between the Subject and the Verb

A **dependent clause** has a subject and a verb, but it does not express a complete thought. When a dependent clause comes between the subject and the verb, it usually starts with the word *who, whose, whom, that,* or *which*.

The subject of a sentence is never in a dependent clause. When you are looking for the subject of a sentence, you can cross out any dependent clauses.

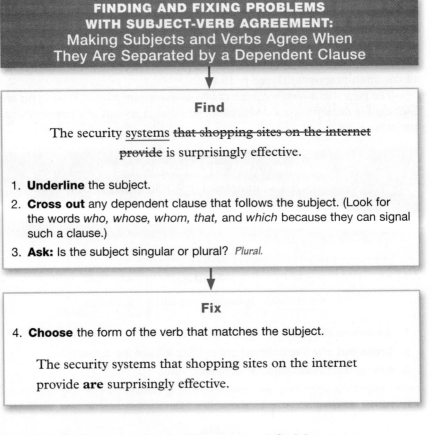

FINDING AND FIXING PROBLEMS WITH SUBJECT-VERB AGREEMENT: Making Subjects and Verbs Agree When They Are Separated by a Dependent Clause

Find

The security <u>systems</u> ~~that shopping sites on the internet provide~~ is surprisingly effective.

1. **Underline** the subject.
2. **Cross out** any dependent clause that follows the subject. (Look for the words *who, whose, whom, that,* and *which* because they can signal such a clause.)
3. **Ask:** Is the subject singular or plural? *Plural.*

Fix

4. **Choose** the form of the verb that matches the subject.

   The security systems that shopping sites on the internet provide **are** surprisingly effective.

3. The Sentence Has a Compound Subject

A **compound subject** is two (or more) subjects joined by *and, or,* or *nor.*

And / Or Rule: If two subjects are joined by *and,* use a plural verb. If two subjects are joined by *or* (or *nor*), they are considered separate, and the verb should agree with whatever subject it is closer to.

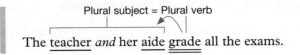

Plural subject = Plural verb

The <u>teacher</u> *and* her <u>aide</u> <u>grade</u> all the exams.

Subject *or* Singular subject = Singular verb

Either the <u>teacher</u> *or* <u>her aide</u> <u>grades</u> all the exams.

Subject *nor* Plural subject = Plural verb

Neither the <u>teacher</u> *nor* <u>her aides</u> <u>grade</u> all the exams.

**FINDING AND FIXING PROBLEMS
WITH SUBJECT-VERB AGREEMENT:**
Making Subjects and Verbs Agree in a Sentence
with a Compound Subject

Find

<u>Watermelon (or) cantaloupe</u> make a delicious and healthy snack.

1. **Underline** the subjects.
2. **Circle** the word between the subjects.
3. **Ask:** Does that word join the subjects to make them plural or keep them separate? *Keeps them separate.*
4. **Ask:** Is the subject that is closer to the verb singular or plural? *Singular.*

Fix

5. **Choose** the verb form that agrees with the subject that is closer to the verb.

Watermelon or cantaloupe **makes** a delicious and healthy snack.

---

4. The Subject Is an Indefinite Pronoun

An **indefinite pronoun** replaces a general person, place, or thing or a general group of people, places, or things. Indefinite pronouns are often singular, although there are some exceptions, as shown in the chart on the next page.

Remember that the verb of a sentence must agree with the subject of the sentence, and the subject of a sentence is *never in a prepositional phrase or dependent clause.*

Indefinite Pronouns

ALWAYS SINGULAR (USE THE *IS* FORM OF *BE*)

anybody	everyone	nothing
anyone	everything	one (of)
anything	much	somebody
each (of)	neither (of)	someone
either (of)	nobody	something
everybody	no one	

ALWAYS PLURAL (USE THE *ARE* FORM OF *BE*)

both	many
few	several

MAY BE SINGULAR OR PLURAL (USE THE *IS* OR *ARE* FORM OF *BE*)

all	most	some
any	none	

FINDING AND FIXING PROBLEMS WITH SUBJECT-VERB AGREEMENT: Making Subjects and Verbs Agree When the Subject Is an Indefinite Pronoun

Find

One ~~of my best friends~~ live in California.

1. **Underline** the subject.
2. **Cross out** any prepositional phrase or dependent clause that follows the subject.
3. **Ask:** Is the subject singular or plural? *Singular.*

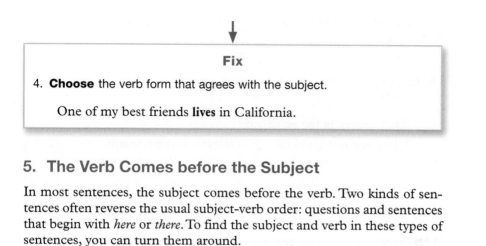

Fix

4. **Choose** the verb form that agrees with the subject.

One of my best friends **lives** in California.

5. The Verb Comes before the Subject

In most sentences, the subject comes before the verb. Two kinds of sentences often reverse the usual subject-verb order: questions and sentences that begin with *here* or *there*. To find the subject and verb in these types of sentences, you can turn them around.

Are you excited? / You are excited.

There are four keys on the table. / Four keys are on the table.

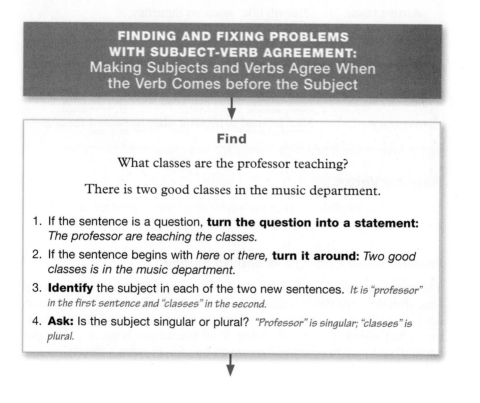

FINDING AND FIXING PROBLEMS WITH SUBJECT-VERB AGREEMENT:
Making Subjects and Verbs Agree When the Verb Comes before the Subject

Find

What classes are the professor teaching?

There is two good classes in the music department.

1. If the sentence is a question, **turn the question into a statement:** *The professor are teaching the classes.*
2. If the sentence begins with *here* or *there*, **turn it around:** *Two good classes is in the music department.*
3. **Identify** the subject in each of the two new sentences. *It is "professor" in the first sentence and "classes" in the second.*
4. **Ask:** Is the subject singular or plural? *"Professor" is singular; "classes" is plural.*

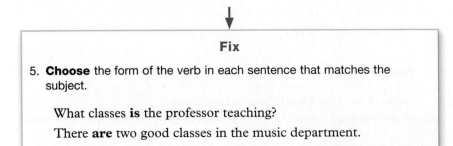

Fix

5. **Choose** the form of the verb in each sentence that matches the subject.

What classes **is** the professor teaching?

There **are** two good classes in the music department.

Problems with Verb Tense

Verb tense tells *when* an action happened: in the past, in the present, or in the future. Verbs change their form or use the helping verbs *have, be,* or *will* to indicate different tenses.

PRESENT TENSE	Rick <u>hikes</u> every weekend.
PAST TENSE	He <u>hiked</u> 10 miles last weekend.
FUTURE TENSE	He <u>will hike</u> again on Saturday.

LANGUAGE NOTE: Remember to include needed endings on present-tense and past-tense verbs, even if they are not noticed in speech.

PRESENT TENSE	Nate <u>listens</u> to his new iPod wherever <u>he goes.</u>
PAST TENSE	Nate <u>listened</u> to his iPod while <u>he walked</u> the dog.

Regular Verbs

Most verbs in English are **regular verbs** that follow standard rules about what endings to use to express time.

Present-Tense Endings: -s and No Ending

The **present tense** is used for actions that are happening at the same time that they are being written about (the present) and for things that happen all the time. Present-tense, regular verbs either end in *-s* or have no ending added. Use the *-s* ending when the subject is *he, she, it,* or the name of one person or thing. Use no ending for all other subjects.

Regular Verbs in the Present Tense

	Singular	Plural
FIRST PERSON	I jump.	We jump.
SECOND PERSON	You jump.	You jump.
THIRD PERSON	She (he, it) jumps.	They jump.
	The child jumps.	The children jump.

Regular Past-Tense Ending: -ed or -d

The **past tense** is used for actions that have already happened. A *-d* or an *-ed* ending is needed on all regular verbs in the past tense.

	PRESENT TENSE		PAST TENSE	
FIRST PERSON	I live.	I walk.	I lived.	I walked.
SECOND PERSON	You live.	You walk.	You lived.	You walked.
THIRD PERSON	He lives.	He walks.	He lived.	He walked.

The past-tense form of regular verbs can also serve as the past participle and be paired with a helping verb such as *have* or *do*. (To learn about when past participles are used, see p. 221.)

PAST TENSE	PAST PARTICIPLE
My kids watched cartoons.	They have watched cartoons before.
George visited his cousins.	He has visited them every year.

Irregular Verbs

Irregular verbs do not follow the simple rules of regular verbs. They show past tense with a change in spelling, or by not changing their spelling. The most common irregular verbs are *be* and *have* (see p. 209). As you write and edit, use the following chart to make sure you use the correct form of irregular verbs.

NOTE: What is called "Present Tense" in the chart below is sometimes called the "base form of the verb."

Irregular Verbs

PRESENT TENSE (BASE FORM OF VERB)	PAST TENSE	PAST PARTICIPLE (USED WITH HELPING VERB)
be (am/are/is)	was/were	been
become	became	become
begin	began	begun
bite	bit	bitten
blow	blew	blown
break	broke	broken
bring	brought	brought
build	built	built
buy	bought	bought
catch	caught	caught
choose	chose	chosen
come	came	come
cost	cost	cost
dive	dived, dove	dived
do	did	done
draw	drew	drawn
drink	drank	drunk
drive	drove	driven
eat	ate	eaten
fall	fell	fallen
feed	fed	fed
feel	felt	felt
fight	fought	fought
find	found	found
fly	flew	flown
forget	forgot	forgotten

PRESENT TENSE (BASE FORM OF VERB)	PAST TENSE	PAST PARTICIPLE (USED WITH HELPING VERB)
get	got	gotten
give	gave	given
go	went	gone
grow	grew	grown
have/has	had	had
hear	heard	heard
hide	hid	hidden
hit	hit	hit
hold	held	held
hurt	hurt	hurt
keep	kept	kept
know	knew	known
lay	laid	laid
lead	led	led
leave	left	left
let	let	let
lie	lay	lain
light	lit	lit
lose	lost	lost
make	made	made
mean	meant	meant
meet	met	met
pay	paid	paid
put	put	put
quit	quit	quit

PRESENT TENSE (BASE FORM OF VERB)	PAST TENSE	PAST PARTICIPLE (USED WITH HELPING VERB)
read	read	read
ride	rode	ridden
ring	rang	rung
rise	rose	risen
run	ran	run
say	said	said
see	saw	seen
seek	sought	sought
sell	sold	sold
send	sent	sent
shake	shook	shaken
show	showed	shown
shrink	shrank	shrunk
shut	shut	shut
sing	sang	sung
sink	sank	sunk
sit	sat	sat
sleep	slept	slept
speak	spoke	spoken
spend	spent	spent
stand	stood	stood
steal	stole	stolen
stick	stuck	stuck
sting	stung	stung
strike	struck	struck, stricken
swim	swam	swum

PRESENT TENSE (BASE FORM OF VERB)	PAST TENSE	PAST PARTICIPLE (USED WITH HELPING VERB)
take	took	taken
teach	taught	taught
tear	tore	torn
tell	told	told
think	thought	thought
throw	threw	thrown
understand	understood	understood
wake	woke	woken
wear	wore	worn
win	won	won
write	wrote	written

Past Participles

A **past participle**, by itself, cannot be the main verb of a sentence. When a past participle is combined with another verb, called a **helping verb**, however, it can be used to make the present perfect tense and the past perfect tense.

The **present perfect** tense is used for an action that began in the past and either continues into the present or was completed at some unknown time in the past.

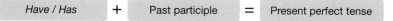

| Have / Has | + | Past participle | = | Present perfect tense |

My <u>car</u> <u>has stalled</u> several times recently.

Use *had* plus the past participle to make the **past perfect tense**. The past perfect tense is used for an action that began in the past and ended before some other past action.

| Had | + | Past participle | = | Past perfect tense |

My <u>car</u> <u>had stalled</u> several times before I called the mechanic.

A sentence that is written in the **passive voice** has a subject that does not perform an action. Instead, the subject is acted upon. To create the passive voice, combine a form of the verb *be* with a past participle.

| *Be* | + | Past participle | = | Passive voice |

PASSIVE The <u>report</u> <u><u>was written</u></u> by the vice-president.

Most sentences should be written in the **active voice**, which means that the subject performs the action.

ACTIVE The <u>vice-president</u> <u>wrote</u> the report.

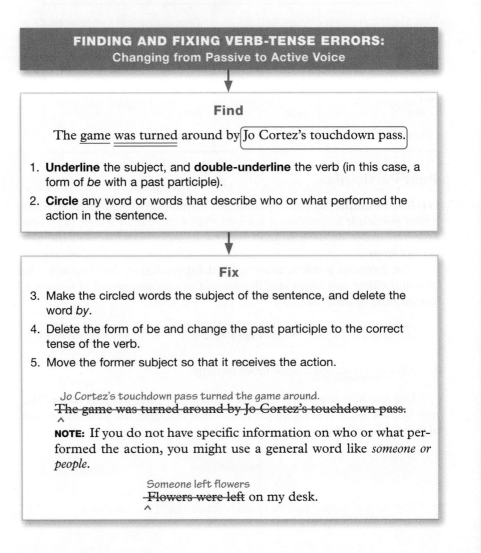

FINDING AND FIXING VERB-TENSE ERRORS:
Changing from Passive to Active Voice

Find

The <u>game</u> <u><u>was turned</u></u> around by Jo Cortez's touchdown pass.

1. **Underline** the subject, and **double-underline** the verb (in this case, a form of *be* with a past participle).
2. **Circle** any word or words that describe who or what performed the action in the sentence.

Fix

3. Make the circled words the subject of the sentence, and delete the word *by*.
4. Delete the form of be and change the past participle to the correct tense of the verb.
5. Move the former subject so that it receives the action.

> *Jo Cortez's touchdown pass turned the game around.*
> ~~The game was turned around by Jo Cortez's touchdown pass.~~

NOTE: If you do not have specific information on who or what performed the action, you might use a general word like *someone or people*.

> *Someone left flowers*
> ~~Flowers were left~~ on my desk.

17

Other Grammar and Style Concerns

In addition to checking your writing for the four most serious errors covered in Chapter 16, you will want to be aware of common trouble spots in other areas of grammar and style: pronouns, adjectives and adverbs, modifiers, coordination and subordination, parallelism, sentence variety, and word choice. Matters of punctuation and capitalization are covered in Chapter 18.

Pronouns

A **pronoun** is used in place of a noun or other pronoun mentioned earlier. In most cases, a pronoun refers to a specific noun or pronoun mentioned nearby.

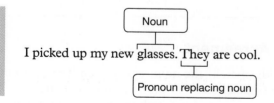

Noun

I picked up my new glasses. They are cool.

Pronoun replacing noun

Common Pronouns

PERSONAL PRONOUNS	POSSESSIVE PRONOUNS	INDEFINITE PRONOUNS	
I	my	all	much
me	mine	any	neither (of)
you	your / yours	anybody	nobody
she / he	hers / his	anyone	none (of)
her / him	hers / his	anything	no one
it	its	both	nothing
we	our / ours	each (of)	one (of)
us	our / ours	either (of)	some
they	their / theirs	everybody	somebody
them	their / theirs	everyone	someone
		everything	something
		few (of)	

Check for Pronoun Agreement

A pronoun must agree with (match) the noun or pronoun it refers to in number. It must be either singular (one) or plural (more than one).

If a pronoun is singular, it must also match the noun or pronoun it refers to in gender (*he, she,* or *it*).

> **CONSISTENT**   Magda sold *her* old television set.
>
> [*Her* agrees with *Magda* because both are singular and feminine.]

Watch out for singular, general nouns. If a noun is singular, the pronoun that refers to it must be singular as well.

INCONSISTENT   Any student can tell you what ~~their~~ least
                                                ^{his or her}
                    favorite course is.
                                    ^

[*Student* is singular, so the plural pronoun *their* must
be replaced with the singular pronouns *his* and *her*.]

To avoid using the awkward phrase *his or her*, make the subject plural
when you can.

CONSISTENT   Most students can tell you what *their* least
                  favorite course is.

Two types of words often cause errors in pronoun agreement: indefinite pronouns and collective nouns.

Indefinite Pronouns

An **indefinite pronoun** does not refer to a specific person, place, or thing: it is general. Indefinite pronouns often take singular verbs. Whenever a pronoun refers to an indefinite pronoun, check for agreement.

The monks got up at dawn. Everybody had ~~their~~ chores for the day.
                                          ^{his}
                                          ^

Indefinite Pronouns

ALWAYS SINGULAR (USE THE *IS* FORM OF *BE*)		
anybody	everyone	nothing
anyone	everything	one (of)
anything	much	somebody
each (of)	neither (of)	someone
either (of)	nobody	something
everybody	no one	

ALWAYS PLURAL (USE THE *ARE* FORM OF *BE*)		
both	many	
few	several	
MAY BE SINGULAR OR PLURAL (USE THE *IS* OR *ARE* FORM OF *BE*)		
all	most	some
any	none	

NOTE: Although grammatically correct, using the pronoun *he* to refer to an indefinite pronoun such as *everyone* is considered sexist. Here are two ways to avoid this problem:

1. Use *his or her.*

> Someone posted *his or her* email address to the website.

2. Change the sentence so that the pronoun refers to a plural noun or pronoun.

> Some students posted *their* email addresses to the website.

Collective Nouns

A **collective noun** names a group that acts as a single unit. Some common collective nouns are *class, committee, company, family, government, group,* and *society.* Collective nouns are usually singular, so when you use a pronoun to refer to a collective noun, it is also usually singular.

>
> its
> The team had ~~their~~ sixth consecutive win of the season.
> ^

If the people in a group are acting as individuals, however, the noun is plural and should be used with a plural pronoun.

                        their
The class brought ~~its~~ papers to read.

Make Pronoun Reference Clear

In an **ambiguous pronoun reference**, the pronoun could refer to more than one noun.

                           dirty
AMBIGUOUS   I put the glass on the shelf, ~~even though it was dirty.~~

           [Was the glass dirty? Or was the shelf dirty? The revision makes it clear.]

In a **vague pronoun reference**, the pronoun does not refer clearly to any particular person, place, or thing. To correct a vague pronoun reference, use a more specific noun instead of the pronoun.

                             the nurse
VAGUE   When Tom got to the clinic ~~they~~ told him it

          was closed.

          [Who told Tom the clinic was closed? The revision makes it clear.]

Repetitious Pronoun Reference

In a **repetitious pronoun reference**, the pronoun repeats a reference to a noun rather than replacing the noun.

The nurse at the clinic ~~he~~ told Tom that it was closed.
The newspaper, ~~it~~ says that the new diet therapy is promising.

Three Important Types of Pronoun

Three important types of pronouns are **subject pronouns, object pronouns,** and **possessive pronouns.** Notice their uses in the following sentences.

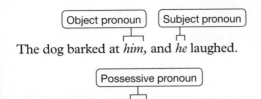

The dog barked at *him,* and *he* laughed.

As Josh walked out, *his* phone started ringing.

Pronoun Types

TIP Never put an apostrophe in a possessive pronoun.

	SUBJECT	OBJECT	POSSESSIVE
First-person singular / plural	I / we	me / us	my, mine / our, ours
Second-person singular / plural	you / you	you / you	your, yours / your, yours
Third-person singular	he, she, it	him, her, it	his, her, hers, its
	who	whom	whose
Third-person plural	they	them	their, theirs
	who	whom	whose

Subject Pronouns

Subject pronouns serve as the subject of a verb.

You live next door to a coffee shop.

I opened the door too quickly.

Object Pronouns

Object pronouns either receive the action of a verb or are part of a prepositional phrase. (For a list of common prepositions, see p. 194.)

OBJECT OF THE VERB	Jay gave *me* his watch.
OBJECT OF THE PREPOSITION	Jay gave his watch to *me*.

Possessive Pronouns

Possessive pronouns show ownership.

> Dave is *my* uncle.

Use the Right Pronoun

Three trouble spots make it difficult to know what type of pronoun to use: compound subjects or compound objects, comparisons, and sentences that need *who* or *whom*.

Pronouns Used with Compound Subjects and Objects

A **compound subject** has more than one subject joined by *and* or *or*. A **compound object** has more than one object joined by *and* or *or*.

> **COMPOUND SUBJECT**   Chandler and *I* worked on the project.
>
> **COMPOUND OBJECT**   My boss gave the assignment to Chandler and *me*.

To decide what type of pronoun to use in a compound construction, try leaving out the other part of the compound and the *and* or *or*. Then, say the sentence aloud to yourself.

> **COMPOUND SUBJECT**
>
> J̶o̶a̶n̶ ̶a̶n̶d̶ (me /Ⓘ) went to the movies last night.
>
> [Think: *I* went to the movies last night.]
>
> **COMPOUND OBJECT**
>
> I will keep that information just between you and (I /ⓜⓔ).
>
> [*Between you and me* is a prepositional phrase, so an object pronoun, *me*, is required.]

Pronouns Used in Comparisons

Using the right type of pronoun in comparisons is particularly important because using the wrong type changes the meaning of the sentence. Editing comparisons can be tricky because they often imply the presence of words that are not actually included in the sentence.

> Bob trusts Donna more than *I*.   [This sentence means that Bob trusts Donna more than I trust her. The implied words are *trust her*.]

> Bob trusts Donna more than *me*.   [This sentence means that Bob trusts Donna more than he trusts me. The implied words are *he trusts*.]

To decide whether to use a subject or object pronoun in a comparison, try adding the implied words and saying the sentence aloud.

> The registrar is much more efficient than (us / we).
>
> [Think: The registrar is much more efficient than *we are*.]
>
> Susan rides her bicycle more than (he / him).
>
> [Think: Susan rides her bicycle more than *he does*.]

Choosing between Who and Whom

Who is always a subject; *whom* is always an object. If a pronoun performs an action, use the subject form *who*. If a pronoun does not perform an action, use the object form *whom*.

WHO = SUBJECT	I would like to know <u>who</u> <u>delivered</u> this package.
WHOM = OBJECT	He told me to *whom* <u>I</u> <u>should report</u>.

In sentences other than questions, when the pronoun (*who* or *whom*) is followed by a verb, use *who*. When the pronoun (*who* or *whom*) is followed by a noun or pronoun, use *whom*.

> The pianist (who / whom) <u>played</u> was excellent.
>
> [The pronoun is followed by the verb *played*. Use *who*.]
>
> The pianist (who / whom) <u>I</u> <u>saw</u> was excellent.
>
> [The pronoun is followed by another pronoun: *I*. Use *whom*.]

Make Pronouns Consistent in Person

Person is the point of view a writer uses—the perspective from which he or she writes. Pronouns may be in first person (*I* or *we*), second person (*you*), or third person (*he, she,* or *it*). (See the chart on p. 224.)

INCONSISTENT	As soon as *a shopper* walks into the store, *you* can tell it is a weird place.
	[The sentence starts with the third person (*a shopper*) but shifts to the second person (*you*).]
CONSISTENT, SINGULAR	As soon as *a shopper* walks into the store, *he* or *she* can tell it is a weird place.
CONSISTENT, PLURAL	As soon as *shoppers* walk into the store, *they* can tell it is a weird place.

Adjectives and Adverbs

Adjectives describe or modify nouns (words that name people, places, things, or ideas) and pronouns (words that replace nouns). They add information about *what kind, which one,* or *how many.*

The *final* exam was today.

It was *long* and *difficult.*

The *three shiny new* coins were on the dresser.

Adverbs describe or modify verbs (words that tell what happens in a sentence), adjectives, or other adverbs. They add information about *how, how much, when, where, why,* or *to what extent.*

MODIFYING VERB	Sharon *enthusiastically* accepted the job.
MODIFYING ADJECTIVE	The *very* young lawyer handled the case.
MODIFYING ANOTHER ADVERB	The team played *surprisingly* well.

Adjectives usually come before the words they modify; adverbs come before or after. You can use more than one adjective or adverb to modify a word.

Choosing between Adjectives and Adverbs

Many adverbs are formed by adding *-ly* to the end of an adjective.

ADJECTIVE	She received a *quick* answer.
ADVERB	Her sister answered *quickly.*

To decide whether to use an adjective or an adverb, find the word being described. If that word is a noun or pronoun, use an adjective. If it is a verb, adjective, or another adverb, use an adverb.

Adjectives and Adverbs in Comparisons

To compare two people, places, or things, use the **comparative** form of adjectives or adverbs. Comparisons often use the word *than*.

> Carol ran *faster* than I did.

> Johan is *more intelligent* than his sister.

To compare three or more people, places, or things, use the **superlative** form of adjectives or adverbs.

> Carol ran the *fastest* of all the women runners.

> Johan is the *most intelligent* of the five children.

If an adjective or adverb is short (one syllable), add the endings *-er* to form the comparative and *-est* to form the superlative. Also use this pattern for adjectives that end in *-y* (but change the *-y* to *-i* before adding *-er* or *-est*).

For all other adjectives and adverbs, add the word *more* to make the comparative and the word *most* to make the superlative.

Forming Comparatives and Superlatives

ADJECTIVE OR ADVERB	COMPARATIVE	SUPERLATIVE
ADJECTIVES AND ADVERBS OF ONE SYLLABLE		
tall	taller	tallest
fast	faster	fastest
ADJECTIVES ENDING IN -Y		
happy	happier	happiest
silly	sillier	silliest
OTHER ADJECTIVES AND ADVERBS		
graceful	more graceful	most graceful
gracefully	more gracefully	most gracefully
intelligent	more intelligent	most intelligent
intelligently	more intelligently	most intelligently

Use either an ending (*-er* or *-est*) or an extra word (*more* or *most*) to form a comparative or superlative — not both at once.

J. K. Rowling is the ~~most~~ richest author in the world.

Good, Well, Bad, and *Badly*

Four common adjectives and adverbs have irregular forms: *good, well, bad,* and *badly.*

Forming Irregular Comparatives and Superlatives

	COMPARATIVE	SUPERLATIVE
ADJECTIVE		
good	better	best
bad	worse	worst
ADVERB		
well	better	best
badly	worse	worst

People often get confused about whether to use *good* or *well. Good* is an adjective, so use it to describe a noun or pronoun. *Well* is an adverb, so use it to describe a verb or an adjective.

ADJECTIVE   She has a *good* job.

ADVERB   Herb works *well* with his colleagues.

Well can also be an adjective to describe someone's health: I am not *well* today.

Misplaced and Dangling Modifiers

Modifiers are words or word groups that describe other words in a sentence. Modifiers should be near the words they modify; otherwise, the sentence can be confusing or unintentionally funny.

Misplaced Modifiers

A **misplaced modifier**, because it is in the wrong place, describes the wrong word or words.

> **MISPLACED**   Linda saw the White House *flying over Washington, D.C.*
>
> [Was the White House flying over Washington?]

To correct a misplaced modifier, place the modifier as close as possible to the word or words it modifies, often directly before it.

> **CLEAR**   *Flying over Washington, D.C.,* Linda saw the White House.

Four constructions often lead to misplaced modifiers.

1. **Modifiers such as *only, almost, hardly, nearly,* and *just.*** These words need to be immediately before — not just close to — the words or phrases they modify.

    > almost
    > Joanne ~~almost~~ ate the whole cake.
    > ^
    > [Joanne actually ate; she did not "almost" eat.]

2. **Modifiers that are prepositional phrases.**

    > in plastic cups
    > Jen served punch to the seniors ~~in plastic cups.~~
    > ^   ^
    > [The seniors were not in plastic cups; the punch was.]

3. **Modifiers that start with *-ing* verbs.**

    > Wearing flip-flops,
    > Javier climbed the mountain. ~~wearing flip-flops.~~
    > ^   ^
    > [The mountain was not wearing flip-flops; Javier was.]

4. **Modifier clauses that start with *who, whose, that,* or *which*.**

    who was crying
    The baby on the bus ~~who was crying~~ had curly hair.
                      ^

    [The bus was not crying; the baby was.]

Dangling Modifiers

A **dangling modifier** "dangles" because the word or word group it modifies is not in the sentence. Dangling modifiers usually appear at the beginning of a sentence and seem to modify the noun or pronoun that immediately follows them, but they are really modifying another word or group of words.

DANGLING	*Rushing to class,* the books fell out of my bag.
	[The books were not rushing to class.]
CLEAR	*Rushing to class,* I dropped my books.

There are two basic ways to correct dangling modifiers. Use the one that makes more sense. One way is to add the word being modified immediately after the opening modifier so that the connection between the two is clear.

                              I   on my bike
Trying to eat a hot dog, ~~my bike~~ swerved.
                         ^   ^

Another way is to add the word being modified in the opening modifier itself.

While I was trying
~~Trying~~ to eat a hot dog, my bike swerved.
^

Coordination and Subordination

Joining two sentences with related ideas can make your writing less choppy.

Coordination

In **coordination,** two sentences can be joined with a comma and a coordinating conjunction, a semicolon alone, or a semicolon and a conjunctive adverb. The coordinating conjunctions are *for, and, nor, but, or, yet,* and *so* (FANBOYS). Conjunctive adverbs are listed in the following box:

Conjunctive Adverbs

also	however	moreover
as a result	in addition	still
besides	in fact	then
furthermore	instead	therefore

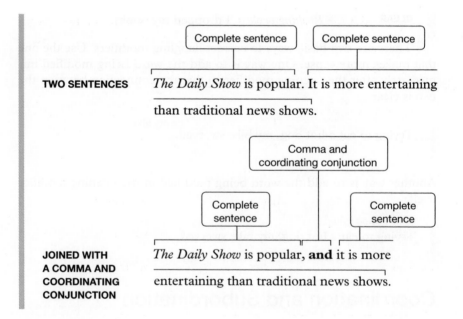

TWO SENTENCES   *The Daily Show* is popular. It is more entertaining than traditional news shows.

JOINED WITH A COMMA AND COORDINATING CONJUNCTION   *The Daily Show* is popular, **and** it is more entertaining than traditional news shows.

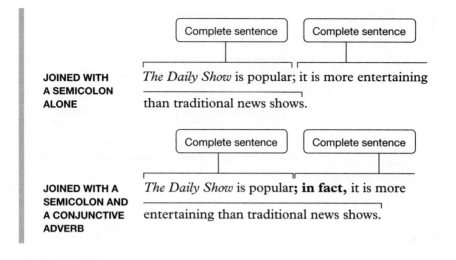

JOINED WITH
A SEMICOLON
ALONE

The Daily Show is popular; it is more entertaining than traditional news shows.

JOINED WITH A
SEMICOLON AND
A CONJUNCTIVE
ADVERB

The Daily Show is popular; **in fact,** it is more entertaining than traditional news shows.

Subordination

With **subordination,** you put a dependent word (such as *after, although, because,* or *when*) in front of one of the sentences, which then becomes a dependent clause and is no longer a complete sentence.

Subordinating Conjunctions (Dependent Words)

after	if	unless
although	if only	until
as	now that	when
as if	once	whenever
because	since	where
before	so that	while
even if / though		

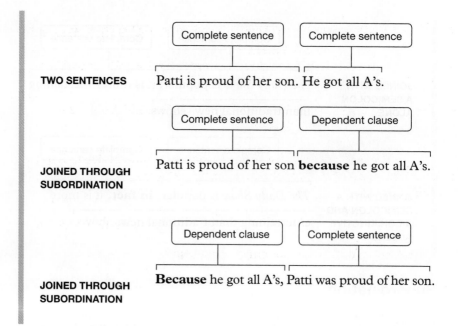

TWO SENTENCES   Patti is proud of her son. He got all A's.

JOINED THROUGH
SUBORDINATION   Patti is proud of her son **because** he got all A's.

JOINED THROUGH
SUBORDINATION   **Because** he got all A's, Patti was proud of her son.

Parallelism

Parallelism in writing means that similar parts in a sentence have the same structure: their parts are balanced. When comparing things or listing items in a series, use nouns with nouns, verbs with verbs, and phrases with phrases.

NOT PARALLEL   I enjoy <u>basketball</u> more than <u>playing video games</u>.
[Basketball is a noun, but *playing video games* is a phrase.]

PARALLEL   I enjoy <u>basketball</u> more than <u>video games</u>.

PARALLEL   I enjoy <u>playing basketball</u> more than <u>playing video games</u>.

NOT PARALLEL   Last night, I <u>worked</u>, <u>studied</u>, and <u>was watching</u> television.
[Verbs must be in the same tense to be parallel. *Was watching* has a different structure from *worked* and *studied*.]

PARALLEL   Last night, I <u>worked</u>, <u>studied</u>, and <u>watched</u> television.

PARALLEL   Last night, I was <u>working</u>, <u>studying</u>, and <u>watching</u> television.

NOT PARALLEL	This weekend, we can go <u>to the beach</u> or <u>walking in the mountains</u>.
	[*To the beach* should be paired with another prepositional phrase: *to the mountains*.]
PARALLEL	This weekend, we can go <u>to the beach</u> or <u>to the mountains</u>.

Certain paired words, called **correlative conjunctions**, link two equal elements and show the relationship between them. Here are the paired words:

both . . . and	neither . . . nor	rather . . . than
either . . . or	not only . . . but also	

Make sure the items joined by these paired words are parallel.

NOT PARALLEL	Bruce wants *both* <u>freedom</u> *and* <u>to be wealthy</u>.
	[*Both* is used with *and*, but the items joined by them are not parallel.]
PARALLEL	Bruce wants *both* <u>freedom</u> *and* <u>wealth</u>.
NOT PARALLEL	He can *neither* <u>fail the course</u> and <u>quitting his job</u> is also impossible.
PARALLEL	He can *neither* <u>fail the course</u> *nor* <u>quit his job</u>.

Sentence Variety

Sentence variety means using different sentence patterns and lengths to give your writing good rhythm and flow. Here are some strategies for achieving more sentence variety in your writing.

Start Some Sentences with Adverbs

Adverbs are words that describe verbs, adjectives, or other adverbs; they often end with *-ly*. As long as the meaning is clear, adverbs can be placed at the beginning of a sentence instead of in the middle. Adverbs at the beginning of a sentence are usually followed by a comma.

| ADVERB IN MIDDLE | Stories about haunted houses *frequently* surface at Halloween. |
| ADVERB AT BEGINNING | *Frequently*, stories about haunted houses surface at Halloween. |

Join Ideas Using an *-ing* Verb

One way to combine sentences is to add *-ing* to the verb in the less important of the two sentences and to delete the subject, creating a phrase.

| TWO SENTENCES | A pecan roll from our bakery is not a health food. It contains 800 calories. |
| JOINED WITH *-ING* VERB FORM | *Containing* 800 calories, a pecan roll from our bakery is not a health food. |

Join Ideas Using a Past Participle

Another way to combine sentences is to use a past participle (often, a verb ending in *-ed*) to turn the less important of the two sentences into a phrase.

| TWO SENTENCES | Henry VIII was a powerful English king. He is *remembered* for his many wives. |
| JOINED WITH A PAST PARTICIPLE | *Remembered* for his many wives, Henry VIII was a powerful English king. |

Join Ideas Using an Appositive

An **appositive** is a noun or noun phrase that renames a noun or pronoun. Appositives can be used to combine two sentences into one.

TWO SENTENCES	Brussels sprouts can be roasted for a delicious flavor. They are a commonly disliked food.
JOINED WITH AN APPOSITIVE	Brussels sprouts, a commonly disliked food, can be roasted for a delicious flavor.
	[The phrase *a commonly disliked food* renames the noun Brussels *sprouts*.]

Join Ideas Using an Adjective Clause

An **adjective clause** is a group of words with a subject and a verb that describes a noun. An adjective clause often begins with the word *who, which,* or *that,* and it can be used to combine two sentences into one.

TWO SENTENCES	Lauren has won many basketball awards. She is captain of her college team.
JOINED WITH AN ADJECTIVE CLAUSE	Lauren, *who is captain of her college team,* has won many basketball awards.

NOTE: If an adjective clause is an essential part of a sentence, do not put commas around it.

Lauren is an award-winning basketball player who overcame childhood cancer.

[*Who overcame childhood cancer* is an essential part of this sentence.]

Word-Choice Problems

Five common problems with word choice may make it hard for readers to understand your point.

Vague and Abstract Words

Vague and abstract words are too general. They do not give your readers a clear idea of what you mean. Here are some common vague and abstract words.

Vague and Abstract Words

a lot	cute	nice	stuff
amazing	dumb	OK (okay)	terrible
awesome	good	old	thing
bad	great	pretty	very
beautiful	happy	sad	whatever
big	huge	small	young

When you see one of these words or another general word in your writing, replace it with a concrete or more specific word or description. A **concrete** word names something that can be seen, heard, felt, tasted, or smelled. A **specific** word names a particular person or quality. Compare these two sentences:

> **VAGUE AND ABSTRACT**   An old man crossed the street.
>
> **CONCRETE AND SPECIFIC**   An eighty-seven-year-old priest stumbled along Main Street.

The first version is too general to be interesting. The second version creates a clear, strong image. Some words are so vague that it is best to avoid them altogether.

> **VAGUE AND ABSTRACT**   It is awesome.
>
> [This sentence is neither concrete nor specific. What is awesome, and why?]
>
> **CONCRETE AND SPECIFIC**   The mountain towered over our heads, its steep sides clothed in dark pine trees, the peak snow-capped and awe-inspiring.

Slang

Slang, informal and casual language, should be used only in informal situations. Avoid it when you write, especially for college classes or at work. Use language that is appropriate for your audience and purpose.

SLANG	EDITED
S'all good.	Everything is going well.
Dawg, I don't deserve this grade.	Professor, I don't deserve this grade.

Wordy Language

Too many words can weaken a writer's point.

> **WORDY**   I am not interested *at this point in time*.
>
> **EDITED**   I am not interested now.
>
> [The phrase *at this point in time* uses five words to express what could be said in one word: *now*.]

Common Wordy Expressions

WORDY	EDITED
As a result of	because
Due to the fact that	because
In spite of the fact that	although
It is my opinion that	I think (or just make the point)
In the event that	if
The fact of the matter is that	(Just state the point.)
A great number of	many
At that time	then
In this day and age	now
At this point in time	now
In this paper I will show that . . .	(Just make the point; do not announce it.)
Utilize	use

Clichés

Clichés are phrases used so often that people no longer pay attention to them. To get your point across and to get your readers' attention, replace clichés with fresh and specific language.

CLICHÉS	EDITED
I cannot *make ends meet.*	I do not have enough money to live on.
My uncle *worked his way up the corporate ladder.*	My uncle started as a shipping clerk but ended up as a regional vice president.
This roll is *as hard as a rock.*	This roll is so hard I could bounce it.

Common Clichés

as big as a house	few and far between	spoiled brat
as light as a feather	hell on earth	starting from scratch
better late than never	last but not least	sweating blood / bullets
break the ice	no way on earth	too little, too late
crystal clear	110 percent	24/7
a drop in the bucket	playing with fire	work like a dog
easier said than done	pull your punches	worst nightmare

Sexist Language

Language that favors one gender over another or that assumes that only one gender performs a certain role is called *sexist*. Such language should be avoided.

SEXIST

A doctor should politely answer *his* patients' questions.

[Not all doctors are male, as suggested by the pronoun *his*.]

REVISED

A doctor should politely answer *his or her* patients' questions.

Doctors should politely answer *their* patients' questions.

[The first revision changes *his* to *his or her* to avoid sexism. The second revision changes the subject to a plural noun (*Doctors*) so that a genderless pronoun (*their*) can be used. Usually, it is preferable to avoid *his or her*.]

18

Punctuation and Capitalization

Commas [,]

To get your intended meaning across to your readers, it is important that you use commas correctly, especially in the following situations.

Commas between Items in a Series

Use commas to separate the items in a series (three or more items), including the last item in the series, which usually has *and* or *or* before it.

▌ We can *sleep in the car, stay in a motel,* or *camp outside.*

Commas between Coordinate Adjectives

Coordinate adjectives are two or more adjectives that independently modify the same noun and are separated by commas.

▌ Conor ordered a *big, fat, greasy* burger.

Note that a comma is not used between the final adjective and the noun it describes.

Cumulative adjectives describe the same noun but are not separated by commas because they form a unit that describes the noun. You can identify cumulative adjectives because separating them by *and* does not make any sense.

The store is having its *last storewide clearance* sale.

[Putting *and* between *last* and *storewide* and between *storewide* and *clearance* would make an odd sentence: The store is having its *last* and *storewide* and *clearance* sale. The adjectives in the sentence are cumulative adjectives and should not be separated by commas.]

Commas in Compound Sentences

A **compound sentence** contains two complete sentences joined by a co-ordinating conjunction: *for, and, nor, but, or, yet, so.* Use a comma before the joining word to separate the two complete sentences.

I called my best friend, and she agreed to drive me to work.

I asked my best friend to drive me to work, but she was busy.

I can take the bus to work, or I can call another friend.

NOTE: A comma alone cannot separate two sentences. Doing so creates a run-on (see pp. 203–08).

Commas after Introductory Words

Use a comma after an introductory word, phrase, or clause. The comma lets your readers know when the main part of the sentence is starting.

INTRODUCTORY WORD	*Yesterday,* I went to the game.
INTRODUCTORY PHRASE	*By the way,* I do not have a babysitter for tomorrow.
INTRODUCTORY CLAUSE	*While I waited outside,* Susan went backstage.

Commas around Appositives and Interrupters

An **appositive** comes directly before or after a noun or pronoun and renames it.

Lily, *a senior,* will take her nursing exam this summer.

The prices are outrageous at Beans, *the local coffee shop.*

An **interrupter** is an aside or transition that interrupts the flow of a sentence and does not affect its meaning.

My sister, *incidentally,* has good reasons for being late.

Her child had a fever, *for example.*

Commas around Adjective Clauses

An **adjective clause** is a group of words that begins with *who, which,* or *that*; has a subject and a verb; and describes a noun right before it in a sentence.

If an adjective clause can be taken out of a sentence without completely changing the meaning of the sentence, put commas around the clause.

> Beans, *which is the local coffee shop,* charges outrageous prices.
> I complained to Mr. Kranz, *who is the shop's manager.*

If an adjective clause is essential to the meaning of a sentence, do not put commas around it. You can tell whether a clause is essential by taking it out and seeing if the meaning of the sentence changes significantly, as it would if you took the clauses out of the following examples.

> The only grocery store *that sold good bread* went out of business.
> Students *who do internships* often improve their hiring potential.

Commas with Quotation Marks

Quotation marks are used to show that you are repeating exactly what someone said. Use commas to set off the words inside quotation marks from the rest of the sentence.

> "Let me see your license," demanded the police officer.
> "Did you realize," she asked, "that you were going 80 miles per hour?"
> I exclaimed, "No!"

Notice that a comma never comes directly after a quotation mark.

Commas in Addresses

Use commas to separate the elements of an address included in a sentence. However, do not use a comma before a zip code.

> My address is 2512 Windermere Street, Jackson, Mississippi 40720.

If a sentence continues after a city-state combination or after a street address, put a comma after the state or the address.

> I moved here from Detroit, Michigan, when I was eighteen.
> I've lived at 24 Heener Street, Madison, since 1989.

Commas in Dates

Separate the day from the year with a comma. If you give just the month and year, do not separate them with a comma.

My daughter was born on November 8, 2004.

The next conference is in August 2019.

If a sentence continues after the date, put a comma after the date.

On April 21, 2020, the contract will expire.

Commas with Names

Put a comma after (and sometimes before) the name of someone being addressed directly.

Don, I want you to come look at this.

Unfortunately, Marie, you need to finish the report by next week.

Commas with *Yes* or *No*

Put a comma after the word *yes* or *no* in response to a question.

Yes, I believe that you are right.

Apostrophes [']

An **apostrophe** (') is a punctuation mark that either shows ownership (*Susan's*) or indicates that a letter has been intentionally left out to form a contraction (*I'm, that's, they're*).

Apostrophes to Show Ownership

Add -'s to a singular noun to show ownership even if the noun already ends in -s.

Karen's apartment is on the South Side.

Chris's house is way over on the West Side.

If a noun is plural and ends in -s, just add an apostrophe. If it is plural but does not end in -s, add -'s.

The *twins'* father was building them a playhouse.
[more than one twin]

The *children's* toys were broken.

The placement of an apostrophe makes a difference in meaning.

> My *sister's* six children are at my house for the weekend.
> [one sister who has six children]
>
> My *sisters'* six children are at my house for the weekend.
> [two or more sisters who together have six children]

Do not use an apostrophe to form the plural of a noun.

> Gina went camping with her *sister's* and their children.
> All the *highway's* to the airport are under construction.

Do not use an apostrophe with a possessive pronoun. These pronouns already show ownership (possession).

> Is that bag *your's*?   No, it is *our's*.

Possessive Pronouns

my	his	its	their
mine	her	our	theirs
your	hers	ours	whose
yours			

The single most common error with apostrophes and pronouns is confusing *its* (a possessive pronoun) with *it's* (a contraction meaning "it is"). Whenever you write *it's*, test correctness by replacing it with *it is* and reading the sentence aloud to hear if it makes sense.

Apostrophes in Contractions

A **contraction** is formed by joining two words and leaving out one or more of the letters. When writing a contraction, put an apostrophe where the letter or letters have been left out.

> *She's* on her way. = *She is* on her way.
> *I'll* see you there. = *I will* see you there.

Be sure to put the apostrophe in the correct place.

▌ It *does/n't* really matter.

Common Contractions

aren't = are not	I'd = I would, I had
can't = cannot	I'll = I will
couldn't = could not	I'm = I am
didn't = did not	I've = I have
don't = do not	isn't = is not
he'd = he would, he had	it's = it is, it has
he'll = he will	let's = let us
he's = he is, he has	she'd = she would, she had
she'll = she will	won't = will not
she's = she is, she has	wouldn't = would not
there's = there is	you'll = you will
they're = they are	you're = you are
who's = who is, who has	you've = you have

Apostrophes with Letters, Numbers, and Time

Use *-'s* to make letters and numbers plural. The apostrophe prevents confusion or misreading.

▌ In Scrabble games, there are more *e's* than any other letter.
▌ In women's shoes, size *8's* are more common than size *10's.*

Use an apostrophe or *-'s* in certain expressions in which time nouns are treated as if they possess something.

She took four *weeks'* maternity leave after the baby was born.

This *year's* graduating class is huge.

Quotation Marks [" "]

Quotation marks always appear in pairs. Quotation marks are used with direct quotations and to set off titles.

Quotation Marks for Direct Quotations

When you write a direct quotation, use quotation marks around the quoted words. Quotation marks tell readers that the words used are exactly what was said or written.

1. "I do not know what she means," I said to my friend Lina.
2. Lina asked, "Do you think we should ask a question?"
3. "Excuse me, Professor Soames," I called out, "but could you explain that again?"
4. "Yes," said Professor Soames. "Let me make sure you all understand."

When you are writing a paper that uses outside sources, use quotation marks to indicate where you quote the exact words of a source.

We all need to become more conscientious recyclers. A recent editorial in the *Bolton Common* reported, "When recycling volunteers spot-checked bags that were supposed to contain only newspaper, they found a collection of non-recyclable items such as plastic candy wrappers, aluminum foil, and birthday cards."

When quoting, writers usually use words that identify who is speaking, such as *I said to my friend Lina* in the first example above. The identifying words can come after the quoted words (example 1), before them (example 2), or in the middle of them (example 3). Here are some guidelines for capitalization and punctuation.

GUIDELINES FOR CAPITALIZATION AND PUNCTUATION

- Capitalize the first letter in a complete sentence that is being quoted, even if it comes after some identifying words (example 2 above).
- Do not capitalize the first letter in a quotation if it is not the first word in a complete sentence (*but* in example 3).

- If it is a complete sentence and it is clear who the speaker is, a quotation can stand on its own (second sentence in example 4).

- Identifying words must be attached to a quotation; they cannot be a sentence on their own.

- Use commas to separate any identifying words from quoted words in the same sentence.

- Always put quotation marks after commas and periods. Put quotation marks after question marks and exclamation points if they are part of the quoted sentence.

Quotation mark   Quotation mark
Lina asked, "Do you think we should ask a question?"
Comma   Question mark

- If a question mark or exclamation point is part of your own sentence, put it after the quotation mark.

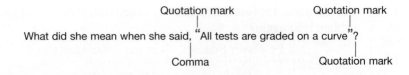

Quotation mark   Quotation mark
What did she mean when she said, "All tests are graded on a curve"?
Comma   Quotation mark

Setting Off a Quotation within Another Quotation

Sometimes, when you quote someone directly, part of what that person said quotes words that someone else said or wrote. Put single quotation marks (' ') around the quotation within a quotation so that readers understand who said what.

> Terry told his instructor, "I am sorry I missed the exam, but that is not a reason to fail me for the term. Our student handbook says, 'Students must be given the opportunity to make up work missed for legitimate reasons,' and I have a good reason."

No Quotation Marks for Indirect Speech

When you report what someone said or wrote but do not use the person's exact words, you are writing **indirect speech**. Do not use quotation marks for indirect speech, which often begins with the word *that*.

INDIRECT SPEECH   The police said that we should move along.

DIRECT QUOTATION   "Move along," directed the police.

Quotation Marks for Certain Titles

When you refer to a short work such as a magazine or newspaper article, a chapter in a book, a short story, an essay, a song, or a poem, put quotation marks around the title of the work.

NEWSPAPER ARTICLE	"Volunteers Honored for Service"
SHORT STORY	"The Awakening"
ESSAY	"Why Are We So Angry?"

Usually, titles of longer works, such as novels, books, magazines, newspapers, movies, television programs, and CDs, are italicized. The titles of sacred books such as the Bible or the Qur'an are neither underlined nor surrounded by quotation marks.

BOOK	*The Good Earth*
NEWSPAPER	*The Washington Post*

If you are writing a paper with many outside sources, your instructor will probably refer you to a particular system of citing sources. Follow that system's guidelines when you use titles in your paper.

NOTE: Do not enclose the title of a paragraph or an essay that you have written in quotation marks when it appears at the beginning of your paper. Do not italicize it either.

Semicolon [;]

Semicolons are used to join related sentences and separate items in lists.

Semicolons to Join Closely Related Sentences

Use a semicolon to join two closely related sentences into one sentence.

In an interview, hold your head up and do not slouch; it is important to look alert.

Make good eye contact; looking down is not appropriate in an interview.

Semicolons When Items in a List Contain Commas

Use semicolons to separate items in a list that itself contains commas. Otherwise, it is difficult for readers to tell where one item ends and another begins.

> For dinner, Bob ate an order of onion rings; a 16-ounce steak; a baked potato with sour cream, bacon bits, and cheese; a green salad; and a huge bowl of ice cream with fudge sauce.

Because one item, *a baked potato with sour cream, bacon bits, and cheese,* contains its own commas, all items need to be separated by semicolons.

Colon [:]

Colons are used before lists, explanations or examples, and subtitles and in business correspondence.

Colons before Lists

Use a colon after an independent clause to introduce a list. An independent clause contains a subject, a verb, and a complete thought. It can stand on its own as a sentence.

> The software conference fair featured a vast array of products: financial-management applications, games, educational CDs, college-application programs, and so on.

Colons before Explanations or Examples

Use a colon after an independent clause to let readers know that you are about to provide an explanation or example of what you just wrote.

> The conference was overwhelming: too much hype about too many things.

One of the most common misuses of colons is to use them after a phrase instead of an independent clause. Watch out especially for colons following the phrases *such as* and *for example*.

> **INCORRECT** Tonya enjoys sports that are sometimes dangerous. For example: white-water rafting, wilderness skiing, rock climbing, and motorcycle racing.
>
> **CORRECT** Tonya enjoys sports that are sometimes dangerous: white-water rafting, wilderness skiing, rock climbing, and motorcycle racing.

Colons in Business Correspondence and before Subtitles

Use a colon after a greeting (called a *salutation*) in a business letter and after the standard heading lines at the beginning of a memorandum.

> Dear Mr. Hernandez:
>
> To: Pat Toney
> From: Miriam Moore

Colons should also be used before subtitles, for example, "Running a Marathon: The Five Most Important Tips."

Parentheses [( )]

Use parentheses to set off information that is not essential to the meaning of a sentence. Parentheses are always used in pairs and should be used sparingly.

> My grandfather's most successful invention (and also his first) was the electric blanket.
>
> When he died (at the age of ninety-six), he had more than 150 patents registered.

Dash [—]

Dashes can be used like parentheses to set off additional information, particularly information that you want to emphasize. Make a dash by writing or typing two hyphens together. Do not put extra spaces around a dash.

> The final exam—worth 25 percent of your total grade—will be next Thursday.

A dash can also indicate a pause, much like a comma does.

> My uncle went on long fishing trips—without my aunt and cousins.

Hyphen [-]

Use hyphens to join words to create single descriptors and to divide words at the end of lines.

Hyphens to Join Words That Form a Single Description

Writers often join two or more words that together form a single description of a person, place, or thing. To join the words, use a hyphen.

> Being a stockbroker is a high-risk career.
>
> Jill is a lovely three-year-old girl.

When writing out two-word numbers from twenty-one to ninety-nine, put a hyphen between the two words.

> Seventy-five people participated in the demonstration.

Hyphens to Divide a Word at the End of a Line

Use a hyphen to divide a word when part of the word must continue on the next line.

> Critics accused the tobacco industry of increasing the amounts of nico-
> tine in cigarettes to encourage addiction and boost sales.

If you are not sure where to break a word, look it up in a dictionary. The word's main entry will show you where you can break the word: *dic • tion • ar • y*. If you still are not confident that you are putting the hyphen in the correct place, do not break the word; write it all on the next line.

Capitalization

If you can remember the following rules, you will avoid the most common errors of capitalization. Capitalize the first letter

- of every new sentence.
- in names of specific people, places, dates, and things.
- of important words in titles.

Capitalization of Sentences

Capitalize the first letter of each new sentence, including the first word of a direct quotation.

> The superintendent was surprised.
>
> He asked, "What is going on here?"

Capitalization of Names of Specific People, Places, Dates, and Things

The general rule is to capitalize the first letter in names of specific people, places, dates, and things. Do not capitalize a generic (common) name such as *college* as opposed to the specific name: *Carroll State College*. Look at the examples for each group.

People

Capitalize the first letter in names of specific people and in titles used with names of specific people.

SPECIFIC	NOT SPECIFIC
Jean Heaton	my neighbor
Professor Fitzgerald	your math professor
Dr. Cornog	the doctor
Aunt Pat, Mother	my aunt, your mother

The name of a family member is capitalized when the family member is being addressed directly: Happy Birthday, *Mother*. In other instances, do not capitalize: It is my *mother's* birthday.

The word *president* is not capitalized unless it comes directly before a name as part of that person's title: *President* Donald Trump.

Places

Capitalize the first letter in names of specific buildings, streets, cities, states, regions, and countries.

SPECIFIC	NOT SPECIFIC
Bolton Town Hall	the town hall
Arlington Street	our street
Dearborn Heights	my hometown
Arizona	this state
the South	the southern region
Spain	that country

Do not capitalize directions in a sentence.

▌ Drive *south* for five blocks.

Dates

Capitalize the first letter in the names of days, months, and holidays. Do not capitalize the names of the seasons (winter, spring, summer, fall).

SPECIFIC	NOT SPECIFIC
Wednesday	tomorrow
June 25	summer
Thanksgiving	my birthday

Organizations, Companies, and Groups

SPECIFIC	NOT SPECIFIC
Taft Community College	my college
Microsoft	that software company
Alcoholics Anonymous	the self-help group

Languages, Nationalities, and Religions

SPECIFIC	NOT SPECIFIC
English, Greek, Spanish	my first language
Christianity, Buddhism	your religion

The names of languages should be capitalized even if you aren't referring to a specific course.

▌ I am taking psychology and *Spanish.*

Courses

SPECIFIC	NOT SPECIFIC
Composition 101	a writing course
Introduction to Psychology	my psychology course

Commercial Products

SPECIFIC	NOT SPECIFIC
Diet Pepsi	a diet cola
Skippy peanut butter	peanut butter

Capitalization of Titles

When you write the title of a book, movie, television program, magazine, newspaper, article, story, song, paper, poem, and so on, capitalize the first word and all important words. The only words that do not need to be capitalized (unless they are the first word) are indefinite articles (*the, a, an*), coordinating conjunctions (*and, but, for, nor, or, so, yet*), and prepositions (e.g., *in, about, after, above, below,* etc.).

> *The Catcher in the Rye* (novel)
> *Beauty and the Beast* (movie)
> "At Least 50 Dead in Las Vegas Shooting" (newspaper article)
> "The Biography of a Cloud" (poem)

Acknowledgments (*continued from page vi*)

Susan Adam, "The Weirdest Job Interview Questions and How to Handle Them," Forbes.com, June 16, 2011. Copyright © 2011 by Forbes. All rights reserved. Used by permission and protected by the copyright Laws of the United States. The printing, copying, redistribution, or retransmission of this content without express written permission is prohibited.

Mary LaCue Booker, "School Rules." Reprinted by permission of Mary LaCue Booker.

Janice Castro with Dan Cook and Cristina Garcia, "Spanglish," TIME, July 11, 1988. © 1988 Time Inc. All rights reserved. Reprinted from TIME and published with permission of Time Inc. Reproduction in any manner in any language in whole or in part without written permission is prohibited. TIME and the TIME logo are registered trademarks of Time Inc. used under license.

Jeremy Graham, "Becoming a Community Leader." Reprinted by permission of Jeremy Graham, youth pastor and motivational speaker.

Oscar Hijuelos, "Memories of New York City Snow" from *Metropolis Found: New York Is Book Country 25th Anniversary Collection* (New York: New York Is Book Country, 2003). Copyright © 2003 by Oscar Hijuelos. Reprinted with the permission of The Jennifer Lyons Literary Agency, LLC for the estate of the author.

Amanda Jacobowitz, "A Ban on Water Bottles: A Way to Bolster the University's Image." Posted by Amanda Jacobowitz on April 28, 2010. Forum Staff Columnists. Reprinted by permission of the author.

"Don't Work in a Goat's Stomach," by Frances Cole Jones, from *The Wow Factor: The 33 Things You Must (and Must Not) Do to Guarantee Your Edge in Today's Business World* by Frances Cole Jones, copyright © 2009, 2010 by Frances Cole Jones. Used by permission of Ballantine Books, an imprint of Random House, a division of Penguin Random House LLC. All rights reserved.

Diane Melancon, "The Importance of Advance Directives." Reprinted by permission of Diane Melancon, MD.

Casandra Palmer, "Gifts from the Heart." Reprinted by permission.

Eric Rosenberg, "How to Start Your Service Based Side Hustle." Reprinted by permission of the author.

Amy Tan, "Fish Cheeks." © 1987 by Amy Tan. First appeared in *Seventeen Magazine* in 1987. Reprinted by permission of the author and the Sandra Dijkstra Literary Agency.

Anne Terreden, "Nursing note." Reprinted by permission of Anne Terreden, Registered Nurse.

Karen Upright, "Memo." Reprinted by permission of Karen Upright.

Commander Kristen Ziman, "Bad Attitudes and Glow Worms," Originally appeared in *The Sun-Times Beacon News*, May 8, 2011. Reprinted by permission of Kristen Ziman.

Index

A

a / an, lowercase in titles, 259
Abstracts, 6
Abstract words, 241–42
Academic courses, capitalization of, 259
account of events, in writing assignment, 67
Action verbs, 191
Active reading, 6
Active voice, 222
Adams, Susan, "The Weirdest Job Interview
  Questions and How to Handle Them,"
  85–87
Additions, transitional words / phrases for, 60
Addresses, commas in, 247
Adjective clauses
  commas around, 246–47
  defined, 246
  joining ideas using, 241
Adjectives, 189, 231–33
  vs. adverbs, 231
  comparative and superlative form, 232–33
  in comparisons, 232–33
  coordinate, 245
  cumulative, 245
  defined, 231
  good / well, 233
  in sentence patterns, 195
Adverbs, 190, 231–33
  vs. adjectives, 231
  comparative and superlative form, 232–33
  in comparisons, 232–33
  conjunctive, 204, 236–37
  defined, 231, 239
  good / well, 233
  -ly ending, 231
  in sentence patterns, 195
  starting sentences with, 239–240
Agreement
  pronoun-antecedent, 224–27
  subject-verb, 208–16
agree or disagree, in writing assignment, 162
"All My Music" (Mattazi), 119
almost, as misplaced modifier, 234
am
  as helping verb, 192
  as linking verb, 191, 192
Ambiguous pronoun reference, 227
an / a, lowercase in titles, 259

Analysis, and critical writing, 16
and
  and commas in joined sentences, 206, 246
  in compound sentences, 246
  as coordinating conjunction, 206, 236
  coordination in sentences with, 236
  in items in series, 245
  lowercase in titles, 259
  run-ons, correcting with, 205–6
  subject connected with, 212–13
  subject-verb agreement with, 212–13
Apostrophes, 248–251
  in contractions, 249–250
  defined, 248
  with letters, numbers, and time, 250–51
  to show ownership, 248–49
Appositives
  commas around, 246
  defined, 240, 246
  joining ideas using, 240
are
  as helping verb, 192
  indefinite pronouns with, 214
  as linking verb, 191, 192
Argument, 161–173
  basics of, 161–63
  concluding sentences / conclusion in,
    164–65
  defined, 161
  evidence in, 163, 166
  main point in, 162–65
  organization in, 166–67
  paragraphs vs. essays in, 164–65
  purpose of, 161, 162
  reading and analyzing, 167–171
  support in, 163, 164–65
  thesis statement in, 163, 165
  topic sentence in, 163, 164–65
  transitions in, 167
  writing, 172–73
  writing situations for, 162, 172
Articles, indefinite, lowercase in titles, 259
Articles, information about, for sources, 178
Assignments, length of, 34–36
Assumptions
  questioning, 27–28
  recognizing and questioning, 1–3
Audience, 7, 20–22
Author, 5

B

bad, comparative and superlative form, 233
"Bad Attitudes and Glowworms" (Ziman), 157–59
badly, comparative and superlative form, 233
"Ban on Water Bottles: A Way to Bolster the University's Image" (Jacobowitz), 11–13
Base for, of irregular verbs, 218–221
be, forms of
  as helping verb, 192, 216
  indefinite pronouns with, 214
  as linking verb, 192
  past participle, 218
  past tense, 209, 218
  present tense, 209, 210
  subject-verb agreement with, 209–10
Beck, Shari, "A Classroom Distraction—and Worse," 170–71
become
  as linking verb, 192
  past participle, 218
  past tense, 218
been, as helping verb, 192
being, as helping verb, 192
Bias, awareness of, 3–4
Bible, 253
Bibliography, running, 178
"Bird Rescue" (Cepeda), 96
Body
  of essay, 23, 52
  of paragraph, 23
Booker, Mary LaCue, "School Rules," 154–55
Books
  information about, for sources, 178
  titles, 253, 259
both . . . and, 239
Brainstorming, 30
Brown, Charlton, "Buying a Car at an Auction," 107–8
Business letters, colon after greeting, 255
but
  in compound sentences, 246
  as coordinating conjunction, 236
  lowercase in titles, 259
  run-ons, correcting with, 205–6
"Buying a Car at an Auction" (Brown), 107–8

C

Call number, 175
can, as helping verb, 192
Capitalization, 256–59
  of names of people, places, dates, and things, 257–59
  of sentences, 256
  of titles, 259
Castro, Janice E., "Spanglish," 131–33

Cause
  defined, 148
  transitional words / phrases for, 60
Cause and effect, 148–160
  basics of, 148–151
  concluding sentences / conclusion in, 152–53
  main point in, 150, 151, 152–53
  order of importance in, 148–49
  organization in, 151, 154
  paragraphs vs. essays in, 152–53
  purpose of, 151
  reading and analyzing, 154–59
  support in, 150–53
  thesis statement in, 150
  topic sentence in, 150, 152–53
  transitions in, 154
  writing, 159–160
  writing situations for, 149, 159–160
CD titles, italics for, 253
Cepeda, Alessandra, "Bird Rescue," 96
Chapter in book, quotation marks for, 253
Checklists
  argument, writing, 173
  cause and effect, writing, 160
  classification, writing, 123
  comparison and contrast, writing, 147
  definition, writing, 135
  description, writing, 100
  draft essay, evaluating, 56
  draft paragraph, evaluating, 51
  illustration, writing, 89
  main point, evaluating, 39
  narration, writing, 76
  narrowed topic, evaluating, 32
  outline, evaluating, 48
  peer review questions, 65
  process analysis, writing, 111
  revised essay, evaluating, 65
  revised paragraph, evaluating, 62
  revising writing, 57
  support, evaluating, 44
Chronological order, 44–45, 66, 68–69
Citations
  in-text, 179–180
  MLA format, 179–180
  works cited list, 180, 185–86
Claims, 162
Classification, 112–123
  basics of, 112–15
  concluding sentences / conclusion in, 116–17
  defined, 112
  main point in, 114–17
  organization in, 115
  organizing principles, 112, 114–15
  paragraphs vs. essays in, 116–17
  purpose of, 115
  reading and analyzing, 118–122
  support in, 115, 116–17
  thesis statement in, 114, 117
  topic sentence in, 114, 116–17

transitions in, 115
writing, 122–23
writing situations for, 113, 122–23
"Classroom Distraction—and Worse, A"
  (Beck), 170–71
Clauses
  adjective, 241, 246–47
  dependent, 211–12
  independent, 203
  introductory, 246
  as misplaced modifiers, 235
Clichés, 243
Closed questions, 176
Clustering, 30–31
Coherence, revising for, 59–61
Collective nouns, 226–27
Colons, 254–55
  in business correspondence, 255
  before explanations or examples, 254
  function of, 254
  before lists, 254
  before subtitles, 255
.com, 177
Commas, 245–48
  in addresses, 247
  after introductory words, 246
  around adjective clauses, 246–47
  around appositives and interrupters, 246
  in compound sentences, 246
  between coordinate conjunctions, 245
  coordination in sentences with, 236
  correcting run-ons using, 205–6
  in dates, 247–48
  between items in a series, 245
  with names, 248
  with quotation marks, 247
  with quotations, 252
  with *yes* or *no*, 248
Comma splices, 203
Commercial products, capitalization of, 259
Comp, concluding sentences / conclusion in,
  140–41
Companies, capitalization of, 258
Comparatives, 232–33
Comparison
  adjectives and adverbs in, 232–33
  defined, 136
  parallelism in, 238–39
  pronouns used in, 229–230
Comparison and contrast, 136–147
  basics of, 136–39
  main point in, 138, 140–41
  organization in, 139
  paragraphs vs. essays in, 140–41
  reading and analyzing, 142–46
  support in, 138–39, 140–41
  thesis statement in, 138, 139
  topic sentence in, 138, 139, 140–41
  transitions in, 142
  writing, 146–47

writing situations for, 137, 146
Complete thoughts, 190, 194–95
Complete verbs, 192
Compound object, 229
Compound sentences
  commas in, 246
  defined, 246
Compound subjects, 193, 212–13, 229
Concluding sentences, 23, 50
  in argument, 164
  in cause and effect, 152
  in classification, 116
  in comparison and contrast, 140
  in definition, 126
  in illustration, 80
  main point, connecting to, 50
  in narration, 70
  in outline, 47
  in process analysis, 104
Conclusion
  in argument, 164–65
  basics of good, 53
  in cause and effect, 152–53
  in comparison and contrast, 141
  in definition, 127
  in description, 93
  of essay, 23, 53
  in illustration, 81
  main point, connecting to, 53
  in narration, 71
  in outline, 47
  in process analysis, 105
Concrete words, 242
Conjunctions, 190
  coordinating, 205–6, 259
  correcting run-ons using, 205–6
  correlative, 239
  subordinating, 199–200, 206, 237
Conjunctive adverbs, 204, 236–37
Context, rhetorical, 5–6
Contractions
  apostrophes in, 249–250
  common, 250
  defined, 249
Contrast
  defined, 136
  transitional words / phrases for, 60
Cook, Dan, "Spanglish," 131–32
Coordinate adjectives, 245
Coordinating conjunctions, 205–6
  in compound sentences, 246
  correcting run-ons using, 203, 205–6
  FANBOYS mnemonic for, 205, 236
  joining sentences with, 236, 246
  lowercase in titles, 259
Coordination, 236–37
  conjunctions for. *See* Coordinating
    conjunctions
  for joining sentences, 236–37
Correlative conjunctions, 239

Costas, Corin, "What Community Involvement Means to Me," 130–31
could, as helping verb, 192
Counterarguments, 163
Counterclaims, 163
Critical reading, 5–13
   example, 11–13
   for main point / support, 6–8
   process, 5–11
Critical thinking, 1–5
   assumptions, questioning, 1–3, 27–28
   bias, awareness of, 3–4
   defined, 1
Critical writing, 13–19
   analysis as, 16
   evaluation as, 19
   summary as, 14–16
   synthesis as, 16–18
Cumulative adjectives, 245

D

-d, past tense regular verbs, 217
Dangling modifiers, 235
Dashes, 255
Dates
   capitalization of, 258
   commas in, 247–48
defend or refute, in writing assignments, 162
Definitions, 6, 124–135
   basics of, 124–29
   concluding sentences / conclusion in, 126–27
   defined, 124
   main point in, 125, 126–27
   order of importance in, 124–25
   organization in, 129
   paragraphs vs. essays in, 126–27
   purpose of, 125
   reading and analyzing, 129–133
   support in, 126–27, 128–29
   thesis statement in, 127, 128
   topic sentence in, 126–27, 128
   transitions in, 129
   writing, 133–35
   writing situations for, 125, 133–34
Dependent clauses
   commas with, 199, 206
   defined, 211
   dependent words in, 199, 206
   between subject and verb, 211–12
   subordination in sentences with, 237
Dependent words
   common, 199
   correcting run-ons using, 206–8
   defined, 199
   in dependent clause, 199, 206
   fragments starting with, 199–200
   list of, 207
   as subordinating conjunctions, 237
describe, in writing assignments, 67
Description, 90–100

basics of, 90–94
concluding sentences / conclusion in, 92–93
defined, 90
main point in, 91, 94
organization in, 94
paragraphs vs. essays in, 92–93
reading and analyzing, 95–98
support in, 92, 94
thesis statement in, 91–93, 94
topic sentence in, 91–93, 94
transitions in, 94
writing, 99–100
writing situations for, 91, 99
Descriptive verbs, 15
Details, supporting. *See* Support
Devil's advocate, 27
"Difficult Decision with a Positive Outcome, A" (Prokop), 156–57
Direct objects, in sentence patterns, 195–96
Direct quotations, 179
Discussing ideas, 30
discuss the causes (or effects), in writing assignments, 149
discuss the meaning, in writing assignments, 125
do, forms of
   as helping verb, 192
   present tense, 210
   subject-verb agreement with, 210
"Don't Work in a Goat's Stomach" (Jones), 120–22
Draft
   basics of good, 49
   defined, 49
   of essay, 52–56
   outline of, 46–48
   of paragraphs, 49–51
   planning, 46–48
   revising, 56–65
   in writing process, 25

E

Editing
   defined, 56
   in writing process, 25
.edu, 177
-ed verb form
   joining ideas using, 240
   past tense regular verbs, 217
Effect. *See also* Cause and effect, defined, 148
either . . . or, 239
"Employee Assistance Program" (Scanlon), 129–130
English, formal vs. informal, 21
-er, in comparative form, 232–33
Essays
   argument, form for, 164
   body of, 23, 52
   cause and effect, form for, 153
   classification, form for, 117
   comparison and contrast, form for, 141

conclusion, 23, 53
definition, form for, 127
description, form for, 93
draft, evaluating, 56
drafting, 52–56
illustration, form for, 81
introduction, 23, 52–53
narration, form for, 71
outlining, 47
process analysis, form for, 105
quotation marks for, 253
revising, 56–65
sample, 54–55
structure of, 23–24
support in, 41–42
thesis statement in, 33, 68, 79
title, 53–54
topic sentences in, 52
topics for, 25–28
-est, in superlative form, 232–33
Evaluation
    and critical writing, 19
    of sources, 176–77
Evidence. See also Support
    in argument, 163, 166
    examples, 166
    expert opinions, 166
    facts, 163
    predictions, 166
    testing, 166
    types of, 163, 166
Examples
    colons before, 254
    as evidence, 166
    fragments that are, 201–2
    in illustration, 79
    in introductions, 53
    transitional words / phrases for, 60
    words signaling, 202
Exclamation points, with quotations, 252
Expert opinions, 166
Experts, interviewing, 176
Explanations
    colons before, 254
    fragments that are, 201–2
    words signaling, 202
"Eyeglasses vs. Laser Surgery: Benefits and Drawbacks" (Ibrahim), 143–44

F
Facts, 163
FANBOYS mnemonic, 205, 236
Feedback, peer review, 64–65
First-person subjects, 209
"Fish Cheeks" (Tan), 73–74
for
    and commas in joined sentences, 246
    in compound sentences, 246
    as coordinating conjunction, 236

lowercase in titles, 259
run-ons, correcting with, 205–6
Formal English, 21
Fragments, 197–202
    correcting, 198–202
    defined, 197
    dependent word, 199–200
    examples or explanations, 201–2
    gerund (-ing verbs), 200
    infinitive (to + verb), 201
    prepositional, 198
Freewriting, 29
Fused sentences, 203
Future tense, 216

G
Garcia, Cristina, "Spanglish," 131–32
Gender of pronouns
    pronoun agreement with, 224
    sexist language, avoiding, 244
Gerunds. See -ing verb form
"Gifts from the Heart" (Palmer), 84
good, comparative and superlative form, 233
Google, 175
.gov, 177
Grammar, 189–196
    adjectives, 231–33
    adverbs, 231–33
    parts of speech, 189–190
    pronouns, 223–230
    sentences, basic, 190–96
Grammatical errors, 197–222
    fragments, 197–202
    misplaced and dangling modifiers, 233–35
    run-ons, 203–8
    in subject-verb agreement, 208–16
    in verb tense, 216–222
Groups, capitalization of, 258
Guiding research question, 175

H
had
    as helping verb, 192
    past perfect, 221
hardly, as misplaced modifier, 234
has
    as helping verb, 192
    present perfect, 221
have, forms of
    as helping verb, 192, 216
    past participle, 219, 221
    present perfect, 221
    present tense, 209
    subject-verb agreement with, 209–10
he
    as subject pronoun, 228
    subject-verb agreement with, 209
Headings, 6
Helping verbs, 192, 221

her
as object pronoun, 228
as possessive pronoun, 228
subject-verb agreement with, 209
Hijuelos, Oscar, "Memories of New York City Snow," 97–98
him, as object pronoun, 228
his
as possessive pronoun, 228
sexist language, avoiding, 244
Holidays, capitalization of, 258
"How to Practice Simple Meditation" (Martin), 106–7
"How to Start Your Service Based Side Hustle" (Rosenberg), 108–10
Hyphenated words, 255–56
Hyphens, 255–56

I

I
as subject pronoun, 228
subject-verb agreement with, 208–10
Ibrahim, Said, "Eyeglasses vs. Laser Surgery: Benefits and Drawbacks," 143–44
Iceberg principle, 1
Ideas, arranging, 44–46
Illustration, 77–89
basics of, 77–82
concluding sentences / conclusion in, 80–81
defined, 77
main point in, 78–79, 80
order of importance in, 82
organization in, 82
paragraphs vs. essays in, 80–81
reading and analyzing, 82–87
support in, 79, 80
thesis statement in, 78–79, 81
topic sentence in, 78–79, 81
transitions in, 82
writing, 87–89
writing situations for, 78, 87–88
Importance
order of. *See* Order of importance
transitional words / phrases for, 60
"Importance of Advance Directives, The" (Melancon), 167–69
"Incident Report: Malicious Wounding" (Roy), 95–96
Incomplete sentences. *See* Fragments
Incomplete thoughts, 194–95
Indefinite articles, lowercase in titles, 259
Indefinite pronouns
agreement with, 225
defined, 213, 225
list of, 214, 224, 225–26
as subject, 213–15
Independent clauses. *See also* Sentences, 203
Indirect objects, in sentence patterns, 196
Indirect speech, 252

Informal English, 21
-ing verb form
defined, 200
fragments starting with, 200
joining ideas using, 240
modifiers starting with, 234
Internet address extensions, 177
Interrupters
commas around, 246
defined, 246
Interviews, 176
In-text citations, 179–180
Introduction
basics of good, 52
of essay, 23, 52–53
Introductory techniques, 49
Introductory words, commas after, 246
Invention strategies, 29–31, 42
Irregular verbs. *See also specific verbs*
defined, 217
list of, 218–221
past participle, 218–221
past tense, 218–221
present tense, 218–221
and subject-verb agreement, 209–10
verb tense, 217–221
is
as helping verb, 192
indefinite pronouns with, 214
as linking verb, 191, 192
it
as object pronoun, 228
as subject pronoun, 228
subject-verb agreement with, 209
Italics, for titles of longer works, 253
its, as possessive pronoun, 228

J

Jacobowitz, Amanda, "A Ban on Water Bottles," 11–13
Jones, Frances Cole, "Don't Work in a Goat's Stomach," 120–22
Journals, 31
just, as misplaced modifier, 234

K

Key words, 61
King, Leigh, "Prom Fashions," 118

L

Language
sexist, 244
slang, 242
wordy, 242–43
Languages, capitalization of, 258
"Learning Tool Whose Time Has Come, A" (Yilmaz), 169–170
Leibov, Brad, "Who We Are," 142–43
Letters, apostrophes with, 250–51

Library resources, 175
Linking verbs, 191–92
Listing, 30
Lists
    colons before, 254
    parallelism with, 238–39
    semicolons with, 253–54
Logical fallacies, 150–51
Lynch, Jelani, "My Turnaround," 72–73

M

Magazine articles, quotation marks for, 253
Magazine titles, italics for, 253
Main point. *See also* Thesis statements; *also*
        Topic sentences, 33–48
    in argument, 162–63, 164–65
    in cause and effect, 150, 151, 152–53
    in classification, 114–15, 116–17
    in comparison and contrast, 138, 140–41
    connecting conclusion / concluding sentence
        to, 50, 53
    in definition, 125, 126–27
    in description, 91, 94
    of essay, 23
    evaluating, 39
    in illustration, 78–79, 80
    in narration, 67–68
    of paragraph, 23
    in process analysis, 102–3, 104–5
    of reading, 6–7
    single, stating, 36–37
    specificity of, 37–38
    support for, 40–44
    in thesis statements, 33–39
    in topic sentences, 33–39
Main verbs, 190
Mapping, 30–31
Marginalia, 6
Martin, Stephen, "How to Practice Simple
        Meditation," 106–7
Mattazi, Lorenza, "All My Music," 119
may, as helping verb, 192
me, as object pronoun, 228
Melancon, Diane, "The Importance of Advance
        Directives," 167–69
Memo, example of (Karen Upright), 82–83
"Memories of New York City Snow" (Hijuelos),
        97–98
might, as helping verb, 192
mine, as possessive pronoun, 228
Misplaced modifiers, 234–35
MLA format, 179–180
Modern Language Association (MLA), 179–180
Modifiers
    dangling, 235
    defined, 233
    misplaced, 234–35
more, 232–33
most, 232–33
Movie titles, italics for, 253

must, as helping verb, 192
my, as possessive pronoun, 228
"My Turnaround" (Lynch), 72–73

N

Names
    capitalization of, 257–59
    commas with, 248
Narration, 66–76
    basics of, 66–69
    concluding sentence in, 70
    conclusion in, 71
    defined, 66
    main point in, 67–68
    organization in, 68–69
    paragraphs vs. essays in, 70–71
    reading and analyzing, 69–74
    in real world, 69
    support in, 68, 70
    thesis statement in, 68, 71
    time order in, 66, 68–69
    topic sentence in, 67–68, 70, 71
    writing, 75–76
Narrowing topic, 26–28
Nationalities, capitalization of, 258
nearly, as misplaced modifier, 234
neither . . . nor, 239
.net, 177
Newspaper articles, quotation marks for, 253
Newspaper titles
    capitalization of, 259
    italics for, 253
no, commas with, 248
nor
    and commas in joined sentences, 246
    in compound sentences, 246
    as coordinating conjunction, 236
    lowercase in titles, 259
    run-ons, correcting with, 205–6
not only . . . but also, 239
Nouns
    adjective clauses as descriptors of, 246–47
    and appositives, 246
    collective, 226–27
    defined, 189
    as subject of sentence, 193
Novel titles, italics for, 253
Numbers, apostrophes with, 250–51
"Nursing Note" (Terreden), 69

O

Object of a preposition, 193
Object of sentence
    compound, 229
    direct, 195
    indirect, 196
    object of the preposition, 228
    object of verb, 228
    pronouns as, 228–29

Object pronouns, 227–28
Online catalogs, 175
only, as misplaced modifier, 234
Open-ended questions, 176
Opinions, in introductions, 53
or
   and commas in joined sentences, 246
   in compound sentences, 246
   as coordinating conjunction, 236
   in items in series, 245
   run-ons, correcting with, 205–6
   subject connected with, 212–13
   subject-verb agreement with, 212–13
Order
   defined, 44
   of ideas, 44–46
   space, 45–46, 94
   time, 44–45, 66, 68–69, 94, 103–5
Order of emphasis, for classification, 115
Order of importance
   in argument, 166
   for cause and effect, 148–49, 151
   for classification, 115
   for comparison and contrast, 139
   for definitions, 124–25, 129
   for description, 94
   to emphasize a point, 46
   in illustration, 82
.org, 177
Organization
   in argument, 166–67
   in cause and effect, 151, 154
   in classification, 115
   in comparison and contrast, 139
   in definition, 129
   in description, 94
   in illustration, 82
   in narration, 68–69
   in process analysis, 103–5
Organizations, capitalization of, 258
Organizing principles, 112, 114–15
our / ours, as possessive pronoun, 228
Outlines, 46–48
Overgeneralization, 166
Ownership
   apostrophes to show, 248–49
   possessive pronouns, 224, 227–29, 249

P

Palmer, Casandra, "Gifts from the Heart," 84
Paragraphs
   argument, form for, 164
   body of, 23
   cause and effect, form for, 152
   classification, form for, 116
   comparison and contrast, form for, 140
   concluding sentences, 23
   definition, form for, 126
   description, form for, 92

draft, evaluating, 51
drafting, 49–51
illustration, form for, 81
main point in, 33
narration, form for, 70
outlining, 47
process analysis, form for, 104
revising, 56–65
sample, 50–51
structure of, 22–23
support in. *See also* Support, 23, 41–42
title, 50
topic sentence, 23
topics for, 25–32
Parallelism, 238–39
Paraphrasing, 9–11, 179
Parentheses, 255
Parts of speech, 189–190
Passive voice, 222
Past participles, 221–22
   joining ideas using, 240
Past perfect tense, 221
Past tense, 216, 217
Pause, during reading, 8–9
Peer review, 64–65
People, capitalization of names of, 257
Periodical databases, 175
Periodicals, 175
Periods
   correcting run-ons using, 204–5
   with quotations, 252
Person
   defined, 230
   pronoun consistency, 230
Personal pronouns, 224
Phrases
   introductory, 246
   prepositional. *See* Prepositional phrases
   transitional. *See* Transitional words /
      phrases
Places, capitalization of, 257–58
Plagiarism
   avoiding, 32, 177–78
   defined, 177
Plural subjects
   pronoun agreement with, 226
   subject-verb agreement with, 208–16
Poems, quotation marks for, 253
Point-by-point organization, 139
Possessive pronouns, 224, 227–29, 249
Post hoc fallacy, 151
Predictions, 166
Prepositional phrases, 193, 194
   defined, 211
   modifiers as, 234
   between subject and verb, 211
Prepositions, 190, 193–94
   fragments starting with, 198
   lowercase in titles, 259
Present perfect tense, 221

Present tense, 216–17
Previewing, in critical reading process, 5–6
Prewriting techniques, 29–31, 42
Primary support points, 40, 43, 68
Process analysis, 101–11
  basics of, 101–3
  concluding sentences / conclusion in, 104–5
  defined, 101
  main point in, 102–3, 104–5
  organization in, 103–5
  paragraphs vs. essays in, 104–5
  purpose of, 102
  reading and analyzing, 106–10
  support in, 103, 104–5
  thesis statement in, 103
  time order in, 101–2, 103–5
  topic sentence in, 103, 104–5
  transitions in, 106
  writing, 110–11
  writing situations for, 102, 110–11
Prokop, Caitlin, "A Difficult Decision with a Positive Outcome," 156–57
"Prom Fashions" (King), 118
Pronouns, 189, 193, 223–230
  agreement, checking for, 224–27
  in comparisons, 229–230
  with compound subjects and objects, 229
  consistency of, 230
  defined, 223
  indefinite, 224, 225–26
  object, 227–28
  personal, 224
  possessive, 224, 227–29, 249
  reference, clarity of, 227
  relative, 206
  sexist, avoiding, 226
  subject, 227–28
  types of, 227–29
  using right, 229–230
  who / whom, 230
Proper nouns
  capitalization of, 257–59
  names, commas with, 248
Punctuation
  apostrophes, 248–251
  colons, 254–55
  commas, 245–48
  dashes, 255
  hyphens, 255–56
  parentheses, 255
  quotation marks, 251–53
  semicolons, 253–54
Purpose
  in argument, 161, 162
  in cause and effect, 151
  in classification, 115
  in definition, 125
  in process analysis, 102
  of writing, 6–7, 20–21

Q

Question marks, with quotations, 252
Questions
  closed, 176
  guiding research question, 175
  in introductions, 53
  open-ended, 176
  for peer reviewers, 65
Quotation marks, 178, 251–53
  commas with, 247
  defined, 247, 251
  for direct quotations, 251–52
  and indirect speech, 252
  single, 252
  for titles, 253
Quotations
  within another quotation, 252
  capitalization and punctuation guidelines, 251–52
  direct, 179, 251–52
  indirect, 252
  in introductions, 52
Qur'an, 253

R

rather . . . than, 239
Reasons, in argument, 163
Reference librarians, 175
Regular verbs
  past tense, 217
  present tense, 216–17
  subject-verb agreement, 208–9
  verb tense, 216–17
Relative pronouns, 206
Religions, capitalization of, 258
Repetitious pronoun reference, 227
report, in writing assignments, 67
Research, 174–188
  basics of, 174–180
  defined, 174
  guiding question for, 175
  reading and analyzing, 181–86
  sources, finding, 175–76
  uses of, 174
  writing, 180, 187–88
Resources, library, 175
Results, transitional words / phrases for, 60
retell, in writing assignments, 67
Revising, 56–65
  checklist for, 57
  for coherence, 59–61
  defined, 56
  for development of support, 59
  peer review, 64–65
  revised essay, evaluating, 65
  revised paragraph, evaluating, 62
  sample essay, 62–64
  sample paragraph, 61–62

Revising, (*continued*)
   tips for, 57
   for unity, 58
   in writing process, 25
Rhetorical context, 5–6
Rosenberg, Eric, "How to Start Your Service
      Based Side Hustle," 108–10
Roy, James C., "Incident Report: Malicious
      Wounding," 95–96
Running bibliography, 178
Run-ons, 203–8
   comma and a coordinating conjunction to
      correct, 205–6
   correcting, 203–8
   defined, 203
   dependent word, correcting with, 206–8
   period to correct, 204–5
   semicolon to correct, 204–5
   types of, 203

S

Salutations, 255
Scanlon, Walter, "Employee Assistance
      Program," 129–130
"School Rules" (Booker), 154–55
Search engines, 175–76
Seasons, 258
Secondary support, 40, 43, 68
seem, as linking verb, 192
Semicolons, 253–54
   coordination in sentences with, 237
   correcting run-ons using, 204–5
   function of, 253
   with items in list containing commas,
      253–54
   to join closely related sentences, 253
Sense verbs, 192
Sentence errors
   fragments, 197–202
   misplaced and dangling modifiers, 234–35
   run-ons, 203–8
   subject-verb agreement problems, 208–16
   verb-tense problems, 222
Sentences
   basic patterns, 195–96
   capitalization of, 256
   complete, in drafts, 49
   concluding, 23, 50
   coordination for joining, 236–37
   run-ons, 203–8
   semicolons for joining, 253
   subjects of, 193–94
   subordination for joining, 237–38
   support, 23
   topic, 23
   verbs in, 190–93
Sentence variety, 239–241
   adjective clause to join ideas, 241
   adverbs, beginning sentences with, 239–240
   appositives to join ideas, 240

-ing verb forms to join ideas, 240
   past participle to join ideas, 240
Sexist language, 244
she, as subject pronoun, 228
Short stories, quotation marks for, 253
should, as helping verb, 192
Slang, 242
Slippery slope fallacy, 151
so
   and commas in joined sentences, 246
   in compound sentences, 246
   as coordinating conjunction, 236
   run-ons, correcting with, 205–6
Song titles
   capitalization of, 259
   quotation marks for, 253
Sources
   citing and documenting, 177–180
   evaluating, 176–77
   finding appropriate, 175–76
   of publications, 5
   recording information from, 32, 178
   synthesizing, 177
Space order, 45–46
   for cause and effect, 151
   for classification, 115
   for description, 94
   transitional words / phrases for, 60
"Spanglish" (Castro), 131–33
Specific words, 242
Statistics, 166
Subject pronouns, 227–28
Subjects, 193–94
   compound, 193, 212–13, 229
   first-person, 209
   identifying, 193–94
   pronoun agreement with, 224–27
   in sentence patterns, 195
   third-person, 209
   verb agreement with. *See* Subject-verb
      agreement
Subject-verb agreement, 208–16
   and compound subject, 212–13
   indefinite pronoun as subject, 213–15
   and irregular verbs *be*, *have*, *do*, 209–10
   and regular verbs, 208–9
   and verbs before subject, 215–16
   and words between subject and verb,
      211–12
Subordinating conjunctions, 199–200, 206, 237
Subordination, 237–38
Subtitles, colons before, 255
Summaries
   and critical reading, 6
   and critical writing, 14–16
Superlatives, 232–33
Support, 7–8
   in argument, 163, 164–65
   in cause and effect, 150–53
   in classification, 115, 116–17
   in comparison and contrast, 138–141

defined, 40
in definition, 126–29
in description, 92, 94
evaluating, 44
features of good, 40
generating, 42
in illustration, 79, 80
for main point, 40–44
in narration, 68, 70
in paragraphs vs. essays, 41–42
primary, 40, 68
in process analysis, 103, 104–5
revising for development of, 59
secondary, 40, 43, 68
selecting best primary, 43
Support paragraphs, 23
Support sentences, 23
Surprises, in introductions, 53
Synthesis, and critical writing, 16–18

T

Tan, Amy, "Fish Cheeks," 73–74
Television programs
capitalization of, 259
italics for, 253
Tense of verb. *See* Verb tense
Terreden, Anne, "Nursing Note" 69
that
in adjective clauses, 246
in dependent clauses, 211–12
with indirect speech, 252
modifier clauses starting with, 235
the, lowercase in titles, 259
their / theirs
in non-sexist language, 244
as possessive pronoun, 228
them, as object pronoun, 228
Thesis statements, 23, 33–39
in argument, 163, 165
basics of good, 33
in cause and effect, 150
in classification, 114, 117
in comparison and contrast, 138, 139
in definition, 127, 128
in description, 91–93, 94
in illustration, 78–79, 81
main point in, 33–39, 68
in narration, 71
in process analysis, 103
single main point for, 36–37
and size of assignment, 34–36
specificity of, 37–38
synthesizing information to support, 177
vs. topic sentences, 34
they, as subject pronoun, 228
Third-person subjects, 209
Time, apostrophes with, 250–51
Time order, 44–45
for cause and effect, 151
for classification, 115

for description, 94
for narration, 66, 68–69
for process analysis, 101–2, 103–5
transitional words / phrases for, 60
Titles
capitalization of, 259
and critical reading, 5
essay, 53–54
paragraph, 50
quotation marks with, 253
Tone, 21
Topics, 7
choosing, questions to ask, 25–26
defined, 25
exploring, 29–32
narrowing, 26–28
researching, 31
Topic sentences, 23, 33–39
in argument, 163, 164–65
basics of good, 33
in cause and effect, 150, 152–53
in classification, 114, 116–17
in comparison and contrast, 138, 139, 140–41
in definition, 126–27, 128
in description, 91–92, 94
in essay, 52
in illustration, 78–79, 81
main point in, 33–39, 67–68
in narration, 70, 71
in process analysis, 103, 104–5
single main point for, 36–37
and size of assignment, 34–36
specificity of, 37–38
vs. thesis statements, 34
Transitional words / phrases, 59–60
in argument, 167
in cause and effect, 154
for causes or results, 60
in classification, 115
for coherence, 59–60
in comparison and contrast, 142
for contrast, 60
in definition, 129
in description, 94
in illustration, 82
list of, 59–60
in narration, 69
for order of importance, 60
in process analysis, 106
for space order, 60
for time order, 60, 69
Twain, Mark, "Two Ways of Seeing a River,"
144–46
"Two Ways of Seeing a River" (Twain),
144–46

U

Unity, revising for, 58
Upright, Karen, memo example, 82–83
us, as object pronoun, 228

V

Vague pronoun reference, 227
Vague words, 241–42
Verbs, 189, 190–93
    action, 191
    active and passive voice, 222
    complete, 192
    descriptive, 15
    helping, 192, 221
    irregular, 209–10
    linking, 191–92
    main, 190
    past participles, 221–22
    regular, 216–17
    sense, 192
    in sentence patterns, 195–96
Verb tense, 216–222
    defined, 216
    finding and fixing errors in, 222
    future, 216
    irregular verbs, 217–221
    past, 216, 217
    past perfect, 221
    present, 216–17
    present perfect, 221
    regular verbs, 216–17
Visuals, 6
Voice, active and passive, 222

W

was
    as helping verb, 192
    as linking verb, 192
we, as subject pronoun, 228
Websites, information about, for sources, 178
"Weirdest Job Interview Questions and How to
        Handle Them" (Adams), 85–87
well, comparative and superlative form, 233
were
    as helping verb, 192
    as linking verb, 192
"What Community Involvement Means to Me"
        (Costas), 130–31
which
    in adjective clauses, 246
    in dependent clauses, 211–12
    modifier clauses starting with, 235
who
    in adjective clauses, 246
    in dependent clauses, 211–12
    modifier clauses starting with, 235
    as subject pronoun, 228
    vs. *whom*, 230
Whole-to-whole organization, 139
whom
    in dependent clauses, 211–12
    as object pronoun, 228
    as subject pronoun, 228
    vs. *who*, 230

whose
    in dependent clauses, 211–12
    modifier clauses starting with, 235
    as possessive pronoun, 228
    as subject pronoun, 228
"Who We Are" (Leibov), 142–43
will, as helping verb, 192, 216
Word-choice problems, 241–44
    clichés, 243
    sexist language, avoiding, 244
    slang, 242
    vague and abstract words, 241–42
    wordy language, 242–43
Wordy language, 242–43
Works cited, 180, 185–86
would, as helping verb, 192
Writer's purpose, 6–7, 20–21
Writing basics, 20–32
    arranging ideas, 44–46
    audience, 20–22
    essay form, 23–24
    paragraph form, 22–23
    plagiarism, avoiding, 32
    prewriting, 29–31
    purpose, 20–21
    topic choice, 25–28
    writing process, steps in, 24–25
Writing patterns. *See also specific types*
    argument, 161–174
    cause and effect, 148–160
    classification, 112–123
    comparison and contrast, 136–147
    definition, 124–135
    description, 90–100
    illustration, 77–89
    narration, 66–76
    process analysis, 101–11
Writing process
    outlining, 46–48
    steps in, 24–25

Y

yes, commas with, 248
yet
    and commas in joined sentences, 246
    in compound sentences, 246
    as coordinating conjunction, 236
    run-ons, correcting with, 205–6
Yilmaz, Jason, "A Learning Tool Whose Time
        Has Come," 169–170
you
    as object pronoun, 228
    as subject pronoun, 228
your / yours, as possessive pronoun, 228

Z

Ziman, Kristen, "Bad Attitudes and
        Glowworms," 157–59

Real Take-Away Points

Four Basics of Good Writing

1 It reflects the writer's purpose and the needs, knowledge, and expectations of its intended audience.

2 It results from a thoughtful writing process.

3 It includes a clear, definite point.

4 It provides support that shows, explains, or proves the main point.

2PR   The Critical Reading Process

1 **Preview** the reading.

2 **Read** the piece, double underlining the <u>thesis statement</u> and underlining the <u>major support</u>. Consider the quality of the support.

3 **Pause** to think during the reading. Take notes and ask questions about what you are reading. Imagine that you are talking to the author.

4 **Review** the reading, your marginal notes, and your questions.

Writing Critically

Summarize

- What is important about the text?
- What is the purpose, the big picture? Who is the intended audience?
- What are the main points and key support?

Analyze

- What elements have been used to convey the main point?
- Do any elements raise questions? Do any key points seem missing or undeveloped?

Synthesize

- What do other sources say about the topic of the text?
- How does your own (or others') experience affect how you see the topic?
- What new point(s) might you make by bringing together all the different sources and experiences?

Evaluate

- Based on your application of summary, analysis, and synthesis, what do you think about the material you have read?
- Is the work successful? Does it achieve its purpose?
- Does the author show any biases? Are there any hidden assumptions? If so, do they make the piece more or less effective?